THE BOUNDARIES OF THE CAMPUS

The Boundaries of the Campus

A History of the
University of Wisconsin Extension Division
1885-1945

Frederick M. Rosentreter

Madison   The University of Wisconsin Press   1957

Published by the University of Wisconsin Press, 430 Sterling
Court, Madison 6, Wisconsin

Copyright © 1957 by the Regents of the University of Wisconsin. Copyright, Canada, 1957

Distributed in Canada by Burns and MacEachern, Toronto

Printed in the United States of America by Cushing-Malloy,
Inc., Ann Arbor, Michigan

Library of Congress Catalog Card Number 57-9812

Preface

This study is a revision of a doctoral dissertation in history. It was made possible by a financial grant from the Extension Division of the University of Wisconsin. For the grant and for the Division's coöperation in opening files and unlocking memories, the writer is deeply grateful.

Although this account of the Extension Division follows by but a few years the history by Merle Curti and Vernon Carstensen, The University of Wisconsin, 1848–1925, the author has been able to make use of papers not previously available. Shortly after the comprehensive history of the University was written, Professor William H. Lighty, longtime secretary of the Division's correspondence study department, turned over his manuscript collection to the Wisconsin State Historical Society. This collection contains what remains of the Division's records from 1906 to 1925. The Lighty Collection consists of those materials which he was able to save from destruction, and is, therefore, sometimes spotty in its coverage. Without it, however, a major part of the Division's history would have had to remain untold.

The writer is indebted to the readers of this manuscript; to the staffs of the Wisconsin Legislative Reference Library, the Historical, University, and Agricultural College Libraries for generous assistance; and to the Wisconsin Historical Society and the President's Office of the University of Wisconsin for the use of materials.

v

Contents

I	Widening Educational Horizons	3
II	The Farmers' Institutes	15
III	General Extension in Wisconsin, First Phase	27
IV	"Revivification"	43
V	Extension's Early Critics	56
VI	Planners and Planning	65
VII	Extension as Teacher	78
VIII	Extension as Humanitarian	96
IX	Problems in Communication	113
X	Competition and Transition	123
XI	Extension in Prosperity and Disillusionment	138
XII	Extension in War and Peace	153
XIII	Balance Sheet	172
	List of Manuscript Sources	181
	Notes	182
	Index	199

THE BOUNDARIES OF THE CAMPUS

Widening Educational Horizons

What is "University Extension?" There is no all-embracing, unequivocable short answer. Any acceptable definition must include reference to time, place and circumstance—must focus, at least for the present, upon specific extension programs. University Extension is a vital, utilitarian concept whose history is one of constant reinterpretation and change. Historically, this vitality has been a product of the dynamics of extension-community relationships. Extension has been an active part of the community even as the community has been an active part of extension.

What is University Extension? Sometimes it is what its label implies, an extension of the educational services of the University of which it is a part. Not all extension divisions, however, have confined themselves to university level instruction. Their offerings have ranged from finger painting for children to bathing a baby, from automobile repair to academic graduate study. Various institutions have at different times stressed one, several, or more of these levels of work. Herein lies one of extension's greatest strengths, or to critics, its weakness: its ready adaptability and the seeds of diletantism lurking within it. In the hands of willing administrators, extension activity can be made to meet quickly the observed needs of many groups. This potential flexibility is rooted in precedent, and freedom from some of the pressures to which the traditional university is subject. There is no interference from alumni organizations; extension has none. On the other hand, extension divisions have had constantly to justify their existence to the institutions of which they are a part, legislatures, or other fiscal agencies, and the public.

What is University Extension? The key word, "extension," implies reaching out, going to or toward. More than any other formally organized educational institution, extension has gone to its public not only with actual instruction, but with the object of convincing the public of the need for that instruction. The word "need" requires emphasis. Extension's home study students have not enrolled simply because of family tradition, the desire to leave home immediately after

high school, or the social glamour which is a part of conventional campus life. They became students because they
were convinced of the value of guided study or discussion
itself. The disadvantageous circumstances under which
much of this study has been done has lent urgency to extension's constant quest for new or revised teaching techniques, for ways in which to employ the most recent developments in mass communication: the mail service, the
railroad, automobile, picture projection, radio, and finally,
television.

What is University Extension? To the historian, it is a
part of the story of Western civilization. Thus its study
brings into association the names of the Greek philosopher-
teachers; the early Christians, who preached to the multi-
tudes; Thomas Malthus, who advocated a formula for
avoiding mass misery; Augustus Comte, who argued that
the means to a better next generation was the education of
the present one; the English Christian Socialists, who
helped found the London Workingmen's College; Professor
James Stuart of Cambridge, who in the 1870's spurned convention and gave women teachers lectures in physical
science; Herbert Baxter Adams, who brought concepts of
mass adult education from England to America; Josiah
Holbrook who founded the American Lyceum movement
during the Jacksonian era; William R. Harper, who made
extension work part of the program of the University of
Chicago; Frederick Jackson Turner and Richard T. Ely,
who helped pioneer the extension movement at the University of Wisconsin. The study would necessarily include the
names of Gustav Langerscheidt and Charles Toussaint, who
took advantage of improved mail service to pioneer correspondence study of languages in Paris in 1856;[1] the British
University Extensionists, who made use of steam railroads
to develop circuits for their traveling instructors; Dr.
Charles McCarthy, who fought for University-sponsored
courses for shop workers; and Louis E. Reber, first dean
of the Extension Division of the University of Wisconsin.

It does not matter that one cannot demonstrate a direct
connection between English Extension and its American
counterpart. It is of little moment that one cannot show an
unbroken and consistent line of thought between Socrates
and Herbert Baxter Adams. These movements and individuals are bound together by a more subtle relationship,
namely their existence within cultures which produced men
who felt the need for change and who viewed mass education

as the means of achieving it. The fact, too, that these
leaders found receptive listeners already prepared to respect the written and spoken word and to see in it a means
of advancement binds them into a group unfettered by time
or space.

Despite this general unity in extension work, each of its
institutionalized manifestations remains somewhat unique.
Each was developed in answer to specific, although rarely
completely isolated, problems. This in itself indicates the
existence of three major variables: time, place, and human
personality. What created the conditions which certain individuals or groups felt called upon to change? Why were
these men able to give their wishes concrete form? Why did
they select popular education as their means, and why did
they give it a particular emphasis? Were their efforts opposed, and if so, why? Is extension work today what it was
a generation or so ago? The immediate answers call for the
study of individual extension movements. This book is a
study of the development of extension work at the University
of Wisconsin. Yet it would be shortsighted to review that
development without preliminary reference to a larger context. At the same time, it will be impossible to generalize
about American extension work until many more individual
case histories have been compiled.

Major American educational developments have never
occurred in complete isolation. The American scene proved
receptive to modifications of German answers to problems
in the fields of elementary and graduate school work. Many
Americans were also inspired by British developments in
part-time adult education. The British efforts evolved along
two major lines: educational programs designed to help
artisans achieve greater skill in discharging their daily
tasks, and programs offering courses of a cultural nature
to workers unable to attend daytime classes. The first reflected interest in the artisan as an artisan, the second in
the worker as a man obliged to play many social roles.

In 1800, Dr. George Birkbeck formalized his impromptu
efforts to teach Glasgow glassblowers the scientific principles of their craft. He had been obliged to spend valuable
hours showing workers how to create special tubes and jars,
and he hit upon an efficient substitute for his personal instruction, namely evening classes grouped within a Mechanics' Institute. Other men appreciated the possibilities of
such instruction, and between 1824 and 1830, the Institutes
spread southward into England. The second line of develop-

ment was shaped by the interacting ideas of the Christian
Socialists, laborers and school teachers who desired instruction, and representatives of established English universities and colleges. The Christian Socialists, fearing a
repetition of the worker violence of 1848, envisaged in
popular mass education a means of encouraging men to lead
spiritually and intellectually fruitful rather than acquisitive
lives. Like Adam Smith, they believed mass ignorance a
threat to public order and national stability. Many workers,
on the other hand, saw in educational opportunities the
means of greater prestige, success, and self-respect.
Women school teachers desirous of a better understanding
of the physical sciences they were required to teach sought
and received instruction from a member of the Cambridge
faculty. The composite result was the establishment in 1875
of the London Society for the Extension of University
Teaching.

The Society was composed of representatives of major
English universities, who supervised the creation of classes
for workers obliged to combine study with wage earning.
The curricula were designed to provide students, many
possessing only the rudiments of education, a unified picture
of the various elements of liberal culture. The goal gave
the work both direction and continuity. This was no popular
one-lecture approach to mass education, but a carefully
planned program consisting of twelve lecture units per
course. Arnold Toynbee, who inspired English settlement
house work, presented a popular series of lectures which
included discussion of free trade and wages, and a critical
examination of the theories of Henry George.

This extension of modified university work to adult
audiences—University Extension—did not attract the numbers anticipated in the London area. Moved elsewhere,
however, where cultural opportunities and diversions were
scarcer, it flourished. University extension "centers,"
staffed by circuit-riding graduate students, were developed
throughout England. The centers offered welcome professional opportunities to the graduates, whose numbers had
come to exceed the positions available in traditional schools.
At the same time, circuit-riding and living in new communities enabled the young faculty members to become con-
versant with local needs. The universities went out to the
people and the people came to these extensions of the universities. By 1899, 10,881 students were enrolled in the
over 100 courses offered through University Extension,

were listening to lectures with the aid of specially prepared syllabi, participating in discussion groups and taking examinations.[2]

American educators were not slow to grasp the impor- tance of the British extension movement. Herbert Baxter Adams of Johns Hopkins University, and Methodist Bishop John H. Vincent, pioneer of the Chautauqua Assembly, ob- served the work at firsthand. Adams described the British program as part of the democratic movement, as related to broadened suffrage, compulsory education for children, and the "emancipation" of Catholics and Jews. Noteworthy, too, was the opening of broad educational opportunities to women, who responded by becoming mainstays of the move- ment. There was yet another aspect which Adams did not miss; by shedding some of their aristocratic aloofness, the universities had become powerful forces in decreasing the antagonism between the rich and the poor.[3] The hopes of Adam Smith and the Christian Socialists had not been vain. Looking to the future, the American observers felt that the English program contained much of value for their own country.

Adams and Vincent enthusiastically sought to transplant these concepts of adult education from the center of the Industrial Revolution to a land which was but beginning to feel the impact of industrialism. It is significant, however, that Adams and Vincent were not introducing anything fundamentally new to the American scene. Chautauqua's foundations, which were built of native materials, were laid in 1874, and earlier generations of Americans had already produced the leaders and audiences for several adult edu- cational movements. To the American ear, "University Extension" may have had a superficially new and exciting ring; but the American mind had long been prepared for the ideals and mechanics which underlay the basic concept.

Many American colonists appreciated the need for both informal and formal instruction along technical as well as general cultural lines. Colonial indigo growers punctuated their convivial gatherings with the reading of technical papers. Other men saw the need of instructing working youths during off duty hours along the lines of their trade, and founders of colleges made plans, which proved either abortive or tardy, to include agricultural courses in their curricula. By 1825, the westward movement and the simul- taneous increase in manufacturing had lessened East Coast demands for agricultural education, but the cry was now to be heard in Pennsylvania, Ohio and Michigan. The answer, given in the establishment of such specialized schools as Rensselaer Polytechnic Institute, revealed that even the "West" was not entirely agricultural. The courses offered included not only natural science, but engineering. During these same mid-century years, Ohio farmers and workers financed the establishment of Farmers' College. Eighteen fifty-five saw the beginnings of Michigan's Agricultural College.[4]

By 1848, the year of the founding of the University of Wisconsin, such states as Indiana, Missouri, Iowa and Michigan already boasted tax-supported universities. The trend toward state supported education, however, did not keep step with the growing demands for vocational training. Denominational colleges still dominated the field of higher education, and continued to dictate its general tone. The tax-supported schools tended to reflect their concept of the educated man as being one steeped in the traditional classical disciplines.[5] Two major factors, however, soon caused state school officials to reconsider their positions: the Land Grant College Act of 1862 with its promise of Federal financial aid to schools offering instruction in agriculture and engineering, and the concomitant pressure of local groups demanding that the schools prepare students for active roles in a society increasing in technical specialization.

The second line of educational development in America was more informal. It consisted of voluntary associations, such as the early agricultural societies whose membership included Robert Livingston, John Marshall, John Taylor, Thomas Jefferson, and Edmund Ruffin. These organizations, which for a time flourished along the entire length of the Atlantic seaboard, were largely gentlemen's societies, social, political, and professional organizations for the operators of extensive acreages. They did not cater directly to the needs and interests of the small farmer or town mechanic. The lyceum movement was designed to fill that gap by attracting, serving, and educating the latter. In that capacity, it served both as a symbol of Jacksonian democracy, and as an effort to prevent popular excesses.

The founder of the lyceum movement was Josiah Holbrook, recent graduate of Yale, who established the "American Lyceum of Science and Arts Composed of Associations for Mutual Instruction and Designed for the General Diffusion of Useful and Practical Knowledge," in Millbury, Massa-

chusetts, in 1896. Holbrook hoped to spread the scientific
knowledge he had come to revere, and at the same time
popularize his own social and political views. His means
were deeply rooted in American ideals and behavior, for
they were based upon the respect accorded the New England
town meeting and material scientific achievement. Holbrook
hoped to spark the creation of a vast network of local
societies affording opportunities for discussion and facilities for study and research.

The Lyceum was designed to encourage the intellectual
mingling of lawyers, farmers, doctors, mechanics, and
housewives—everybody over the age of eighteen. Each individual was assumed to possess some knowledge valuable to
his contemporaries; here was a means of pooling information gleaned from formal study and actual experience.
Everyman an educator; everyman a student. Holbrook's
proposals, however, were not an attack upon formal education. Rather were they an attempt to make available to all
the advances in the broad field of learning. Holbrook saw in
Lyceum the means of forcing a reorganization of the existing public school system along those lines, and of improving
the professional preparation of teachers.

Holbrook looked beyond individual advantage, and saw
within the framework of the Lyceum possibilities for developing community spirit based upon democracy and mutual
respect. There could be no class hatred, no gross factionalism among men and women who knew one another and
understood one another's problems. Association was assumed to develop "good moral" and "good political" tendencies, to enable people "to view the principles of their
constitution as inviolable" and encourage them to "defend it
with the same boldness and energy as the hands that drew
it."[6] Here was Holbrook's answer to President Washington's
warning against the government's being undermined by "the
spirit of innovation upon its principles," and "constitutional
alterations that will impair the energy of the system...."
Here was Holbrook's contribution to the fight to keep political and social changes within prescribed limits. Education,
broadly considered, was seen as a weapon against impetu-
ous change.

Lyceum, however, did not flourish in the manner envisioned by its founder. The very word became, instead,
synonymous with popular lectures. The first centers of such
platform activity were in the vicinities of Boston and
Philadelphia, where enthusiastic audiences heard Wendell

Phillips, James Russell Lowell, Henry Ward Beecher, Ralph
Waldo Emerson, and Daniel Webster. But Lyceum also
moved westward with the settlers. By 1835, it was an important phase of the cultural life of at least fifteen states
and in evidence on the very fringes of settlement. Holbrook's
optimism had not been entirely misplaced, however. While
Alexis de Tocqueville deemed the American tendency to
enjoy using and hearing generalities as reflecting a desire
for effortless success, for gaining "information without
labor," he also concluded that the development of the doctrine of intellectual equality inherent in speaker-audience
relationships presaged the decline of the innovator and the
threat of "sudden intellectual revolutions."[7]

Established as well as newly created schools experimented with programs in popular adult education. In 1869,
Cornell University sponsored a short-lived extension lecture program featuring appearances of Louis Agassiz,
James Russell Lowell, and Theodore Dwight. The effort
was timid and was launched without the prior establishment
of definite goals. About the same time there appeared a
correspondence school, the Society to Encourage Studies at
Home. While these ventures quickly collapsed, the
Chautauqua Movement, begun in 1874 as a development of
Dr. John H. Vincent's instruction of Sunday School teachers,
became a permanent landmark in the history of adult education. The summer open air meetings excited the imagination of an Ohio businessman, who helped finance their
expansion into a large scale adult education enterprise. The
popularity of the sessions on the shore of Lake Chautauqua,
New York, and the subsequent appearance of related tent
schools throughout the country, led the German-born
historian, H. Von Holst, to describe Chautauqua meetings
as the most characteristic of American sights.[8]

The contact enjoyed by Adams and Vincent with the English extensionists, therefore, but amplified and refined
existing American adult education efforts. Vincent and
Adams incorporated into Chautauqua the teaching techniques
of lecture, syllabus, and examination. In 1887, Adams encouraged the American Library Association to sponsor
library extension courses. In 1890-91, American enthusiasts, aided by British extensionists, established in Philadelphia the American Society for the Extension of University Teaching. Before the decade was half over, major
universities in both the East and the West were also offering
extension programs.[9]

The value of the English influence must not be slighted, for it had two major effects upon the American scene. It boosted the already existing enthusiasm for adult education, and it gave the latter greater depth, continuity and direction. The extensionists had no doubt that an eager public would grasp at the opportunities they offered. If your universities won't serve you in this regard, Adams advised his readers, protest to your legislatures and draw upon local talent and that of nearby colleges. Were not the universities created for the people, began another argument. Then why bar from their benefits those who cannot attend campus classes? The concept of the university as a place for the gathering of youth for a specified period of concentrated study seemed obsolete; the universities would now go to the people. Education was to be no longer for the few, but a "natural and inalienable right;" "utter neglect of intellectual capacity is immoral," wrote Dr. Vincent. The enthusiasm of these pioneers was as boundless as their faith in man's essential goodness.[10]

Extension work, by whomever offered, possessed discipline and continuity hitherto not observed in American adult education programs. Chautauqua, which hoped to serve as a link between the colleges and the people, required "Home Papers" of those working for one of its "College Certificates." Whatever its value as a testimonial of scholarship, the certificate represented attendance at six-, eight-, or twelve-unit lecture courses, and recognition of some outside preparation. Library extension work was generally presented in twelve-lecture units, the number to which the British had gradually advanced. University-sponsored extension, however, began by offering six-lecture units, and rarely succeeded in enlarging them. While this resulted from a lack of popular interest, the enthusiasm of some students led to the permanent establishment of correspondence study in America. Chautauqua language students who voluntarily continued their study at home during the winter months wrote repeatedly for advice from their summertime instructor, William R. Harper. To expedite his replies, Harper worked out study aids for distribution by mail. In 1882, Chautauqua formally adopted correspondence as a method of instruction, preceding comparable British developments by about five years. When in 1891, Harper became president of the University of Chicago, he added extension work, including correspondence courses, to the school's program.[11]

The lists of extension courses reflect the primary interests of extension pioneers. They reveal an emphasis upon
general rather than specialized, vocational education. This
does not mean that work with immediate job value, other
than to teachers, was entirely neglected, but offerings in
algebra, chemistry and strength of materials were overshadowed by those in history, economics, and political
science. The problem of recruiting faculties to teach these
courses was sometimes difficult, for extension still had an
aura of newness and vulgar popularization. The names of
young men who were later to hold high rank in American
education, however, appear frequently in such positions —
Charles M. Andrews, Edward Bemis, Richard T. Ely,
William Harper, E. P. Cheyney, J. C. Freeman and
Frederick Jackson Turner —a brilliant array of promising
talent which represented such varied schools as Princeton,
Harvard, Bryn Mawr, Johns Hopkins, and the Universities
of Pennsylvania and Wisconsin.

The appearance and actions of many of these men defied
the popular stereotype of the academician as a stuffy gray-
beard. They dared not only to lecture outside their university classrooms, but to challenge assumptions accepted by
many as hallowed truths. Among these innovators were
Edward Bemis and Richard T. Ely. Bemis pioneered
Buffalo library extension work in the winter of 1887/88,
presenting a series of twelve lectures on contemporary
problems: "Causes of Discontent," "Socialism and Anarchy,"
"Henry George's Theory of Rent Taxation," monopolies,
immigration, labor organizations and legislation. During
subsequent winters, he presented his course in Canton, Ohio,
and St. Louis. Bemis did not confine his efforts to the lecture room. He visited such politically prominent men as
William McKinley, whom he found "ready to listen attentive-
ly" to his arguments in support of municipal ownership of
public utilities. He also maintained close contact with his
friend and sometime colleague, Richard T. Ely, professor
of political economy at Johns Hopkins.[12]

Ely's name was already likely to provoke heated controversy. Views expressed in his Johns Hopkin's seminars had
been spread through lectures at Cornell, whose President
Andrew D. White encouraged him to publish them. Ely challenged the deterministic doctrines of both the Right and the
Left. He denounced laissez faire as an embodiment of selfishness that could but lead to destruction, and "atheistic
materialism" as but a means of using "pretended natural

law" to consecrate slavery. Ely urged the churches to as-
sert themselves in social matters by developing "productive
and cooperative associations on a Christian basis." The
result would be the rewinning of the respect and allegiance
of the masses. Ely's views helped to round out the teachings
of the Social Gospel, and were given concrete expression in
the efforts of the American Home Missionary Society to
employ "the evangelization of the foreign element" in combatting the spread of European radicalism in America.[13]

On another level, Ely and like-minded young economists
and churchmen organized the American Economics Association. The Association served as a rallying point in the fight
against the doctrines of the classical economists, the advocates of Social Darwinism, and those who found comfort or
a rationale in their views. Bemis organized local chapters
of the Association and left them in the wake of his extension
courses. Ely augmented his own work at Chautauqua
sessions by helping to bring in such exponents of the Social
Gospel as Washington Gladden and Josiah Strong, who characterized Ely as "doing much to hasten the kingdom where-
in dwelleth righteousness."[14]

The ideals and goals of these American extensionists
sprang from their discontent with industrial society's tendency to produce concentrations of wealth and the power
based upon them. They sprang from their discontent with
the world of Carnegie and Rockefeller as defined by Herbert
Spencer and William Graham Sumner and from their unwillingness to accept the definitions of Marx and Engels.
The extensionists were buoyed by optimism and faith—optimism regarding the goodness and capability of men, and
faith in the ability of education to emphasize these qualities;
optimism regarding the future and faith that Christianity
and democracy contained the seeds of a social milieu in
which reason and humanitarianism could become dominant.
The histories of societies were not inescapably predeter-
mined; men were not necessarily the helpless pawns of
"forces" over which they had no control. It was important
to the extensionists that many people be educated to share
this outlook, for was not the success of the broadened
franchise dependent upon a high "general intelligence?" How
better could this be developed than by bringing churchmen,
statesmen and humanitarians to public platforms from which
they could "mold and inspire for the right?" Adams saw in
Chautauqua work "religion realized in life and culture in
practical, not merely theoretical ways or barren creeds."

Theodore Roosevelt, still to enunciate his New Nationalism, saw such efforts as "fraught with good to the nation."[15]

The extension movement was not without its critics. To the skeptical, Chautauqua was a "mixture of science, fresh air, flirtation, Greek reminiscences, and devoutness .... a guerilla high school." University Extension was a "guerilla college" which fruitlessly drained the energies of the nation's educators. From another point of view, one of Ely's readers concluded that he was either a socialist or "the most cold-blooded social anatomist in existence." Those whom Bemis described as "selfish" upper class groups, deemed his and Ely's doctrines subversive.[16] Extension work was to come under increasing fire both for its strenuous popularization and for the views given currency by some of its leaders. Extensionists did not pretend that their courses were of university grade. De Tocqueville's appraisal of the American intellectual character seemed borne out half a century later in Dr. Vincent's instructions to Ely regarding plans for a Chautauqua text book. Specifications included securing an author with a national reputation who would present in popular fashion whatever material he had at hand, stressing principles without presenting "too many facts to be remembered."[17] On the other hand, the contact, however brief and limited, which countless thousands gained with higher education through the various adult education programs helped pave the way for the increased college enrollments of the future. Many adults who had glimpsed new intellectual horizons resolved that their children would enjoy the educational opportunities they had missed. Regarding the charge of partisanship, there was no doubt that some extensionists were popularizing theses abhorrent to many. This criticism was soon to be complicated by the direct and indirect subsidies provided extension by several states. This brought legislatures and interested tax-payers into the picture. Ely's coming to the University of Wisconsin paved the way for the state's first experiment with University Extension, but also touched off significant discussions regarding the place of the school and the professor in American society.

The Farmers' Institutes

The farmer today furnishes the brawn and the strength
of the community, but he is not a manager, he does not
make the laws, he does not move the forces of society
... and why? Because of his mistaken notion that farming is a work of the hands purely, and not a work of the
head.

—William D. Hoard, 1885

In these words addressed to the Wisconsin State Agricultural Society, William Dempster Hoard, dairyman and agricultural publicist articulated the feelings of those farmers who
were beginning to believe that the solution to their economic
problems lay elsewhere than in longer and harder hours of
work or direct political action.[1] The men and women who
farmed the sandy soil along Lake Michigan and the richer
land of the hills of southern and western Wisconsin had in
large part fought their own battles to achieve whatever
place they held on the economic and social scale. Agricultural skills were handed from the older to the younger
generations, and with them philosophies of life—and often
mortgages. The maxim "Find what's selling and grow all
you can" led many Wisconsin farmers into almost frenzied
concentration upon the growing of hops and then wheat.
Plant diseases and the opening of new agricultural areas in
the West hurt many of these growers badly, leaving them
unable to pay for the new lands and machinery they had purchased in their ill-advised optimism. Individual futures and
a way of life were threatened, not only in Wisconsin, but by
similar circumstances elsewhere. Desperately, some farmers turned to third parties, but such movements did not
flower in Wisconsin as they did in neighboring states. A
partial explanation lies in the successful efforts of those
who encouraged farmers to build more satisfactory economic
bases of diversified farming and dairying. By the time
Populism had developed as a major political movement,
Wisconsin was well on its way to assuming the title "America's Dairyland." This development was not achieved, however, without an answer being provided to Hoard's original
challenge and to its corollary: "We hear a good deal said
about improving the breed of cattle. But what shall we do to

15

improve the breed of farmer? The agricultural brain must
be stimulated to understand the great destiny which lies before it, and the responsibilities that bear upon it."[2]

Hope lay in an organized program of rural adult education.
Hoard and men who paralleled or sympathized with his point
of view—Professor W. A. Henry, Director of the University
of Wisconsin Experimental Station, C. E. Estabrook,
member of the state legislature from Milwaukee, Governor
Jeremiah Rusk, William F. Vilas, lawyer, politician, and
University regent—formulated from their Wisconsin experiences and observations plans similar to those of Josiah
Holbrook in Massachusetts earlier in the century. There
was, however, a major difference between the programs of
Holbrook and of Hoard. Whereas the former programs
centered about private contributions and self-help, the latter, while begun under private auspices, were brought to
fruition within a tax-supported institution, the state
University.

The roles played by the University administration and
faculty were forced upon them by community pressures.
For years, University men had periodically entertained the
idea of preparing students for the seemingly ungenteel vo-
cations connected with farming and industry. Fear of a loss
of students to Michigan State College, which was pioneering
an agricultural curriculum, and desire for Land Grant College funds had proved but temporary spurs to such planning,
however. Limited offerings in business and general science
were made available, but the curriculum remained predom-
inantly classical.[3] The school remained aloof from the
everyday life of the state; the professor seemed to possess
a status remote from that of the farmer, the clerk, or the
factory worker. The fewer than 500 students annually enrolled in the University before the mid-1880's represented
still fewer communities. Though even well into the new
century an investigator could define the campus as still
somewhat isolated from the larger community,[4] town and
gown relations had by then virtually been revolutionized.

For several decades, the University of Wisconsin claimed
Land Grant College funds without adequately fulfilling the
obligations imposed by the Act. The three-year course
offered farm boys in 1867 was based primarily upon existing general science courses, a situation which the school
tried to justify by explaining that it was giving farm youth
instruction which they could not receive at home. A two-
year course open to farm boys proficient in reading, spell-

ing, penmanship, geography, grammar, and history proved
no more popular.[5] Farm leaders grew impatient with the
University's failure to grant youths planning to be farmers
opportunities similar to those available to students interested in the humanities. Many farmers were already aware
of the advantages and opportunities available through edu-
cation-research programs. The University Experimental
Stations' published reports had proved invaluable to them.
So, too, though in a much more limited sense, had the work
of the Wisconsin Dairymen's Association, which privately
was attempting to popularize dairying. The latter work was
restricted in scope and effectiveness, and success awaited
more adequate sponsorship.[6]

Late in 1884, rural impatience for University aid led to
demands for the establishment of a separate agricultural
college. The alarmed University regents hastened to block
the move, which threatened an end to federal funds and a
decrease in the institution's influence. The secession attempt was checked by the regents' promise to introduce a
practical course for agricultural students, and legislative
action establishing University sponsored Farmers' Institutes.[7] The University Catalogue of 1885–86 acknowledged
that the old agriculture course had been too expensive to be
popular. Now a twelve-week winter short course costing
about $60 was opened to farm boys over the age of sixteen.
Until 1889, when the College of Agriculture was established,
this and related work was administered by the College of
Arts and Letters. Though the action of the regents led to
ill-feeling in the faculty that was to be felt for years, it is
significant that the agricultural program was to be conducted
"under the auspices of the University."[8] The highest of the
state's educational institutions had been launched upon a
course which if decried as undignified, was, in answer, expedient, practical, and democratic. Thus did the University
of Wisconsin inaugurate a program which was to pave the
way for its leadership in the fields of agricultural education
and the off-campus instruction of men and women not formally enrolled in the institution itself.

Legislative support of the Farmers' Institute was generous. The initial appropriation of $5,000 per year was
more than doubled at the next session, surpassing by more
than half the appropriation made for similar work by the
Michigan legislature almost a decade later.[9] Attendance
records and popular reception of the work justified this
support. In 1885, the first year of Institute work, the

number of separate meetings numbered about 30. By the
end of the decade, the number had been increased to
64, and in 1910, 132 Farmers' Institutes and related
cooking schools were sponsored. The number of Institute
programs operating simultaneously in different parts of the
state was increased from two to six, and still greater expansion was checked only by a lack of money and trained
personnel. Institute records showed an attendance variation
from 20 to 1500.[10]

On foot, by horseback, buggy, and train, farmers struggled
over roads often snow-blocked and icy to attend the Institutes. At times they filled the Opera House at Hudson, over-
flowed the Salvation Army rink at Beloit, and packed town
halls, court and school houses throughout the state. The
effect of the sessions was not limited to those in actual attendance. By the mid-nineties, 60,000 Institute Proceedings,
costing the purchasers about what was received wholesale
for a dozen eggs, were distributed at the meetings and
through creameries and schools. Institute conductors understood that size alone was not a reliable index to effectiveness. One of the most successful Institutes was a two-day
session attended by twenty farmers in a private home.[11]

The popularity of the Institutes hinged in large part upon
the solution, locally provided, for a perennial problem.
H. E. Huxley, Head Worthy Master of the Wisconsin Grange,
phrased it affirmatively when he stated that "farmers as a
class work too hard and think too little." But think along
what lines? American farmers heard the question debated
on many occasions. The farmer must think beyond making
two blades of grass grow where there had been but one, ran
one argument. He has many roles to play, and must be prepared for all of them. As a producer, he should be versed
in economics; as a citizen, in political science; but above
all, as a "man," he must maintain a close relationship with
the great thinkers of all ages. Combining his normal out-
door labor with a study of literature, he stood to become a
tower of physical strength, character, and resolution which
the sedentary city dweller could but envy. The counter argument asserted that such knowledge left "scant room for
common sense," that mathematics and science were the
keys both to immediate success and to an expanded "moral
nature."[12]

The Wisconsin Farmers' Institute programs were divided
into day and evening meetings. The former were clearly
"practical sessions" devoted largely to agricultural proce-

dure. The latter were general in nature, featuring music
and novelty acts, but also including discussions of school,
road, and market matters. The Wisconsin farmer felt that
his concrete problems called for concrete solutions, and he
was prone to define "concrete" in terms of time and money.
When Institute speakers seemed to lack "common sense,"
as did one who told a Green Bay audience that forty two-ton
loads of manure were necessary to start a one-acre garden,
the resulting skepticism dampened the effectiveness of
whatever else Institute men had to say.[13]

This rural preoccupation with "practicality" led a northern editor friendly to the Institutes to attack rumors that
the programs were conducted by "theoretical rather than
practical farmers." They were, he argued, supervised by
the owners and tillers of farms who had dedicated themselves to explaining in popular terms not only the "scientific mysteries of agriculture," but their own successful
careers.[14] By and large, Institute conductors and their
assistants were Wisconsinites with an intimate knowledge
of local conditions and problems, men like George Wylie of
Leeds, Charles Thorp of Burnett, and Charles Everett, who
was recruited as a staff member after making well-received
comments on the growing and use of clover. The backgrounds of Institute superintendents, however, suggest the
increasing professionalization of agriculture. W. H.
Morrison, the first Superintendent, brought to his post not
only his experience as a farmer, but as agricultural society
leader and publisher. C. P. Norgord, who resigned in 1915
to serve on the University Board of Regents, had been on
the staff of the College of Agriculture. His successor, E. L.
Luther, was a graduate of the Michigan College Agricultural
Long Course and had become State Supervisor of Wisconsin
County Agents. The list of guest speakers is also revealing;
it included Professor Stephen Babcock, Henry Wallace,
Iowa farm editor, and agricultural specialists from various
American and Canadian universities and colleges. Beneath
the homey exterior of the Institutes lay a hard core of in-
tensive specialization.

Efforts were made to keep the Institutes from seeming
pedantic and superimposed. Initiation of the sessions was
made to appear to be the work of interested local groups.
Local committees made the arrangements for the meetings,
and local ministers, editors and teachers provided the publicity. Conductors tried to impart to the Institutes the flavor
of a community festival. The popularity of two of the con-

ductors was based in no small part upon their ability to sing
well together. William D. Hoard, an ever welcome speaker,
drove home his points with shirtsleeve illustrations. Cross
breeding, he argued repeatedly, was like mixing brandy,
sugar and water. The end product was acceptable, but at
what cost to the individual ingredients! As Wisconsin farmers were urged to concentrate upon dairying, the problem
of the best corn for that purpose became a hotly debated
one. Robust "Uncle Charlie" Beach championed native
yellow dent, while his Institute colleague, wiry H. C. Adams
held forth in favor of earlier maturing southern varieties.
During one exchange, Beach petulantly referred to Adams
as being similar to his corn: early matured, but small.
Adams countered with the suggestion that Beach was like
the corn he favored: large, but never matured.[15] This was
the kind of debate that could hold the attention of the least
sophisticated members of the audience. If on the surface it
appeared unnecessarily coarse, it differed from residence
faculty rivalries in choice of words rather than in spirit.

Though the University proved sufficiently adaptable to
meet the demands and problems thrust upon it by Institute
work, its initially reluctant role led to much confusion in
statements about the venture. This confusion resulted from
the attempts of University administrators to explain what
had been done, and to lend it a dignity which they felt was
lacking. Many American educators, including those at Wisconsin, had shown increasing interest in the development of
University Extension in England. Its international popularity
became such that its label was at times attached to efforts
which bore but slight resemblance to it.

Wisconsin's President John Bascom, who resigned in
1885, understandably took little interest in the Institutes.
His successor, Thomas C. Chamberlin, however, described
them as surpassing even the English University efforts to
exert an "all-pervasive educational influence upon . . . [the]
patron community."[16] The University Catalogue, through
which President Chamberlin often expressed himself, observed that while some features of the British program
were still impractical for Wisconsin, the University had independently pioneered a movement "that may, in its full
organization and development, be not less conducive to the
common end sought." Once skeptics had doubted the feasibility of a common school education for the masses. Now
Wisconsin's success in the difficult field of agriculture
pointed the way toward almost unlimited future developments

in mass education. In line with this new approach, which
added popular education to the traditional university functions of teaching and research, President Chamberlin suggested two other steps be taken: the establishment of
Mechanics' Institutes as urban counterparts of the work
being done in rural areas, and lecture courses to meet the
needs of still other groups.[17] Whatever scope he hoped to
give the University's off-campus work, the Institutes proved
more in the tradition of the original American Lyceum
movement than in keeping with the academic and cultural
courses being offered in and around London.

Work in local communities sometimes involved the University in local bickerings, but on the whole, enabled it to
gain rapport with a new public.[18] University and farm
groups shared the rewards of favorable comments on Institute work in the British and American press, and the knowledge that other states were patterning programs upon Wisconsin's. Farmers had little chance to forget the
University's role in staving off threatened foreclosures by
enabling them to produce more efficiently.[19] In other ways,
too, the Institutes helped to bring the University and the
rural population closer. Venerable University President
C. K. Adams, who had gained prominence in agricultural
experimentation before coming to Wisconsin, used Institute
platforms to give farmers a friendly picture of the distant
and seemingly remote campus. In school, rich and poor
mingled fraternally, he asserted, and impecunious students
often had the stimulus of knowing they must do well in their
classes if they hoped for success in later life. Was the
campus atmosphere hostile to rural youth? Adams pointed
out that a plurality of students in the Colleges of Engineering and Letters and Arts listed farming as the occupation
of their fathers. Did the University overburden the tax-
payers? Adams recalled the legislator who commented that
the amount he paid in taxes each year for University support added up to the price of a glass of beer and a cigar.[20]
In deed and word, the University donned overalls to make
farmers less suspicious of the academic gown.

The first University-sponsored Farmers' Institute was
held in Hudson, St. Croix County, November 24-5, 1885.
The fall work was done; it was the Thanksgiving season.
Days in advance, local committees planned and worked to
make the "mutual exchange of thought among farmers" attractive to farm wives as well as their husbands. Coöperation came from many quarters. Hotels promised reduced

rates, the railroads, long criticized by Wisconsin farm
groups, announced special round trip fares.[21] The Hudson
program was a forerunner of many hundreds and set the
pattern of business and discussion sessions interspersed
with music and other entertainment. Politicians and well-
known farm leaders mingled with crowds in holiday mood.
The Insitutes offered not only information, but release from
the narrow contacts of pre-automobile rural life.

Institute programs were geared to local needs, but local
problems tended to fall within certain broad categories.
Wisconsin farmers were becoming ever more painfully
aware of competition from outside the state, from the owners
of the vast, new wheat fields of the West and from the manufacturers of "bogus butter," oleomargarine. Prices for farm
products were low, those for what the farmer bought, high.
Farm boys and girls were leaving for the city in increasing
numbers. Should the affected farmers cease the struggle
here and try again elsewhere? Was there a way to make
farming pay a satisfactory return?

Institute speakers tried to make farm life both attractive
and profitable, and in so doing indirectly insured the social
and political conservatism of the Wisconsin farmer. On this
latter point, the Institutes paralleled British extension and
Lyceum. Speakers urged farm boys to "begin to dig right
where you are and stick to it," to take the fullest advantage
of the timber and water which were more abundant in Wisconsin than in many other states. Cities were painted as
places whose bright lights but beckoned to degradation,
poverty, and prostitution.[22] And yet, country life had to be
improved as well as defended if the young were to be encouraged to use their talents for rural rather than urban
development. Rural schools had to stress not only the subjects whose application would lead to fine homes and good
clothes, but also the nobility of work.[23] All this the Institutes
urged, and more.

Increasing attention was paid to the roles of farm wives
and mothers in preserving and encouraging family coöperation and values. Through the regular programs and finally
special cooking schools, women received information not
only about gardening and dairying, but about modernizing
their homes and making them attractive. How should
mothers deal with boys caught using tobacco? Invite them to
sit in the most comfortable chair in the living room and
provide them with cuspidors, they were advised, and
chances were that the offenders would abandon the practice.

In more serious vein, women were encouraged to make their
meals both interesting and nutritious. One might question
the effects upon hearty and largely self-sufficient farm
wives of a Milwaukee cooking teacher's advice to hold the
egg beater "as nearly horizontal as possible" and on how to
cook eggs, but it was at these sessions that many received
their first information about calories and food values. It
was here, too, that they were briefed with arguments to convince their husbands that kitchen sinks were as necessary
as windmills and field machinery. The conspiracy against
farm husbands was complete. While their wives were being
taught the value of serving fish balls and asparagus, the
men were being told of the necessity of home refrigeration
units and how to make them.[24] The Institutes were concerned with the technology of the kitchen and pantry as well
as that of barn and field, with the mechanics of family relations as well as of prices.

However wide their range, the Institutes focused
primarily upon placing Wisconsin farming on a
firmer basis. In urging farmers to abandon wheat raising
and to turn to dairying, the Institutes became a tax-supported amplification of the Wisconsin Dairymen's Association. In this regard, Institute work was divided into two
major parts: popularizing or improving dairying, and helping convinced farmers meet the new problems for which
their training had ill prepared them. The advantage of raising cattle instead of wheat was hotly debated at the first
Institute, but gradually more attention could be given the
problems of transition. The Adams-Beach debates were a
part of the adaptation process; so, too, were the blunt statements that the popularity of butter substitutes resulted from
the inferiority of much of the butter placed on the market.
Institute meetings offered correctives, along with information on stable management of cattle, milk handling and
principles of breeding—the latter meeting open to men only.
W. C. Bradley, for many years the oldest of the Institute
conductors, advised farmers in the use and care of farm
machinery. The silo, that adjunct and symbol of dairy farming, was introduced widely by the Institutes.[25]

In some circumstances, the Institutes urged farmers to
greater economic surety through growing foodstuffs for
home consumption, raising hogs, or breaking the businessman's monopoly on horse breeding.[26] Whatever the emphasis, however, Institute men insisted on the necessity of
applying business methods to agriculture, of planning in

advance and selling as skillfully as possible. "The businessman is no brainier than we," one speaker assured his
audience, and by using his methods, farming can be made
the safest of enterprises. Competition was inevitable, but
worthwhile, for in it lay the spur to success.[27] At the same
time that the farmer was urged into more purposeful individual action, even the early Institutes demonstrated the
advantage of collective activity in the fields of marketing
and the securing and improving of roads. And were not the
Institutes themselves group-sponsored for individual and
ultimately group benefit?

Some farmers remained unconvinced that Institute-type
advice was an answer to their problems and looked instead
toward political action. Since the Civil War, the federal
government had served the large financial and industrial
interests well; perhaps agriculture's interests could be
similarly advanced if farmers could win control of the
national political machinery. Increasing numbers of farm
foreclosures made the matter more than academic. Although
Wisconsin farmers did not turn to direct political action
with the same fervor as some of their neighbors, there
were those who counselled such action. Many sympathized
with the Brodhead farmer who championed the People's
Party as offering a solution to the problem created by merchants whose retail prices were double those paid the farmer. In 1894, however, when South Carolina sent Ben Tillman
to the United States Senate to sit beside five other Populists,
Wisconsin voters returned the state to a Republican administration. Improved economic conditions—in which the
Farmers' Institutes played a vital role—were in part responsible. Institute Superintendent William H. Morrison
estimated that if the Institutes had contributed but one-tenth
to the increased value of the state's annual butter production, they had contributed $80,000 to the industry. Also
involved were the efforts of men like William D. Hoard, who
saw in compulsory school attendance a means of buttressing
conservatism.[28]

On the surface, the Farmers' Institutes were nonpolitical,
and recent students have repeated the statement that Institute leaders consciously sought to avoid those pitfalls into
which the Grangers had fallen.[29] Yet so interwoven were
economics, outlook on life, and politics, that any discussion
of farm problems was bound to have implicit or explicit
political overtones. Improved economic status, aided by the
Institutes, undoubtedly played a role in the political con-

servatism exhibited in rural Wisconsin. So, too, did the
linking of the terms "business" and "farmer," and attempts
to make the farmer feel a kinship with the businessman.
One Institute speaker pointed out that the mercantile business, no less than farming, had its disagreeable aspects,
not the least of which was tedious routine. H. S. Adams,
dairyman, fruit grower, and politician who had helped pass
the bill establishing the Institutes, defended the political
status quo by telling farmers that their painted barns and
good fences invalidated complaints about economic distress.
If the farmer envied the businessman, he admonished
further, he would do well to recall that he had had the same
chance to make money. If the farmer berated the politician,
he would do well to recall that the average politician was no
less honest than the average farmer.[30]

As the Populist movement began to take concrete form,
Charles Beach sternly rebuked those farmers who regarded
it as the means to a panacea. Dissecting the Populist platform, he accepted its planks opposing alien land ownership
and demanding a more equitable tax structure. He approved
government-financed roads and education programs, but
denounced attacks upon trusts and corporations and the proposals that the railroads be nationalized. How could farmers legitimately demand an end to existing monopolies while
planning their own, he asked. How could they demand special privileges when it was a truism that there can be "no
real antagonism between the legitimate business interests
of any country." As for the railroads, had they not been
brought to time within the existing political framework, and
were not their rates lower than those in England? And what
of the hope that political control would lead to economic advantage? Beach concluded that "Government never has nor
ever can have any power over the law of supply and demand."
Briefly, Populism was selfish, unworkable, and unrealistic.[31]

As the nation neared the presidential election year of
1896, General Lucius Fairchild told Wisconsin farmers that
their grumblings about hard times did not square with the
facts, that their pleasure carriages and musical instruments
were indexes of prosperity that by far surpassed that enjoyed in Europe. On the eve of the election, another Institute speaker reiterated this thesis and urged his audience
to "make amends for our past shiftlessness" and to trans-
form their farms into "the dwelling places of a self-depend-
ent, a self-centered, happy people." [32] It is true that these
were the views of individuals, many of whom were not either

farmers or on the University payroll. But these statements
of political and economic morality were addressed to Farmers' Institute audiences and, more important, were included
in the Institute Handbook issued by the University of
Wisconsin.

The popularity and success of Institute work demonstrated to the University not only that it could meet the non-
academic educational demands of its patron community, but
that it could use such efforts to effect closer contact with it.
For their part, participating farmers gained economically
and socially. Through the more skillful selection and efficient production of crops, many approached the ideal busi-
nessman-farmer described by Institute speakers. While the
early Institutes tended to foster economic individualism
and competition on the one hand, they did much to promote
a quickening of community life. Their festival atmosphere
and exhortations to take certain types of common action
typified the latter stress. So, too, did the efforts to improve
rural home life, to give the farmer broader geographical
and intellectual horizons, and to encourage the public appearances of local people with information to impart or
talent to display.

To some observers, the Institutes constituted "about the
only direct cash appropriation for the sole benefit of farmers," or at least the rural equivalent of the city night
schools. By all means, let us keep the Institute program,
opined one farmer, but only until something better can be
developed. Then "crowd it out." The Farmers' Institutes
were to remain an important part of the Wisconsin agricultural scene for several decades more. Changing times were
to result in a lessening emphasis upon laissez faire, until
immediately preceding World War I, merchants and pro-
cessors were to condemn the coöperative marketing and
purchasing advice of the Institute speakers. Meanwhile, the
University had launched upon a second phase of its off-
campus work, University Extension.

General Extension in Wisconsin First Phase

[The mission of University Extension is the] extension of knowledge among people too old to go to school and who are unable to give their entire time to study; the cultivation of habits of useful reading, correct thinking and right conduct; the stimulation of intellectual life, for the purpose of making better citizens, inducing social progress and rendering the conditions of society at large more interesting and enjoyable.

—Professor J. C. Freeman, 1895

It is understandable that farm folk flocked to the sessions of the Farmers' Institutes. Mingling with neighbors ordinarily isolated by rural travel conditions was itself rewarding, and attentive listening could be translated into future profits. But even amidst the talk of animal husbandry and silos appeared evidence of interest in more than the immediate and material. Perhaps the entertainment programs lacked sophistication, but they were not directed at a sophisticated audience. As yet, neither agricultural technology nor the revered red school house afforded conditions conducive to the deeper development of esthetic interests. It would be the grossest error, however, to dismiss the farmers as clods. They insisted upon a degree of formal education for their children, owned books and musical instruments, and were enthusiastic about elocution. Some few even attended the adult education programs that later developed in Madison.

Wisconsin's towns and cities, however, housed concentrations of people possessing the backgrounds and leisure for at least probing areas deemed cultural. Numerous literary, debating and music societies testified to this interest, as did the continued popularity of the platform lecture. Reformers, critics, and travellers could usually attract appreciative audiences, and speaking programs were still a successful means of raising money. While most people came simply to listen, not all audiences were passive. In 1886, a group of Madison women assembled for an enthusiastic and sustained study of European history. Mrs. Anne

Sheldon's Monday Afternoon History Class became one of
the city's cultural landmarks as year after year interested
students assembled not only to hear lectures, but to read
papers and to discuss their assignments. The tenor of the
work and the way it was received is revealed in a notation
by the group's secretary.

> We have visited quaint old Nuremberg and beautiful
> Carcasonne. We have been in Paris with Julius Caesar
> and under Catherine de Medici. We have triumphed with
> Richelieu and plotted with Mazarin . . . and as a result
> . . . . We are happier women—we should be better and
> nobler women for having felt the beat of life with noble
> hearts that have throbbed in past centuries and for
> having caught the glow of their inspiration.[1]

It is impossible to separate satisfactorily the desire for
the rewards of serious study from the desire for learning
as "ornament," but here was a field which the commercial
booking agents could not supply. While Madison was fortunate to possess the academic leadership to fill such needs,
elsewhere culture seekers often had to rely upon occasional
guest lecturers and upon leaders whose chief qualification
was enthusiasm. As the century entered its last decade,
however, Wisconsin University, state normal school, and
private college faculties, for reasons of their own, decided
that this was a field worth exploiting.

Both the normal schools and the University already had
experience with nonresidence students. The audiences had
been composed of teachers, who, in view of the sketchy
requirements for teaching eligibility, had few years of advanced formal education. Around the time of the Civil War,
the legislature, Normal School Board and State Superintendent had coöperated in reviving the Teachers' Institutes of
early statehood days. Though in the beginning the work was
valuable, lack of funds with which to bring in first-rate conductors, and the development of an unfortunate attitude
among the participants, led to its degeneration. In 1892,
The Wisconsin Journal of Education, organ of the State
Teachers' Association, complained that the institutes had
become Meccas for those seeking advanced certification
without accompanying effort. Women and education students
lacking serious purpose had come to dominate the audiences, and fruitful discussion had disappeared.[2]

Creation of the normal school system temporarily curtailed, but did not terminate, the University's role in

teacher training. Desire to eliminate its student prepara-
tory program while maintaining a smooth flow of well-
prepared entering freshmen led in 1880 to inspecting and
accrediting of high schools. As in England, supervision led
to teacher education. In 1884, a chair of Science and Art of
Teaching was established on the campus, and three years
later, the legislature authorized institute classes which
President Thomas C. Chamberlin regarded as essentially
University Extension work.[3] With the inauguration in 1888
of summer classes for teachers, the University was again
deep in the field of teacher training. This extension of its
work into fields for which specialized schools had already
been created added the normals to the list of institutions
with which the University seemed to be competing for
students and influence. Even before it was formally organized as a branch of the University, extension work served
as the University's field representative and provoked the
hostility of those whose positions it appeared to jeopardize.

In 1888, too, University faculty members took other as-
pects of University activity beyond the campus. Professor
William F. Allen, who had helped stimulate the thinking of
Frederick Jackson Turner, suggested initiation of popular
history lectures similar to those already common in the
East. With the aid of Turner, who as a graduate student at
Johns Hopkins had had close contact with its extension program, and Reuben Gold Thwaites, Secretary of the State
Historical Society, he presented six lectures on the History
of the Northwest to the Contemporary Club of Madison. The
success of the initial effort assured its continuation. In
1890/91, Turner's lecture series on North American Colo-
nization attracted encouraging audiences in cities near
Madison.[4]

The value of these programs as indexes of interest in adult
education was limited. Although reading lists and syllabi
similar to those used in English university extension accompanied these lectures, there was no way of determining the
extent of their use. The fact that audiences did turn out to
at least listen, however, led President Chamberlin to
believe that cultural off-campus work could be successfully
added to the major functions of the University. Early in the
development of the Farmers' Institutes, he had felt that
English-type extension was as yet impractical in Wisconsin.
But late in 1890, he cautiously informed the State Teachers'
Association that the state seemed ready for such a "diversion from daily work." For the cities, he envisioned

University-based lecture courses; for sparsely settled
areas, correspondence lessons. President Chamberlin
warned that while such work might place undue strain upon
the parent body, its potential rewards made it worth the
risk.[5]

Chamberlin and his colleagues saw in extension more
than an instrument for carrying culture into the hinterland.
It could serve to better prepare young men and women for
later work at the University, an end the school was already
indirectly pursuing through its Education Department. In
addition, Chamberlin and Turner had reached the same
conclusion as President William R. Harper of the University of Chicago, namely that extension could advertise the
University, increasing both its prestige and its enrollment.[6]
The Farmers' Institutes had proved a means of bringing
together the University and one segment of the state's
population. Now a still broader meeting ground could be
developed.

From yet another point of view might Turner have been
interested in such activity. He had not yet gained national
recognition, but widely read Wisconsin observers were already anticipating aspects of his work. An 1887 editorial in
the Milwaukee Journal warned of the danger to American
institutions posed by the great influx of immigrants unacquainted with American traditions. Several years later
Turner wrote of the need for forging America's new millions
into a "national unity" based upon the "working out of original social ideals and social adjustments." From either
standpoint, the situation called for enlightened leaders and
an enlightened citizenry. A far-reaching extension program
could help provide both.[7]

In June, 1891, the University regents acted favorably
upon faculty recommendations for a limited extension program. Though no funds or full-time administrators were
provided, the future held promise. The effort had a potentially receptive audience, the active support of the president, and a strong faculty upon which to draw. Two crucial
questions remained to be answered, however. Would the
work, as Chamberlin hoped, prove so popular as to become
administered in large part by interested local groups?
Were the stipulations which limited University faculty to
weekend extension appearances adequate to prevent interference with campus obligations? Wisconsin optimists assumed affirmative answers. But even as the University's
experiment was unfolding, George Herbert Palmer, writing

in the Atlantic Monthly on extension work generally could
not agree. In terms of genuine benefits gained, extension
was not worth the drain upon the parent body, he warned.[8]

But there was no time for foreboding. Adult education
enthusiasts developed and popularized countless programs
throughout the country, in time competing for the leisure
interests of men and women of all walks of life. Amidst
fanfare and fluttering banners, Madison itself became a
summertime haven for these devotees. Besides the University program, the Monona Lake Assembly, tearing a page
from Chautauqua's history, offered a combined summer
outing and what one observer called a "grand intellectual
banquet." The fare was varied. William Graham Sumner
and Washington Gladden presented their opposed views on
laissez faire. Professor John Fiske of Harvard lectured
on Virginian and early American history; Hamilton W.
Mabie theorized about American society and literature.
From the same platform General John B. Gordon effusively
relived the last days of the Confederacy, and a speaker
wearing chains described prison life in Siberia. Adult education opportunities were still further increased when in
the mid-nineties Madison became the meeting place for
the Columbian Catholic Summer School. Boasting a faculty
recruited from church schools both in the United States and
Europe, the program added color to the Madison scene. The
University, Extension, the Monona Lake Assembly, the
Catholic Summer School and the springtime appearances of
Ella Wheeler Wilcox—little wonder that Herbert Baxter
Adams described the city as one of the "best centers of
academic and popular education in the great Northwest,"
and an exuberant journalist labeled it the "Western
Athens."[9]

The University extension programs offered the state at
large were sober by comparison with the summer revivals.
Frederick Jackson Turner continued his lectures in American History, and other residence faculty members were
convinced of the value of offering courses. Professors J. C.
Freeman and Julius Olson made available series in English
and Scandinavian literature; Professor F. L. Van Cleef
presented Greek governments; Professor J. B. Parkinson
lectured in economics; Dr. H. C. Tolman, on the antiquities
of India and Iran. There were offerings, too, in the
sciences: Professors C. R. Barnes, E. A. Birge, R. D.
Salisbury, and Dr. H. B. Loomis were available for courses
in the physiology of plants, bacteriology, geology and

electricity.[10] It remained, now, for local communities to
demonstrate their receptivity.

Chamberlin and Turner attempted to insure widespread
interest by bringing in a widely recognized scholar to supervise the work. The newcomer's role would be a complex
one, for it was also intended that he make the University
the leading graduate school in the Northwest, freeing it
from serving as a "feeder to Chicago." Here, too, extension
could help to win popular support for an undertaking that
would require additional legislative appropriations. One
must not lose sight, however, of the planners' enthusiasm
for spreading knowledge. Turner's work in many adult
education programs, some of them outside the state, and
his reputation as a residence teacher are evidence enough
of his sincerity as an educator.

The man chosen for the extension post was Richard T.
Ely of Johns Hopkins, a well-known scholar, Chautauqua
pioneer, close associate of Social Gospel leaders, and one
of Turner's former teachers. His rich background and
known energy promised much. Ely was attracted to Wisconsin with promises of chairmanship of a department of his
own creation. The department of Civics, Sociology and
Historical Science was the result. In addition, Turner
worked closely with him through correspondence, paving
the way for the work ahead. Ely hoped to win powerful state
interests to the support of his work, and Turner made numerous, though futile, efforts to gain the financial backing
of "hard headed Wisconsin capitalists."[11] At the same time,
however, Turner found an eager extension supporter in
R. C. Spencer, founder of the People's Institute of
Milwaukee. The Institute was an outgrowth of the Working
People's Reading Room, which had been founded after an
outburst of labor unrest to teach workers that the rewards
of education were life's most worth-while goals. In the
interests of social peace, Spencer was now trying to take
this message to all groups, and saw in extension a means
of integrating the activities of all of the city's scientific,
artistic, literary and industrial organizations in a manner
reminiscent of the Lyceum efforts of Josiah Holbrook.[12]

Ely's arrival was heralded by an enthusiastic press and
celebrations on the one hand, and misunderstandings on the
other. His addition to the University staff upset the system
of faculty promotions. Even his relations with Chamberlin,
who was leaving Wisconsin for a post at the University of
Chicago, and with Turner became strained after his charges

that they had failed to satisfactorily prepare the way for
him. Observers outside the University were both hopeful
and cynical regarding the future. Spencer felt that his
prayers for the "rejuvenation and elevation" of the community were about to be answered; " . . . the spirit seems to be
moving upon the face of the deep," he noted. To George
Herron, a Social Gospel leader, however, things were
doubtful. "Wisconsin is a state pronounced for its secular-
ities," he warned Ely, and "Milwaukee is a city of infidels
and brewers" who control both political parties.[13] Certainly
these forces would not tolerate Ely's brand of economic
evangelism.

Ely quickly placed his stamp upon extension. With him
came two of his Johns Hopkins students, F. W. Speirs and
Lyman P. Powell. Speirs supervised the People's Institute-
Extension work in Milwaukee. Powell served as part-time
extension lecturer and secretary, with the first task of
organizing extension class centers throughout the state.
The mechanics of the program were based upon Chautauqua
precedents.[14]

Powell worked to persuade local groups to sponsor extension programs on community-wide bases. Since extension was without direct state subsidy, financing was a local
responsibility. Despite advice from extension headquarters,
this responsibility was often hard to discharge. Fees of
$60 per six-lecture series were eventually raised to
$70 or $100 depending upon the rank of the lecturer. In an
effort to raise these sums, several devices were attempted.
The wealthy sponsors upon whom Ely and Powell counted
failed to appear. In Milwaukee, Speirs tried to develop a
"distinctly fashionable" series of lectures appealing to the
well-to-do, but found a singular lack of interest among
"prominent society women."[15] It quickly became apparent
that the range of extension enthusiasts was limited, and
that the financial burden would be borne by an handful of
people. The local mainstays of extension were the teachers
and church and social clubs whose members made house to
house ticket sales and opened their homes to the speakers.
Help came, too, from the railroads, which allowed extensionists special rate privileges even after the practice had
become embarrassing to both the University and the carriers
themselves.[16]

The lectures which Wisconsin audiences attended in
church parlors, public school and municipal auditoriums, a
room in the State Capitol building, and in one instance a

blacksmith shop were designed to treat a branch of literature or science in a manner "lying between classroom work
and popular lectures." Each presentation was complete in
itself, while remaining an integral part of a six-lecture
unit. Extension lecturers found it necessary to break further
and further from their classroom methods. Technical
terms and references were abandoned in conscious efforts
to present the thoughts of the academicians in the vernacu-
lar of the layman.[17] If the lecturers hoped to reach their
audiences, they had to meet them at least halfway. Here
there were no means of forcing class members to meet
certain standards; they had to be enticed into the spirit of
the course. In the long run, it was a losing struggle. A few
students attended for the University credit available upon
the completion of certain additional requirements. Not
many more, the professors found, were sufficiently interested to do other than listen politely. Efforts to promote
class discussion were fruitless, a situation reminiscent of
the revived Teachers' Institutes. Members were eager and
voluble concerning personal experiences or current events,
but silent on the major issues at hand.[18] During the first
year of the program, 8,500 persons attended the lectures.
Of these, 4,500 participated to some extent in class work,
but a mere 127 took final examinations. Of the latter, only
93 received credit should they ever enroll at the University,
indicating, at least, that academic standards were not
lowered in order to promote campus attendance.[19]

In line with President Chamberlin's original plans, correspondence courses were finally offered in 1896. They,
too, could be undertaken for University credit or not and
could reasonably have been expected to attract more serious students than the lectures. The two-dollar fee per eight-
lesson unit placed the offerings within the range of many,
and even work toward the Ph.D. was available. In this case,
however, it was extension rather than the audience that
proved disappointing. Faculty members who were cajoled
or badgered into presenting such courses in addition to
their campus duties were often remiss about correcting
and commenting upon submitted lessons. While some students appreciated the attention shown them, more grumbled
about slowness in returning their papers or the lack of
criticism accorded them. The extension office was virtually
helpless in the matter, and was forced to concede failure.
Its quick withdrawal of the work was entirely warranted.[20]

Whatever the failure of the lecture program to meet an

ideal set of standards, as long as people kept attending
there was hope that something beneficial was being
achieved. Until the middle of the decade, people did come,
and for a few years, in increasing numbers. They heard
Professor Freeman's stereopticon lectures on literature,
M. V. O'Shea argue that the public schools be responsible
for a return to the Greek ideal of physical education, and
George C. Comstock, the perenially popular director of
Washburn Observatory speculate on the "cold, dark, and
lifeless condition" toward which the earth was heading.
Through the economics classes of Professor William A.
Scott many received their first introduction to the works of
Richard T. Ely, Washington Gladden, Edward Bemis, T. V.
Powderly, Edward Bellamy, Karl Marx, and the Fabians.
Under other instructors, they became acquainted with bac-
teriology, geology, and indeed a fair sampling of the work
offered in residence.[21]

Through their campus and extension work, Ely and his
closest aides brought economic, social and political theory
into everyday life. Ely's study of public utilities provided
arguments for those favoring municipal ownership. Officials
of state institutions attended Ely's Madison classes, and
the State Conference of Charities and Corrections was
organized as a link between the campus and these institutions. Wisconsin's first woman Ph.D., an Ely student, went
at once into settlement house work in Pittsburg. Another
student, H. H. Jacobs, helped establish the University-
sponsored settlement house in Milwaukee, and became its
warden. Amos P. Wilder's classes heard lectures on "The
Government of Cities," and discussed such municipal problems as the relationship between "organized saloon power
and inferior officials." Wilder went beyond description, and
urged "municipal patriots" to establish reform clubs and
to Americanize the people of the slums.[22] University professors as such were going beyond classroom teaching and
deliberately entering political life.

Ely's public lectures on socialism were important in an
era of much loose talk about foreign ideologies. One prominent businessman and community leader wrote that before
attending the four-lecture series, he had been unaware of
the differences between socialism and anarchism. Ely
weighed socialism, with its promises of brotherhood and
more efficient production and distribution, and found it
wanting. It was too radical for any but distant realization,
he argued, threatened liberty and freedom in the "higher

pursuits," underestimated the contributions of capital, and
ignored the possibilities of the development of a "social
side" to property. Ely, a land owner, regarded enlightened
self-interest as beneficial to society and urged that taxes
serve to lessen the gap between the rich and the poor. Such
an attitude would, he claimed, constitute a phase of self-
interest, because social stability was impossible while any
group remained "materially and morally wretched." To Ely,
hope for the future lay in development of a corps of trained
and dedicated public servants working within a government
that was more positive than representative. Ely liked to
regard himself as an "aristocrat"—one dedicated to the
"fulfillment of special service."[23]

There was nothing new in a man with University status
expressing himself on current matters. President Bascom
had done so to the point of supporting the strike as a
weapon of organized labor, and further had inspired in such
students as Robert M. La Follete a desire to dedicate themselves to the public service.[24] Bascom, however, had retired in the mid-eighties, when Wisconsinites viewed
management-labor violence and the other attendants of
developing industrial capitalism as remote. Since that time,
however, Wisconsin workers had demanded such threatening measures as payment in cash on specified days.
Municipal ownership had become a hot political issue, and
now state farmers seemed enamored of the doctrines of
Populism. To the apprehensive who deemed their interests
best served by maintenance of the status quo, all of this
seemed somehow related to the discussion of socialism,
the University, and extension. From his observation point
in Milwaukee, Speirs noted, "It is discouraging to find how
persistently the term Socialism is applied to all attempts
to enlarge the industrial functions of the state or munici-
pality." Because it had sponsored Ely's lectures, even the
People's Institute had become suspect of laying the ground-
work for revolution.[25]

As frightening to others was the extent to which the University had made other aspects of its influence felt throughout the state. Its success in gaining legislative appropriations
and in recruiting students within the shadows of state normals
and colleges brought understandable repercussions. In 1895, a
supporter of Lawrence University at Appleton informed Ely in
Spenserian tones that he refused to join those panicked by reports of the University's "absorbing tendencies." Certainly, he
hinted, the University would never veer from its course of "re-

search and truthseeking to engage in petty warfare." At the same time, he concluded, if Methodism allowed Lawrence to be destroyed it ought to be destroyed.[26] Obviously the Methodists had no such intentions.

The growing suspicion and resentment toward the University culminated in a public attack upon Ely. It originated in a letter written by Oliver E. Wells, Superintendent of Public Instruction, to the Nation. Quickly the charges grew to include Ely's advocacy of a strike, espousal of socialism and support of Populism. Speirs was likewise denounced for "Socialist tendencies."[27] At the same time, left-wingers who wore their badges proudly, repudiated both men. A single-tax enthusiast criticized Speirs for failure to carry his ideas to a "logical conclusion." Socialists felt that Ely's advocacy of municipal ownership of power and related services did not qualify him as one of their number. An anarchist fumed that Ely was attempting to curry favor with the "respectable classes." Ely described himself as advocating a "program of conservative social reform."[28]

Ely's supporters advised him to carry the matter completely into the open. Speirs advocated an increased program of lectures, for he was certain that the people alarmed by the charges were not those who had heard Ely personally, but those who had read of his activities in hostile newspapers. Another friend wrote that there was no minimizing the fact that many people took the charges seriously, and urged Ely to answer them squarely and without his usual meaningless qualifications.[29] These observers overestimated public interest in the matter. Despite the general public apathy, however, the Board of Regents decided to investigate. Wells was unable to prove Ely's connection with the labor outburst and indeed was able to show no more than that Ely's economics text had been used and recommended in University extension and summer school classes. The case against Ely faltered and died, but not that against the University and extension.[30]

Within a year, the University was again under fire, this time not for its radicalism, but as an aristocratic institution staffed by sinecurists. The author of this attack, too, was a man connected with the public schools, Oscar Pederson, Winnebago County Superintendent. As before, the original charges grew, this time including a denunciation of the campus as a place of debauchery. Public airing of the matter revealed the roles played by public school, normal school, and college men jealous of the University's financial

support and influence.[31] Answers to the charges were as
varied as the allegations. If the United States was to compete successfully with German industry and commerce, ran
one, she needed a similar quota of university-trained young
men. A public school principal who had been a steady supporter of extension classes suggested that if immorality
was rampant among University students, the homes from
which they came were a more logical source than was the
school.[32]

Again the regents met, investigated, and reported. The
original charges were dismissed as groundless, but in the
course of the matter, extension, the University's arm
throughout the state, was subjected to considerable attention. Recognition was granted its role in stimulating thought
and discussion, but its effect upon residence work was
seriously questioned. Rather than generally underworked,
it appeared that faculty members who engaged in extension
activities were overworked to the detriment of their residence activities. As a result, there was to be no further
expansion of extension until a permanent staff could be engaged.[33] Whatever the political expediency of the move,
here was also an assertion that the University and extension
represented different phases of public education, and that
separation would benefit both. The following year, 1897, the
regents removed the work entirely from Ely's hands,
placing it under the supervision of the University Department of Education.[34]

By this time, however, other circumstances had heralded
the conclusion of this phase of extension work. It made
little difference that the men now charged with its continuation were too busy with teaching and school inspection to
promote it. By 1901, public enthusiasm had so waned that
even legislature-approved public financing of individual
courses failed to attract sufficient attendance at lectures.[35]
The original goal had been to take the University to the
people. Clearly they were no longer interested in receiving
it.

Professor Ely had tried to stem this disintegration by
creating a permanent extension administration. Jerome T.
Raymond, long an admirer of Ely and equipped with extension experience gained at the University of Chicago, was
employed. Enthusiastically he sought and secured engagements for the participating professors. In his zeal, however,
he ignored the lesson learned in England and repeated by
Herbert Baxter Adams: create a demand for your work

rather than superimpose it. As a result, Raymond placed
lecture series in communities too small or not ready to
support them. More than once was he to hear charges
echoing the sentiments of the high school principal who
grumbled, "If it is University policy to fasten lecture
courses upon a community as you did, I want no more deal-
ings with University Extension."[36]

Extension's failure to fulfill the hopes of its initiators
even regarding mere attendance lay deeper than organiza-
tional or promotional shortcomings. Though the number of
lecture courses reached its peak of fifty-nine in 1895/96,
an increase of nineteen over the previous season, important centers like La Crosse reported that the popularity of
the program had been decreasing steadily for the previous
three years. G. S. Albee, president of the Oshkosh State
Normal, who had shown sympathy with extension, observed
that year after year it was the same people who supported
it, some of them openly admitting that they did so only because they felt they ought to. A spokesman for a local
literary society complained that it could no longer "mother
the University Extension movement." More and more centers began to report deficits—$12 at Naceeda, $30 at
Waupun, $10 at Wausau—which the local sponsors grudging-
ly paid from their own pockets.[37]

Extension had never become an integral part of community life, had never succeeded in cutting across class
lines. Speirs's failure to win the support of Milwaukee
society women was matched by failure to secure the support of the workers. Schedules had to be constantly adapted
to square with athletic contests, ladies aid and prayer
meetings. Politics proved a much greater attraction, accounting in part for the marked decline in attendance in the
election years of 1892 and 1896. In times of political or
economic tension, there was little interest in what was regarded as basically a "diversion," a luxury. " . . . it would
be a waste of time to try to arrange for a course of lectures
until we see what the crops are going to bring," wrote a
central Wisconsin farmer amidst the Bryan-McKinley
campaign.[38] School teachers, culture-seeking housewives,
a handful of business and professional men and students
from small colleges who took extension work for credit
were unwilling or unable to keep the program active. Once
the initial attraction had worn off, so did attendance. Adult
workers were unwilling to cap their days with class prep-
arations. As yet, too few high school students anticipated

college careers to make them a source of constant support.
The University planners had failed to realize that the
campus was not the state.

Just as extension students were willing to discuss current events, they were willing to discuss and comment upon
their classes or lecturers. Their appraisals reveal the
spirit in which they participated in the programs. While
discontinuation of one course given by an inexperienced instructor in Milwaukee was justified on grounds of "lack of
substance," and in another case the lecturer appeared
somewhat the worse for drink, the usual criticisms had
another ring: "The lecturer is repetitious and draws out
his words"; "he chooses his words from the Latin instead
of the Anglo-Saxon"; "his words are sometimes too big";
"he must harangue if we are to continue selling tickets";
"he lacks animation"; "she is too scholarly and depends too
much upon her notes"; "we like those lecturers who make
us money." As for course content: "The lecturers were
fine for the historical student, but not of the popular kind."
"We couldn't give away tickets for the Turner course"; "no
subject appeals so little to the average business man as a
study of Greek life."[39]

Wisconsin generously sampled its extension program and
found it too "didactic and encyclopedic," not sufficiently
removed from the atmosphere of the classroom. If groups
occasionally desired serious speakers, they could secure
them more reasonably elsewhere. The normals developed
extension services of their own, and Lawrence successfully
underbid the University's offerings. But even this was not
crucial, for English-type extension had fallen from popularity not only in Wisconsin, but throughout the entire nation.
The programs undertaken with such visions of mass enlightenment sputtered and died as the century drew to a
close. Like their neighbors, Wisconsinites wanted "entertainments" and these were readily available through the
Redpath Agency and the Y.M.C.A. Oshkosh Normal students
who deemed it financially impossible to continue their support of extension classes were able to arrange a speaking
engagement by Booker T. Washington.[40] George Herbert
Palmer, the critic whose pessimistic predictions regarding
the future of extension had been lost amidst the early
enthusiasm, had been right. Yet he had gone no further than
de Tocqueville in characterizing Americans as predomi-
nantly passive in the academic game.

What of the deleterious effects of extension upon resi-

dence work suggested by Potter and more recent critics?
Even enthusiasts like Ely found that it interfered. Others,
too, became apprehensive of its inroads upon their time and
energies, or those of their colleagues. Charles R. Van Hise,
who in the future, as president of the University, would
preside at extension's rebirth, was too immersed in his
geological surveys and rock studies even to consider the
suggestion he give extension lectures.[41] On the other hand,
the names of Wisconsin extensionists appeared regularly
on the rosters of adult education programs outside the state.
Had Ely, Turner and Freeman been more concerned about
the demands of residence work as they grew older, they
would have been less prone to have their names sandwiched
between the bell ringers and bird imitators who made up a
portion of those summer rosters. In their enthusiasm, they
attempted too much.

Raymond's attempts to expand extension activities signaled the departure of the older and relatively popular
professors. Birge, Turner and Scott were among the first
outstanding teachers to remove their courses from the extension lists. The trend they started only hastened the collapse already underway. "Indeed, I do not know but that we
have taken all the best things you have to offer," wrote a
regular extension sponsor in 1897.[42] At the same time, it
is a distortion to blame extension's decline upon the young
lecturers marshalled to meet the demands of the peak year
of 1895, and who replaced the resigning veterans. The seeds
of decay had been sown before 1895, during the era of the
campus giants. When the University revived extension work
on what, to the public, appeared to be sounder bases, young
instructors proved that they could successfully handle a
live program.

Speirs had glimpsed the basis for such a program, but
its development was delayed by his departure from Wisconsin. His observations of the successful operation of the
Drexel and Armour Institutes seemed to belie President
Chamberlin's explanation for the failure of the Mechanics'
Institutes attempted as counterparts to the Farmers' Institutes. If the diverse and routine nature of factory work left
worker students with few common interests and thus hard
to teach in great numbers, why had the private institutions
succeeded? The University itself was not satisfied with
Chamberlin's appraisal, and in 1901 boasted a "new departure" by announcing condensed courses for electric and
steam plant managers. Here was something a public active-

ly wanted, something in line with the growing concern about young men and women with "heads full of knowledge, but with helpless hands."[43] Here was a program in which businessmen could be interested.

Whatever else had been gleaned from the first experiences of Wisconsin extensionists, this was clear: To be successful, a far-flung extension program needed not only an enthusiastic and specialized faculty, but a permanent and dedicated administrative organization. It was clear, too, that efforts designed to be of lasting significance must be based upon premises that distinguished fad from sustained interest. One of the greatest weaknesses of the extension program had stemmed from the assumption that with but minor changes the campus could be made to embrace the state. The University could not remake public taste through casual off-campus contacts; it would be doing well to be able slowly and carefully to direct that taste into channels assumed desirable. If, moreover, University-sponsored programs brought that institution into conflict with political groups and rival institutions, the University would have to expect them to defend their position by striking back. And lastly, if the University wanted to popularize, it could not disdain the popularizer.

"Revivification"

It seems to me that a state university should not be
above meeting the needs of the people, however elementary the instruction necessary to accomplish this.
                              —Charles R. Van Hise, 1905

The turn of the century brought an intensification of the
problems envisioned and defined by Professors Richard T.
Ely and Frederick Jackson Turner. The value of the state's
annual industrial output was surpassing that of its forests
and fields. Wealth, like population, was becoming ever
more concentrated, the distinction between economic and
social groups ever more clear. Capital and labor were
moving into antagonistic camps, and worker organizations
coming to challenge the traditionally preferential place
held by business in local and state government.

As the skies along Wisconsin's lakeshore became hazy
with factory smoke, the state began to experience situations
already common in the East. The age-old apprentice system proved inadequate, and Wisconsin mill and foundry
owners echoed the editor of the organ of the National Manufacturers' Association: "Workmen—Where Can We Find
Them." Ordinary workmen were not enough; employers
wanted skilled laborers who would remain aloof from the
unions which companies were striving so desperately to
break. Large companies like General Electric and Union
Pacific could afford their own training and indoctrination
programs, but smaller concerns could not. Perhaps their
problems could be partially solved by an increased public
school emphasis upon manual training, or by the creation
of free, tax-supported industrial high schools. Wisconsin,
however, seemed unready for such a program, and in 1906,
the Milwaukee Merchants and Manufacturers' Association
created its own industrial training school. Student fees and
private contributions financed the effort.[1]

Workers, too, were beginning to glimpse the advantages
of formal training for their jobs. Some, it is true, continued
to fight the introduction of shop courses into the public
schools, insisting that their children have the same courses,
and, therefore, presumably the same chances for future
success as the children of their employers. On the other

43

hand, many spokesmen for organized labor accepted the
proposition that the sons of wage earners would also be
wage earners. What, they asked, were the educators doing
for the ninety per cent of their students included in this
category? Even when they did offer industrial training
courses, it was suspected that the work was accompanied
by anti-closed shop propaganda. There was no doubt in labor
leaders' minds about the school sponsored by the Milwaukee
Merchants and Manufacturers' Association. It was openly
labeled a "school for scabs."[2]

Professional educators, too, were pondering the problems
of the industrial scene. The positive correlations between
lack of education and social waste, and between individual
and group problems were generally accepted, and provided
principles for action. Like London, New York and Chicago,
Milwaukee developed its settlement house with a betterment
program ranging from handicraft classes to an employment
service. Few would disagree with a National Education
Association committee's conclusions that modern education
"should give efficient aid in reducing the friction inevitable
in human society as industrial and social changes occur."[3]
But how was "aid" to be defined? To some, it meant giving
youth a chance to become "self-sufficient and law abiding."
Steep a boy in knowledge of the craft he will pursue as an
adult, the argument ran, and thereby insure his steady employment and ability to play a useful role in the industrial
community.   Skilled hands lead to full dinner pails; full
stomachs, to a contented working class. Professor S. H.
Goodnight of the University of Wisconsin, however, warned
that separation of the schools into worker and professional
training institutions threatened to stifle individualism and
to create a caste system based upon money.[4] Certainly the
division could not be tolerated in a country which still
prided itself on maintaining a fluid social order.

Whatever their emphases, employers, workers and educators desired some sort of formal training for the operators
of lathes and steam boilers. Would some new educational
agency have to be created, or could an existing one be
adapted to the purpose? The University of Wisconsin was
already preparing young people for certain of the professions, and through its institutes had gone out to the farmers.
Where did its obligations end? If the University assumed
responsibility for the economic betterment of the cattlemen
and buttermakers, what of its responsibility to the Wisconsin industrialist, who often had to search abroad for his

skilled workers, only to find that some brought with them
ideologies hostile to his own? What did the University owe
the city boy seeking employment, or the worker who hoped
to better himself? Were only the socialists and advocates
of unionism concerned with the future of such workers?
The success of the Farmers' Institutes had demonstrated
the possibilities of off-campus training and perhaps social
and political indoctrination. The University already had
some experience upon which to draw should it attempt to
play a similar role in the urban community.

The extension and expansion of state-supported services
was characteristic of the era. Though the city of Milwaukee
remained for a time in the hands of a reactionary political
machine, the state as a whole had turned to the Progressives and elected Robert M. La Follette to the governorship. La Follette had accepted President Bascom's challenge to University students that they dedicate themselves
to the public service. Now as governor he turned to the
school and its corps of academic specialists. He invited the
professors to posts on state advisory boards and commis-
sions, and personally attended graduate seminars to participate in discussions of railroad rates and public utilities.
On another level, men from the Capitol and men from the
University met informally at the Saturday Lunch Club to
exchange ideas and sometimes verbal punches. This was
one aspect of the Wisconsin Idea in action, a means of
making the state University the university of the state.

Governor La Follette felt that tax money spent for education was returned many fold in terms of successful
research and creation of a citizenry jealous of "popular
government in its best form." In his 1905 message to the
legislature he requested increased University and agricultural education appropriations. Men politically close to him,
however, were discussing the possibilities of tax-supported
specialized education for the state's workers. They were
the men of the Wisconsin Free Library Commission,
created in 1895 as a book-lending service for the state's
smaller communities. Under the leadership of its founder
and head, Frank A. Hutchins, and his aid, Dr. Charles
McCarthy, the Commission also collected published materials for the Farmers' Institutes and established a public
postal information service. More dramatic was its Legislative Reference Library, Dr. McCarthy's special interest,
which provided legislators with a working library at the
Capitol, and in addition offered them a unique bill-drafting

service. This was the "people's lobby," which attempted to
provide elected officials with the type of advice and aid
hitherto available only to the corporation lobbyists. Here
was yet another phase of the Wisconsin Idea in action.

Frank Hutchins, son of the president of a small college,
and himself a former teacher and newspaper editor, was
primarily a man of ideas, a detached man whose forte was
suggestion rather than action. His hints and proddings led
to creation of the State Park Service, the Library Commission, the Legislative Reference Library, and the state-wide
service to debating and public discussion groups which became a basis for the revival of University extension in
1906. To one extension pioneer, it seemed "as natural for
ideas to scintillate from his brain as ... for sparks to fly
upward." Hutchins "cast his seeds in political fields, social
service, recreation, indeed in all upland fields, but never
... [had] he ventured into the mire." [5]

Charles McCarthy, University of Wisconsin Ph.D., was
primarily a man of action. The causes he adopted became
crusades to which he devoted himself with single-purposed,
tireless, self-denying militancy. The son of Irish immigrants, he had worked as a youth in a Massachusetts shoe
factory, and then briefly at sea. Determined to enter Brown
University, he argued school authorities into waiving the
usual entrance and curriculum requirements on grounds
that their seventeenth century origin made them obsolete.
At Brown, McCarthy distinguished himself in the social
studies and athletics, and added John D. Rockefeller, Jr.,
to his life-long list of acquaintances. Upon graduation, he
came to Madison for advanced study and to coach football.
Markedly impressed by Professor Ely, he developed an
intense interest in "social engineering." It was a short step
to part-time campus teaching, and then to work in the Legislative Reference Library. Here the Ely influence was somewhat tempered by the more self-effacing benevolence of
Frank Hutchins. [6]

McCarthy's personal background, code of sportmanship,
and ideas of public service made it easy for him to see in
a tax-supported, job-training program material worthy of a
crusade. Besides the immediate advantage such would
provide both workers and employers, he felt that it would
discourage labor's interest in socialism, even as the partially state-financed rural prosperity had rendered rural
areas resistant to radical philosophies. Through his study
of history and political science, McCarthy had developed an

intense respect for German political and industrial efficiency, which he attributed in large part to the interrel-
ationship of the universities, government and industry. Wisconsin had already witnessed university-government
coöperation; why not carry the matter still further?
Unmindful of warnings such as Goodnight's, McCarthy was
to pursue that goal with such zeal that a German language
newspaper chuckled at his enthusiasm,

> Til Dr. Charles McCarthy came
>   To make me understand
> How the Germans beat the Irish—
>   Horse and foot and sea and land,
> I was crazy over Ireland,
>   But I've switched to beat the band,
> For now my only mania is Ger-mania. [7]

Hutchins and McCarthy often discussed the need for mass
urban adult education, only to run up against the difficulty
of implementing their ideas. In casting about for a basis
upon which to operate, they considered the possibilities of
using the moribund University extension program. They
even toyed with selecting a name for the venture, settling
upon John Bascom College.[8] Although it was then a part of
the University's Department of Education, Extension consisted of little more than a few pages in the University
catalogue. A. W. Tressler, nominally in charge of its administration, was unaware of the few lectures still being
given in its name.[9] The structure was there, but for the
moment there seemed no means of occupying and remodel-
ing it.

In 1904, an answer to the problem was suggested in the
speeches celebrating the University Jubilee and the inauguration of President Charles R. Van Hise. Van Hise was a
Wisconsin alumnus and a geologist of national repute. Like
La Follette, he had heard President Bascom urge students
to dedicate themselves to public service. The addresses of
the governor and the new president reflected a common outlook. "The state welcomes the efforts of the University to
assist... the people of the state," La Follette observed,
and asks in return "men and women strong in honesty and
mental character, who shall appreciate the obligations they
owe of loyalty to the state."[10] In establishing the keynote of
his administration, Van Hise rearticulated the theme that
Germany's greatness stemmed from the active participation
of the universities in daily affairs. Wisconsin boasted a

somewhat similar situation, but the University's role could
well be broadened. Van Hise announced plans to augment
the existing program of preparing students for the professions, later adding that the University "should extend its
scope until the field was covered from agriculture to the
fine arts," until in addition to becoming the nation's leading
graduate school, it attacked the cultural backwardness
which made America seem a nation of "money grubbers."[11]

Van Hise had made no specific mention of extension—had
not gone so far in this regard as President Chamberlin.
Within a year, however, he was vigorously and publicly
championing University-sponsored short courses and educational programs at all levels. In 1906, the University
Catalogue proclaimed the institution's desire to be of
service to all who wished to learn—to extend off-campus
aid not only to teachers and farmers, but to everyone interested in self-education. In that same year, Van Hise affirmed that he could never rest until the "beneficient influence of the University was made available in every home in
the state."[12]

President Van Hise's developing enthusiasm for broadened University activity can be traced in part to his interest in the conservation of both material and human resources. But of more immediate importance were the
activities of Hutchins, McCarthy, and Henry E. Legler.
Legler, a former committeeman on the State Conference of
Charities and Corrections which had linked Professor Ely's
classes and the state institutions, had succeeded Hutchins
in the Library Commission when in 1903 ill-health forced
the latter's temporary retirement. Of the three, McCarthy
was the driving force. Though never officially connected
with extension, he adopted its development as one of his
major interests. Ely and Hutchins had brought his ideas
into focus, centering them around the people's need for enlightened positive leadership and the possibilities of util-
izing extension for this end. The Wisconsin manufacturers'
search for trained workers and the German answer to a
similar problem provided him with other points of departure. In 1905, using as a lever Van Hise's casually uttered
words about the field and scope of the University, he forced
upon the president and the faculty the question of reviving
extension. Both proved indifferent,[13] but McCarthy was not
to be deterred. His zeal and powerful position in the state
made it impossible to ignore him. In November, Van Hise

gave the McCarthy demands his verbal approval. The
following month, the regents stepped gingerly into the picture, voting $250 to be used in reviving extension. In Janu-
ary 1906, Edwin H. Pahlow, a history instructor, was
engaged as secretary of the Extension Department.[14]

The major task assigned Pahlow by Van Hise was to study
the possibilities of reorganizing and reinstituting extension
work. The president's actions belied the eagerness of his
words. The Daily Cardinal, campus newspaper, described
the new activity as part of Van Hise's policy of bringing
the University to the people. More accurate from the standpoint of immediate offerings was the announcement in a
city newspaper that extension courses would "again" be
offered. Neither in administrative procedure, instructional
staff or curricula were there evidences of a break with the
nineties. Even Hutchins' aid to debaters was but a further
development of the earlier effort. Extension lecturers continued to operate almost independently, giving the regents
ten per cent of the collected fees in order to meet administrative expenses. The names of Ely-era veterans like
Professors J. R. Freeman and M. V. O'Shea again dominated extension lecture lists. Among the newcomers, however, was Henry Legler. McCarthy marked time. When
Pahlow left his post at the end of the academic year,
McCarthy had Legler groomed and waiting as his replace-
ment. With Legler's appointment as secretary, Extension
headquarters were moved to the offices of the Free Library
Commission.[15] Dr. McCarthy's battle to shape extension
policy was but beginning, however. He controlled the secretary and part of the physical plant, but it remained to
convince President Van Hise of the merit of the program
he had in mind.

The major outlines and McCarthy's plans for extension
were contained in a memorandum to the president urging a
thorough revision and expansion of extension goals and
acitivities. Abandon the "scattered and sporadic lectures"
which the University has been superimposing without benefit on the state's communities, McCarthy advised, and place
major emphasis upon engineering courses. Work in the
cultural fields could be added later. As for the mechanics
of presentation, McCarthy visualized coöperation with local
public libraries. As for financing, he was certain that the
great numbers of Wisconsin residents enrolling in private
correspondence school courses in carpentry, boiler tending

and related work indicated the pressing need and desire for
them and the public's willingness to pay fees. A personally
financed survey alleged that 35,000 state citizens were
spending over $800,000 per year for private instruction, an
amount that would soon be flowing into Extension if it would
but revamp its emphasis.[16] The procedure proved to be
typical of McCarthy in action: selection of a goal, followed
by endless debate, browbeating, and self-justifying surveys.
McCarthy left Van Hise little time for reflection, little
time to try to define for himself what he had meant by
"field" and "scope" in his inaugural address.

While McCarthy was hammering at Van Hise, William
Henry Lighty was applying for the post held by Legler.
Not completely aware of the nature of the situation developing in Madison, he sought the position of "Head of the
Department of University Extension." Lighty had graduated
from Cornell, where, like Ely, he had come under the influence of President Andrew White. From college, Lighty
went into settlement house work in St. Louis, becoming
superintendent of the Ethical Society's Self Culture Hall
Association.[17] He had some familiarity with Wisconsin; he
maintained a summer camp in the northern part of the state
and was acquainted with Professors Turner and Ely. Mrs.
Lighty had been a student and assistant of the latter. In
July, Ely invited Lighty to Madison to confer with McCarthy
and Legler about the position. After the interview, McCarthy
escorted his visitor to President Van Hise; Lighty's appointment as Assistant Professor in charge of Correspondence Courses soon followed. To Lighty, this came to mark
the "revivification" of extension at the University of Wisconsin.[18] The nature of his appointment, however, suggests
that his qualifications did not fully satisfy either Van Hise
or McCarthy. The president was doubtful because of
Lighty's recent illness and seeming physical frailty.
McCarthy perceived in him too much of the spirit of the
original extension movement to entrust him with policy
making powers in the new. For the time, McCarthy kept
extension where he could watch it. Lighty and his secretary,
Miss Julia Flisch, took up their duties in the offices of the
Library Commission. The arrangement made possible
McCarthy's supervision of Lighty's preparation, and even
the interviewing of professors he was trying to "wheedle"
into offering correspondence courses.[19]

The next development in McCarthy's crusade revealed
his coöperation with forces outside the University. In 1907,

the legislature was asked to appropriate $40,000 for exten-
sion and off-campus agricultural teaching. Significantly,
powerful support was given the measure by the Milwaukee
Merchants and Manufacturers' Association. The Association's interest rested upon the need for trained workers
which had inspired establishment of the Milwaukee trades
school. That effort had proved expensive, and both its sponsors and organized labor approved its being taken over by
the city. Now McCarthy and members of the Association
planned to secure state aid in developing an extensive program of job training to be carried on within the factories.
Not only would employers and workers enjoy immediate
benefits, but the University would be able to work out its
"broad social purpose" of making the workers "better and
more intelligent citizens."[20] Two years later McCarthy
amplified his views:

> Our artisan classes ... are not contented. It is there
> where Socialism and disorder and anarchism have their
> roots. We cannot give them money or divide our wealth
> ... [the University can help] ... break up the masses of
> the unintelligent ... make them better individuals ...
> [and more] ... efficient. This is the true equality which
> they desire.[21]

Together with manual skills, conservative ideologies were
to be imparted. Once the Wisconsin Dairymen's Association
had helped force the University—and hence the state—to
take over the program the Association had inaugurated;
now the industrialists were similarly engaged.

The appropriation bill passed with the active support of
the Merchants and Manufacturers' Association of Milwaukee
and those of other lake shore cities. When Governor James
O. Davidson threatened to veto the measure on grounds that
it duplicated work already undertaken by private agencies,
the Milwaukee pressure group persuaded him to change his
mind.[22] For the first time extension rested upon a stable
financial base, and those responsible were adamant that the
existing program of lectures and related educational aids
be abandoned or augmented by shop training. McCarthy
resolved not to allow passage of another year without
achieving the "reorganization that is absolutely essential."[23]
He conferred fruitlessly with Van Hise on the eve of the
latter's departure for an Eastern vacation. If the president
hoped to avoid further haranguing by leaving Madison, he
had misjudged McCarthy, who continued his case by mail.

Soon, Van Hise's vacation became a hectic campaign to maintain his prerogatives in making extension policy.

McCarthy goaded Van Hise into seeking an engineer to take charge of extension. He forced the action by threatening first to cease championing extension, thereby jeopardizing its entire program, and then to appeal directly to the people of the state. McCarthy clinched his effort by nominating his own candidate for the headship, Frederick McKenzie, a recent University graduate and journalist closely associated with the Milwaukee Merchants and Manufacturers' Association and other state business groups. The cornered president played for time by stipulating that the new man be such as to inspire the respect of the University deans, and he cast about frantically for a man of that stature. Working as he was against time, Van Hise considered himself fortunate in finally securing the service of Louis E. Reber, Engineering Dean of Pennsylvania State College.[24] The victory was not entirely McCarthy's, however. Reber was hired with the understanding that he develop extension in "the broadest sense . . . to include correspondence work."[25]

Reber was an honors graduate of Pennsylvania State College, had done advanced work at the Massachusetts Institute of Technology, and had returned to his undergraduate school to head the department of Mechanic Arts, which during his tenure became the School of Engineering. Besides his work as an academic administrator, Reber had supervised the preparation of his school's engineering exhibits for the Paris Exposition of 1889, the Columbia Exposition of 1893, and the Louisiana Purchase Exposition of 1903, at which he was cited for having presented the best state mining exhibit. At the time Van Hise approached him, state political developments threatened his position in Pennsylvania and encouraged his acceptance of the president's offer.

Reber took up his duties at Wisconsin late in 1907. Though his original title was that of "Director of Extension," he was promised a deanship and drew a salary equal to that of the dean of the School of Engineering. Reber set about adding the program demanded by McCarthy and the manufacturers to the existing correspondence, debaters' aids, and Milwaukee settlement house work. While en route to Madison, he hurriedly had studied the methods of the International Correspondence School, which he used as one point of departure. In its broad outlines, however, the program presented was that long urged by McCarthy.

Extension served the state's manufacturers briefly but well. Coöperating employers in Milwaukee, Beaver Dam, Wauwautosa and other cities helped employees pay for extension courses, encouraged continuation of work undertaken, and provided rooms in their plants where students and traveling instructors could meet. The extension courses were basically correspondence work, the lessons being sent to Madison for correction. Circuit-travelling instructors met with the students regularly, however, helping them with problems in elementary shop mathematics, blueprint reading, mechanical drawing and similar subjects. It was this corps of traveling teachers which made the Wisconsin program unique in the correspondence field, and attracted nationwide and even international attention to this further development of the Wisconsin Idea.[26]

The success of the work led manufacturers to ask for either an intensification of the program, or development of an even more extensive one. Conservative implications were readily apparent. A resolution adopted by the National Society of Stationary Engineers praising Extension observed that its popularity demonstrated to employers that workers were not primarily interested in striking, but in increasing their efficiency. As for organized labor at home, however, McCarthy had virtually to dictate a testimonial from Fred Brockhausen, Secretary of the Wisconsin State Federation of Labor, who begged off from further endorsements on grounds that union men were unacquainted with extension services.[27]

Early in the 1909 session of the state legislature, the Merchants and Manufacturers' Association again endorsed generous appropriations for extension. Governor Davidson grumbled briefly that the department's work was too comprehensive, that there should be greater concentration upon the shops and foundries. Reassured as to extension plans for the future, he, too, proved friendly toward the $150,000 request phrased by McCarthy, Hutchins, Reber, and to a lesser extent, Van Hise.[28] This time, however, extension's critics were ready and attempted to sabotage the measure. Some, like Regent G. D. Jones, conservative Wausau attorney who had been an extension faithful of the Ely era, desired to discredit Van Hise for alleged socialistic tendencies. Jones was aided by the politically conservative Regent William D. Hoard, who had sparked the creation of the Farmers' Institutes, and who was now determined to

restore agriculture's waning influence in University affairs,
especially regarding appropriations.[29] Also among Extension's critics were University professors who deemed its
work unworthy, a disgrace to one of the greatest of the
state universities. And there were those who had tasted the
bitterness of Reber's sarcasm or who otherwise disap-
proved of him personally.

Much of the campaign against the Extension appropriation
consisted of rumors and innuendoes. Suggestions of mis-
handled Extension money, hints that Reber was innately incompetent, and charges that Extension was without basic
plans for the future were whispered through Capitol cor-
ridors. Denial by the Dean of the College of Agriculture of
one such story attributed to him was to no avail. McCarthy's
attempted countermoves bordered on the frantic, and provoked threats that he would be charged with lobbying unless
he acted with more discretion.[30]

At a critical point in the debate, the Milwaukee Merchants
and Manufacturers' Association withdrew its support of the
original measure, agreeing to a compromise bill which
eventually assured Extension $50,000 for the first year of
the new biennium, and $75,000 for the second. Given the
curtailment of the University building program by the
budget conscious legislators, and the appropriation of but
$30,000 for the Farmers' Institutes, Extension had fared
well. And again, outside aid had helped place its entire program on a firmer footing.

The Merchants' and Manufacturers' Association's shift
on the money bill stemmed in part from its defense of other
measures in which it was interested. At the same time, it
was aware of a move to create a state-wide system of
vocational schools. This matter bore the McCarthy stamp
as clearly as had Extension. In the spring of 1909, a Milwaukee businessman, August S. Lindemann, had aroused
McCarthy's enthusiasm and enlisted his aid in mapping a
technical education program of such proportions that extension work was counted but a "drop in the bucket."[31] In
the months that followed, McCarthy solicited statements in
support of the goal and dramatized his efforts by making an
investigative trip to Europe. He returned with increased
respect for German efficiency, and armed with materials
for a public report which proved at least as objective as
that on the private correspondence schools. The bill which
he finally framed was a faithful reproduction of his correspondence with Lindemann, and the result was the legisla-

tive creation of a state system of vocational training schools
and a complementary compulsory school attendance law.
At Van Hise's and Reber's insistence, provision was made
for Extension to supply instructors should the need arise.[32]
Years later this portion of the law proved of greatest significance, but at the time it seemed but a conciliatory
gesture. The new system had its own teacher-training
school, Stout Institute. For a few months, Extension did
help prepare a handful of teachers, but in the future its role
in the field was confined to offering home study courses
and the preparation of shop procedure and technical textbooks. Extension's first major role in the industrial life of
the state had been played. It had been of stopgap nature, but
it had demonstrated the worth of such work. The episode
had significance, too, as a venture into a new field of state
service and as one more example of how such service
might be actively sought by the champions as well as critics
of laissez faire. Popularity of the shop courses had been
anticipated by Ely's assistant, Frederick Speirs, almost
two decades earlier. The realization of such courses, however, had awaited the forcefulness of Charles McCarthy.
His coöperation with non-University groups gained for extension that kind of support for which Ely had hoped in vain,
and the appropriations necessary for future development.
When the industrial classes were abandoned, Extension was
financially and administratively poised for a successful
continuation of its remaining program and the originating
of new ones. Although not always mutually congenial on the
personal level, Extension's policy makers and faculty exhibited enthusiasm and varied talents which promised much.
And yet, Extension's future was not wholly assured. Its
very existence was challenged by those who considered it
outside the legitimate scope of University activity, or who
viewed it as either worthless or a threat. If Extension was
to continue, it had to demonstrate the need for its work,
watch constantly for new areas to exploit, and remain ever
flexible.

Extension's Early Critics

Are you not afraid of a "University-State" instead of a State University?... Such a conception suggests that the University is the Octopus with frightful tentacles sucking the life blood of the state, or like Caesar, it is a Colossus which doth bestride the state.

—William Kittle, 1911

The main outlines of the extension program which emerged within the University of Wisconsin in 1906 were neither unique nor new. It was the combination of the various activities that made the experiment noteworthy. During the preceding decade, numerous universities—Wisconsin's among them— had offered watered down educational programs. Private schools had already developed industrial training courses, and though F. W. Speirs' suggestions in the nineties that Extension follow suit went largely unrecognized, the University was even then sponsoring agricultural education of such grade. President Chamberlin's outline in 1892 for future extension work built around lecture and correspondence courses of a cultural nature described a major portion of the program launched more than a decade later. The past also contained a lesson for the future. If the University and its Extension Department were resolved to make their influence widely felt, they could anticipate embroilment in the state's political controversies.

As had Presidents Bascom and Chamberlin, President Charles R. Van Hise spoke freely on current and controversial matters. In his commencement address of 1904, he defined as the "wisest philanthropist" the man who advanced himself in order to elevate others, and labeled self-centered men of business modern "bucaneers" upon whom legal restraints should be imposed. Though a few months later a spokesman for the Milwaukee Merchants and Manufacturers' Association characterized the "new commercialism" as disdaining greed and selfishness, Van Hise was accused of exhibiting tendencies toward socialism. The charges jeopardized not only his position, but that of Extension. To men like University Regent G. D. Jones, from small industrial cities, the president's remarks seemed a threat to established order.[1]

In other ways, too University and Extension men became actively associated with the life and consequently the con- flicts of the state. The turn of the century witnessed in- creasing demands for civic reform and resulting action which encouraged both widespread approval and concen - trated attack. Efforts to benefit individuals through planned group living were not new to Wisconsin. Before the indus- trial era, model community experiments had been conducted near Ripon and Waukesha. These efforts had failed, while more loosely organized towns and cities which remained integral parts of the prevailing economic and political cli- mate had thrived. The growth of these towns, however, had usually been chaotic, and some municipal governments had been captured by political machines unconcerned with the public welfare. To those with faith in reason and govern- ment for as well as by the people, the situation demanded enlightened planners and planning.

1898 was a year of hopeful anticipation. Millions of Amer- icans gained comfort and pride in the thought that their nation had plunged to the defense of democracy and the underprivileged in Cuba and the Philippines. In that year, too, Wisconsin mayors who had gathered in Madison to celebrate the state's fiftieth birthday, helped launch the League of Wisconsin Municipalities. The organization was designed as a clearing house for information about local government, and as a means for conducting related discus- sions.   Men from the University were asked for aid; Pro- fessors Richard T. Ely from social studies and Frederick E. Turneaure from engineering were generous with advice in their respective fields.[2]

Groups of private citizens, too, began to view their cities critically, and to form study and lobbying groups. In Madison and Milwaukee, City Clubs sponsored investigations of city planning, public health, utilities, and the discussion of "live questions." The situation in Milwaukee had become especially alarming. The Democratic administration headed by Mayor David Rose was openly and disdainfully robbing the taxpayers through its mishandling of street railway and paving contracts and the school and tax systems. The abuses eventually touched off protests, and finally concert- ed action. In 1906, the Milwaukee Journal announced editor- ially that the "day of the unrestrained, uncontrolled public service corporation must be brought to an end." A year earlier, The Wisconsin Journal of Education bluntly traced the degeneration of the city school system to the rottenness

of the city administration. In 1908, Protestant ministers devoted a Sunday to sermons denouncing Rose for fostering
conditions which threatened to produce a popular reaction
against the traditional American way of life.[3] Two years
later, a coalition of reformers, including the Merchants
and Manufacturers' Association, backed Emil Seidel, Social
Democratic candidate for mayor. Seidel campaigned on
promises of clean government by experts. The incumbents'
attempts to depict the contest as one between "Patriotism
or Anarchy, the Stars and Stripes or the Red Flag" availed
little. The voters overthrew "City Hall" and awaited Seidel's
concrete definition of good government. At the next election,
the Social Democrats were defeated, but thereafter were
returned repeatedly to power.

The new administration acted vigorously to improve the
public health, uproot graft and corruption, and bring efficiency into government. True to campaign pledges, Seidel
and the Common Council created a Bureau of Economy and
Efficiency patterned after the pioneer New York Bureau of
Municipal Research. Within days of the election, Professor
John R. Commons of the University of Wisconsin accepted
an invitation to conduct an economic survey of the city
which led him beyond ledger books to questions of industrial
hygiene and education, working conditions and hospitals.
With the aid of Professors S. W. Gilman and B. M. Rastall,
who administered University Extension business courses,
Commons set up a city system of cost accounting. Deans
Frederick Turneaure, Harry L. Russell and Louis E. Reber
aided in the solution of municipal health and sanitation problems. New bureaus were created; existing bureaus and departments made more efficient.[4] Building upon plans formulated in 1909, E. J. Ward of University Extension and H. H.
Jacobs, Ely-trained University Settlement House leader,
prepared the way for city parks similar to those of Chicago's
South Side. Jacobs also expanded his original settlement
work into a community-wide program operating through
social centers located in public school buildings. The city
government welcomed the University specialists, and the
University welcomed the opportunity to demonstrate its
worth in the solution of individual and group problems.

It was apparent that however coöperative the University
and Extension proved, they could not carry the whole burden,
nor was it desirable that they do so. A local leadership
training program was clearly in order, and an anonymous
donor provided $3,000 for the purpose. When Mayor Seidel

found the Central Council of Philanthropy uninterested, he
again turned to University Extension. The result was organization of the Institute of Municipal and Social Service. The
Institute was supervised by a local committee of three, the
Reverend Frederick Edwards of St. James Episcopal Church,
Nathan Pereles, who was well known in banking and legal
circles, and H. H. Jacobs. Mrs. Anna Garlin Spencer of the
New York School of Philanthropy, a friend of Lighty's,
supervised the class work conducted in rooms provided in
the City Hall. Formal, fee courses were offered afternoons;
free evening lectures were open to the public. Classes and
audiences heard a variety of social service, political and
business leaders: Mrs. Spencer, associates of Hull House,
E. J. Ward, H. H. Jacobs, Dr. Charles McCarthy, Senator
A. W. Sanborn, and William George Bruce of the Merchants and Manufacturers' Association. Many of these
speakers had causes to champion, as did McCarthy and
Bruce, who used their engagements to support the Workmen's Compensation Bill. [5] The Institute perished with the
change in city administrations in 1912, but Extension's
William H. Lighty helped to perpetuate its work through the
Wisconsin Conference of Charities and Corrections, which
was connected with the State Board of Control.

The relationship between the Social Democrats and the
University inspired charges that the University was a cap-
tive of the socialists. Did not Extension sponsor classes
meeting near the office of the Social Democratic mayor?
The reply that the City Hall belonged to the people and not
to a party did not seem assuring. After all, was there not a
student Socialist Club—however small—on the Madison
campus? Attacks of this nature had hastened the end of the
first phase of extension, as had jibes that the University
faculty was too steeped in theory to make sense in the world
of practical affairs. Now again were heard attacks upon
"experts." This time, however, the main question was
"whose experts?" Specialization and efficiency had become
respected as ends in themselves, and blanket indictments
of specialists could be embarrassing. Accordingly, experts
were likely to be judged bad or good, the latter often
being those who buttressed the public's preconceptions with
graphs and statistics.

In the autumn of 1910, the Wisconsin Federation of Catholic Societies, meeting in New London, adopted resolutions
urging members to investigate local social questions as a
basis for helping spread the spirit of Christianity. In Mil-

waukee, the Catholic Social Union studied housing and labor
problems, and sponsored lectures by anti-socialists. Others
who opposed the Social Democratic administration engaged
in similar activity. When the breakup of reform groups resulted in the temporary dislodging of the Social Democrats
in 1912, the City Club voted to sponsor a municipal survey
of its own, employing Dr. W. H. Allen of the New York
Bureau of Municipal Research. Twenty private $500 contri-
butions financed the work of the new group of experts, who
assembled in the wake of the departing University men.
Professor Commons noted that he would have served the
conservatives, but that they had never asked him.[6] The
reason for this stemmed in part from the distrust of the
academic diploma as opposed to articles of incorporation,
in part from the distrust of those with no sum of money at
stake. It might be well enough to tolerate the sometimes
painful probing of the professors, but only as long as they
confined it to their libraries and classrooms.

Political developments in Milwaukee were but part of a
state-wide picture. The unity which, strained though it was,
had made the Republican party powerful in Wisconsin was
fast disappearing as its Stalwart and Progressive wings
found continued coöperation impossible. They came to grips
over the Wisconsin Idea, especially in the form of the Legislative Reference Library, the University, and Extension.
The clash was symbolized by conflicting attitudes towards
the theme of Lincoln Steffens' article, "Sending a State To
College," which appeared in the American Magazine. La
Follette's Weekly Magazine quoted with approval the conclusion that the University was developing a "public mind,
conscious of a common purpose," was "coördinating all the
resources, efforts and powers . . . to the service of the welfare of all." To Stalwarts like Regent Jones, however, this
meant creating a political machine for the benefit and per-
petuation in office of the Progressives, now led by Governor
Francis McGovern.[7] What seemed democratic to the Progressives seemed demagogic to the Stalwarts.

The battle churned through many phases of the life of the
state. Dr. Charles McCarthy's legislation-drafting department was denounced as a "bill factory," and great emphasis
was placed upon the individual mistakes it had made. Conveniently overlooked were the purpose for which it had been
designed and the service it had rendered. The attacks were
clearly part of the Stalwart drive for supremacy. State
Superintendent of Schools Charles P. Cary, who had freely

employed his position to attack University Extension, was
suggested as a logical opponent of McGovern, as the man
who could best make a bid for office on an anti-University
platform.[8]

Members of the University Extension staff moved quickly
to defend their work and attack Cary. Paul H. Neystrom, an
early correspondence student and now Extension representative in Oshkosh, enlisted the aid of city school officials and
normal school faculty in answering the charges that the University cost too much and was but a cog in the La Follette
political machine.[9] Early in 1912, William H. Lighty used
his position as secretary of the Saturday Lunch Club to set
the stage carefully for a discrediting of Cary and a defense
of the Wisconsin Idea. Evan A. Evans, University alumnus
and Baraboo attorney, and George E. Vincent, president of
the University of Minnesota, were selected to deliver the
blows. Using materials prepared and sent him by Extension,
Evans described the current attack upon the University as
understandable only against the background of the Stalwart-
Progressive split. In his turn, President Vincent defended
the role of the expert in government with salty vigor, but
warned that in the interests of democracy, a sharp division
be maintained between research and administration, that
the University must remain the servant of the people.[10]
Whatever the effect of the program, Emanuel Philipp
rather than Cary was selected to head Stalwart opposition
to McGovern. Cary and Lighty were left beyond reconcili-
ation, and Extension had been publicly committed to a politically partisan role.

There was no doubt as to President Van Hise's stand.
Publicly he observed:

> ... the spirit of the University is in irreconcilable con-
> flict with those who hold that the present state of affairs
> is the best possible, who believe that existing conven-
> tions, morals, political and religious faiths are fixed.
> All are fluid. For one nation they are not the same as
> for another. For each nation they are modified from
> generation to generation. This will continue as long as
> the race endures. In the University, one of the chief
> functions of which is to inquire, ever to adjust, ever to
> improve, ever to advance knowledge, the flux is greatest,
> the progress most rapid; and, therefore, these institu-
> tions are the very centers of disturbance.[11]

The Stalwart answers were sharp, and, if not penetrating,

picturesque. In June, 1914, the temporary chairman of the
Republican State Convention scored the University lobby at
the Capitol and the manner in which it had made Wisconsin
"the final depository of the theories, vagaries, quack
nostrums, isms, fads ... and Utopian dreams ." How dearly
it had cost the taxpayer to watch University experts attempt to "jungleize" northern Wisconsin for the benefit of
Chicago and Milwaukee sportsmen. Henceforth, the University could expect Stalwart support only if it would educate
instead of play politics, only if it would cease interfering
with the "natural laws" which governed economic development. The Stalwarts could and would save the University
from the visionaries, he concluded. [12]

The attack upon Extension was aimed at its allegedly un-
orthodox, inefficient, and useless expenditures, and its promotion of Progressivism. Since it was not doing work of
university grade, why maintain it within the University? Its
social centers and community arts programs were termed
"rat holes" down which the "thoughtless" were encouraged
to pour money. Through these activities, the charge continued, Extension had spread its "pernicious influence"
throughout the entire state school system. Let the legislature set it straight or abolish it! Even the shop-training
program did not escape attack. Milwaukee industrialist,
Thomas J. Neacy, who had opposed city planning and even
street lighting on grounds that the resulting increased taxes
would drive out industry, employed letters to the press to
describe his experience with the work. He characterized
the instructors as "dubs" working without supervision, and
the students as swaggering back from their classes with
the idea that the world owed them a living. In fine, Extension was the "dump of the University and an object lesson in in-
efficiency to divert patronage to private correspondence
schools." Neacy also used his verbal lash upon the University resident staff, which he accused of teaching "soap box
oratory." No professor, he argued, can "fulfill his obligations to the University, (especially if he is on five or six
payrolls at once) while delving through the archives to find
ingredients for his sure cure for trusts." The situation was
made the more tense for off-campus work generally by the
revelation that Agriculture College men had distributed
price lists showing the savings available through mail
order house buying. In large part, too, attacks upon
McCarthy and upon Extension became so interwoven as to
be indistinguishable. [13]

The University reply came in various forms. The Wisconsin State Journal printed a series of articles favorably describing Extension activity written by "Karl B. Weinman," an alleged pseudonym for the University Press editor himself.[14] At the same time, state papers carried reports of a University survey being conducted by William H. Allen, who had earlier administered the study of Milwaukee. Was Extension efficient? queried a reader. Allen replied that in the years 1912-13 Extension (exclusive of Agricultural extension) cost $153,197.13. During the biennium, it had reached 176,000 people, 6,000 by correspondence lessons, 50,000 by lectures, 85,000 by aids to debating and public discussion groups, and 35,000 through its general welfare work. At the same time, however, Van Hise pointed out that calculations based on cost per student were worthless as indexes of Extension's value, and Dean Reber felt that no survey could possibly enumerate the numbers of people indirectly influenced and aided. Given the circumstances, however, Neystrom warned his superiors that failure to present a statistical defense would weaken Extension's position in the eyes of the public.

Wisconsin's voters decided in favor of the Stalwart candidate for the governorship. Governor Philipp immediately attempted to reduce taxes by consolidating state bureaus, departments, and services. The plan of placing all state schools under one administrative board was in keeping with this effort. The reasons for the latter move went beyond the matter of economy, however. To some of the governor's supporters it provided a means for controlling the "educational High-Muck-a-Mucks" who had been feeding at the "public crib" and making the University a "Tyrant." A college president wrote the governor that the consolidation would end overlapping of functions, and raise the efficiency of the entire school system. Another Stalwart, viewing the matter from a political angle, saw in the success of the measure a means of demonstrating the solidarity of the new administration.[15]

With the change in the political situation, Extension could have expected that its financial requests would receive less friendly consideration than before. Dean Reber's plans for developing the department called for over $200,000. The new state administration, however, favored reducing the amount by $63,000, a cut which the governor argued any alert business could absorb without curtailing its activities. A storm of protest arose, some of it clearly political in nature. Spokesmen from the Vilter Manufacturing, Cutler-Hammer, and the Milwaukee Electric Railway and Light Companies testified publicly to the high quality of Extension instruction in their plants, and asked that it not be hampered by lack of funds. H. E. Miles, President of the State Board of Industrial Education, sought to quash vague rumors that Extension had cost the state $600,000. The mayor of Beloit voiced his appreciation for Extension aid in the conduct of his office, and a Winnebago County Assemblyman described the immense popularity of Extension work throughout the state. At the same time, the Socialist Milwaukee Leader attacked Governor Philipp as hostile toward all public education, and warned that "Ignorance of the masses means rulership of the classes."[16]

The Extension appropriation was finally settled at $205,110 per year, an amount in line with the original request. At the next session, the legislature allocated Extension an annual sum of $173,110, also directing that the fees it collected be placed in the University fund and appropriated therefrom for Extension work. An additional $25,000 was set aside for Medical extension and war work, with the provision that $20,000 be used exclusively to meet the demands posed by the war emergency.[17] Given the plans and ambitions of administrators everywhere, no appropriation is sufficient. Now some extensionists voiced that feeling, but in view of its political adventures, Extension had fared well. It had made enemies and critics, but it also had won staunch friends. Perhaps there is no better index to Extension having become an integral part of the state.

Planners and Planning

University Extension must be so organized as to adapt itself readily to changing conditions. It must be prepared at any time to take up whatever new work falling within the legitimate scope of university service is demanded by the people, and on the other hand, must discontinue established activities if the time comes when a local or other state agency has become better prepared to give the service.

—President Charles Van Hise, 1916

Industrial education carried on in factories and foundries was but the most dramatic and support-winning activity of the University's new extension program. While the shop-training effort was being conceived, developed, and then smothered by its very sponsors, extensionists made concrete the general education program envisioned by Frank Hutchins and suggested as Extension's raison d'etre in 1906. Though temporarily eclipsed by shop education, this broader program proved more enduring and hence a more potent factor in the life of the state.

Dr. Charles McCarthy prepared the brief for industrial education; Frederick Jackson Turner drew up that for the training of teachers; Frank A. Hutchins and William H. Lighty presented the cases for broadly conceived programs for mass enlightenment and uplift. The efforts of all were channeled and made effective by Dean Louis E. Reber, who came to Madison in 1907, more than a year after Lighty's arrival and Extension's reactivation. Extension offered a broad program of service to those whose tax dollars helped to support it. Extension went further and successfully educated people to use its services. Within a decade it was established upon a broad popular basis, the absence of which had caused the collapse of extension work in the 1890's.

The decreased popularity of the first extension program did not mean that extension had lost all appeal. There remained a sporadic demand for the lecture series still listed in the University Catalogue. Milwaukee teachers were particularly anxious that University credit courses be offered, and one teacher pointedly reminded Turner of the courses' favorable effect upon residence enrollments. Turner weighed

the matter and considered reviving the lecture-correspondence work he had helped introduce into Wisconsin during
the previous decade. The 1906 appointment of William H.
Lighty to administer correspondence study established the
medium through which such activity could be undertaken
and developed. Turner argued long and plausibly to bring
this about.

Turner rearticulated the position which had inspired his
earlier coöperation with Professor Richard T. Ely. Before
Dr. Charles McCarthy, Henry Legler, and Professor
Edward C. Elliott, members of the Sub-Committee on Credit
for University Extension Work, he built his argument
around the role and future of the University. Its influence
was beneficient, he affirmed, and could be made state-wide
by teachers brought into contact with it through summer
school and Extension. Even yet, the University's prestige
was tenuous; even yet the University might serve as a mere
"feeder" of students and faculty to the University of Chicago.
Although the latter's reputation in the Northwest suffered
from its association with John D. Rockefeller, Wisconsin
could not depend upon this advantage forever. High school
administrators were increasingly demanding teachers with
advanced degrees. Teachers themselves were active in the
"spontaneous formation of classes." If the University of
Wisconsin would not reach out to them, other schools would.
The University must act; through its own staff and coöperating agencies it must make itself a positive force in the
intellectual life of the state.[1]

The committee's discussions provided the framework for
an extensive correspondence study program. The projected
services were designed to carry the University into all
corners of the state, to bring as many people as possible
into contact with the University. Men and women of varied
backgrounds could find educational aid—and in specified
cases University credit—among courses ranging from the
elementary to the graduate level. The plan was tentative,
but this point was stressed: the students enrolled were to
be classified as Extension students, whatever their purpose,
whoever their instructors. McCarthy glanced hurriedly at
this "experiment," and plunged ahead with his plans for industrial education. To Lighty, however, here were possibilities of greater magnitude. Once he had helped bring the
advantages of the settlement house to the underprivileged
of St. Louis; now he was determined to bring the University
way of life to the people of Wisconsin.

In line with the procedure of Ely-era extension, campus faculty members were persuaded to add correspondence teaching to their regular duties. When it seemed evident that University standards were not being destroyed by the home study conducted in its name, hitherto reluctant residence departments offered their coöperation. By 1908, the scope and recognized importance of correspondence study were such that a specialized faculty was indicated. Supervision of the work underwent a change, too, the residence departments gradually confining their interest to University credit courses. As the extension program matured and demonstrated its worth, even skeptics like Dean Frederick Turneaure of the Engineering School and Professors George Hohlfeld and Edgar Snow of the German and Physics departments, became its supporters.[2] The spirit which Lighty infused into his department was vibrant. Dean Reber's first biennial report gave him full credit for establishing correspondence study on such a broad and comprehensive basis that growth was a matter largely of expansion.[3]

From the start, the correspondence department was more than a well-intentioned educational institution. Democratically, it offered home study opportunities for $20 per course, an amount which was payable in installments and which barely covered the cost of instruction. Extension's efforts also made the Division a competitor of the private schools, and even of the state colleges and normals. Fittingly, Frank Hutchins, one of the architects of the Division, also became its first Field Organizer.

The name of Frank Hutchins loomed large in the planning of the other programs, which together with correspondence study, came to constitute Extension. In line with his discussions with McCarthy in the days of the Legislative Reference Library, he created the department of Debating and Public Discussion. Its work was a logical development of the activities of the Free Library Commission, and Hutchins' enthusiasm for it is to be seen in his preparation of debators' guides even before the work of the correspondence department was formally blocked out. Aided by his capable and practical assistant, Miss Almere Scott, Hutchins compiled "package libraries" which were loaned by mail and consisted of collections of clippings and articles on matters of current interest. Lighty enthusiastically termed these libraries a "social invention" of greatest importance in an evolving democracy.[4] Certainly in a day before the development of contemporary mass media, they had great potentialities as molders of public opinion.

The work of the department of Debating and Public Discussion paved the way for direct and indirect Extension
activity in politics. From its files came much of the material used in the Saturday Lunch Club attack upon the Republican Stalwarts in 1912. Even keeping its patrons informed on current events involved more than the assembling
and editing of materials to be loaned. Through the records
of the department can be traced those matters in which
earlier generations showed keenest interest—reciprocity,
imperialism, the status of nonwhites in the American ter-
ritories. There was nothing radical or startling in either
the debaters' handbooks or the package libraries, save,
perhaps, that they presented at least two sides of a given
question. This in itself took them beyond the usually partisan expositions of the press or the political speech, sometimes giving their readers a grasp of affairs that roused
the resentment of office seekers and policy makers. The
success of the glittering generalization and emotion-arous-
ing slogan was challenged in a manner reminiscent of the
Biblical quotation appearing at the masthead of La Follette's
Weekly Magazine: Ye Shall Know the Truth, and the Truth
Shall Make Ye Free.

To the written words of Extension were added the spoken.
Taking another leaf from the history of the Ely effort, the
revived program included platform lectures. This effort was
not pushed, however, until adequate funds assured the success of the venture. In addition, an elastic department, that
of General Information and Welfare, was planned to care for
loose ends and to be alert for new departures. Like the other
departments, it was founded upon faith in the roles of information and reason in promoting the general welfare.

Mass enlightenment, enhancement of University prestige
and influence through correspondence study, encouragement
of public discussion, modified lyceum and ultimately social
service, this was the legacy handed Reber upon his arrival
in Madison in 1907. In his official report of the following
year, he spoke of the "progressive development of the work
of University Extension." [5] In 1922, he noted that since 1906
the work of the Division had remained "fundamentally" the
same: "extension of the campus to the farthest boundaries
of the state, or the greatest possible enlargement of the
student body; . . . the lengthening of the period of education
for the individual; and . . . the expansion of the services of
the University to include educational opportunities other

than those offered in the academic curricula."[6]

There were those, however, who came to feel that in 1907 "Reber found a community spirit and association of social and political ideas headed up a blind alley... [and that] he established... [Extension] as a permanent institution the people of Wisconsin will not willingly let die," and that the work begun in 1906 and 1907 had placed "University Extension in real danger of succumbing to soothing syrup methods and to ex cathedra methods of handling down knowledge from on high...."[7] These charges were leveled at Lighty, Hutchins, and kindred reformers who sought to universalize their concepts of the good life, defined in humanistic terms. To their critics, they seemed to be developing an extension program based upon the limited appeal of the work of the previous decade, and a program assured a similar fate. In an age when empiricism and efficiency were so generally accepted as keys to the future, Reber's position seemed clearheaded and practical. The dean echoed McCarthy in conceiving of extension as a means of providing "equality of opportunity" after a study of community needs, not "absolute ideals," had indicated the course to be taken. Idealism was inherent in extension, he continued, but must be subordinated to "the same common sense that must be applied to any business project. Fine sentiment is not enough."[8] From another point of view, Lighty conceived of his work as dedicated to the development of the whole man. Given his background and responsibilities, it is understandable that Reber stressed vocational education and a program that was assured of both popular and legislative support. The clash between these frames of reference led to bitter factionalism, but in the long run achieved a degree of balance that would otherwise have been lacking.

These circumstances complicated Reber's inherently difficult task of administering Extension. He had been brought into a situation that already had begun to crystallize and had been placed over men who had been making and administering policy for more than a year. This in itself helps to account for the development of cliques centering around Lighty and around Reber. Contention was manifested in various ways. When Reber noted that he had patterned the routine aspects of his administration after those of a commercially operated correspondence school, his critics cited this as evidence of his lack of sympathy with the Wisconsin Idea. His policy of institutional flexibility was labeled opportunism. In view of these circumstances and given his

own considerable ambition, Reber adopted the easy route of
administration by injunction. Luncheon conferences with
his aides were soon discontinued, as were the Madison
briefings of the Extension field representatives. These developments caused the opposition faction to tag the dean
"Czar" and "The Great Surveyor and Purveyor." His out-
bursts of temper and seeming lack of sympathy for the
Lighty ideals prompted repeated protests to the University
regents. In 1918, while Reber was away on war service and
Lighty was made acting dean, an informal hearing was given
the charges. Reber's supporters naturally viewed this as a
stab in the back. But his critics genuinely believed that such
an investigation was vital to the well-being of Extension and
that the facts could only be thoroughly aired when the dean
was not present. The hearings led to the conclusion that
while the dean's personality and temper had made things
difficult for some staff members, there had been no interference with the working out of Extension's major purposes,
and consequently no action was taken. Even Lighty, who
symbolized the opposition to Reber, testified to his "peculiar administrative genius."[9]

Although Reber had been brought to Madison primarily
because of his engineering background, he was not oblivious
to the value of the other aspects of extension. While he was
never enthusiastic about Hutchins, and once instructed
Lighty to "hold him down," he was publicly appreciative of
the significance of debating and open discussion in a democratic society. Furthermore, he worked personally in the
coöperative Milwaukee-Extension program, and during his
deanship, Extension became involved in the rough and
tumble of local politics in many Wisconsin areas. Though
projected before his arrival, the department of General
Information and Welfare and its Community Institutes were
formally launched during his tenure.

Dean Reber's insistence upon Extension's constant alert-
ness for new opportunities was firmly rooted in the institution's early experience. When the vocational schools provided employers with trained men, and when social service
work was taken over by newly created state agencies, Extension re-entrenched, abandoning these fields of activity
and directing its attention toward students seeking vocational work of "higher grade" and toward citizenship education.
When budget stringencies necessitated curtailment of non-
fee-producing activities, greater emphasis was immediately
placed upon those which produced income. Extension could

not remain static; to do so was to die. It could not compel use of its facilities; it had to seek out those areas in which there was already a popular interest, or in which such interest could be readily stimulated. Much depended upon the imagination and far-sightedness of those responsible for policy.

Reber's insistence upon flexibility clashed with his tendency to favor vocational education when, in 1914, the findings of a survey of the University were published. The survey had been inspired in large part by Extension's midwife, Dr. Charles McCarthy. After crusading for vocational schools, he had assumed responsibility for a still more ambitious project, the reform of the educational system of the entire state. His method was his by then familiar procedure of investigating a problem to which he already had an answer, dramatizing the "findings" in a public report, and then struggling to secure legislative sanction and appropriations.

McCarthy began with the rural schools, which he planned to make counterparts of Extension's urban community centers. Coöperating with pioneer rural sociologists, he urged vigorous concentration upon agricultural technology, methods of coöperative marketing, and Extension-sponsored courses of a general nature. The vocational schools were next on McCarthy's list; from them he wanted increased emphasis upon business training and domestic science, and the addition of citizenship classes taught by Extension staff members. The final step consisted of an investigation of the normal schools and the state University by the staff of Dr. William H. Allen of the New York Bureau of Municipal Research. Allen and his aides were already well-known in Wisconsin, a result of their study of the city of Milwaukee. McCarthy considered Allen a "narrow man," but felt that his work could serve as a means of launching an improved state-wide vocational education program.[10]

McCarthy's definition of "improved" had not changed since the days when he had pushed extension work into the shops and the factories. He admitted a "belief" in "cultural value," but asked what it was.

> Is it . . . set by someone outside the state, set by someone who lived a hundred years ago, or does it reside in better homes, better inspiration, better earning capacity, better farms and better work-shops? [If community needs so dictate, we must] cut at the top the so-called cultural

studies and provide solidly and surely for the real
workers of the state.... If we find that our University
and our schools turn out boys and girls who are not in
sympathy with the democratic principles upon which the
state is founded, we ought to find out exactly what is the
matter. Evidently if we are turning out snobs who are
out of sympathy with the great mass of people of our
state, we ought to find out what is the matter.[11]

The survey of the extension phase of University activity
was supervised by Paul H. Neystrom, a former Extension
administrator who had joined the faculty of the University
of Minnesota. Extension staff members were requested to
evaluate their own courses and methods, to report on their
hours of work and the way in which they were spent. What
texts were used, what references? What kinds of questions
were the students asked? What did their answers reveal
regarding grasp of the subject, clarity of expression, use
of English, spelling, punctuation, and penmanship? It was
hoped that such analysis would aid the instructors as well
as contribute to the completion of a mosaic of University
activities. As the related investigations proceeded, reports
released to the press hinted at the outcome. An investigator
of the normal schools found the class work tending toward
pedantry and beyond the grasp of youthful minds which were
forced to wrestle with such terms —gleaned by the investigators from class lectures —as "selective attention" and
"empirical psychology."[12] The McCarthy plan was proceed-
ing on schedule; a blow was being prepared for increased
emphasis upon practical courses, defined as those which
were materially productive.

The section of the published report dealing with Extension
solemnly revealed that while some educators deemed its
work valuable, others did not. Instead of attempting to il-
luminate this conclusion, the report endeavored to show
that Extension's work was over 90 per cent vocational
(courses in commercial and engineering subjects), the remaining efforts being devoted to such "general" work as
courses in social psychology, rural sociology, elementary
French, and literature. This, the report interpreted as
indicating that Wisconsin wanted more vocational work, and
that Extension should develop its program in that direction.[13]
The McCarthy plan now had been advanced through the stage
of public report and recommendation. This time, however,
he was checked with weapons of his own design.

When Extension administrators learned of the nature of the findings, efforts were made to suppress them. Lighty hastened to Minneapolis to urge Neystrom, in a nightmarish hotel room scene, to revise the "offensive pages," which were, Lighty claimed, misleading and injurious to Extension.[14] The report was not altered to the Extension Division's satisfaction, however, and Extension was forced to meet its critics publicly. Reber denied the validity of the survey's findings on grounds that the investigation had been conducted within a mold preconceived by Dr. Allen. Allen replied that Neystrom, who had been approved by Reber and was sympathetic to Extension, bore the responsibility for the work. The general attack upon the Allen Survey, he charged, was but an attempt to becloud the fact that the need for changes and improvements had been indicated.[15]

The University as a whole was justifiably indignant over the way it had been handled in the Allen report, and segments of Extension especially so.[16] When the matter was probed, it was found that the Allen staff members had skewed their findings by only partially quoting their informants, quoting them out of context, and giving the testimony of recent or disgruntled Extension staff members the same weight as that accorded veterans. More serious was the way in which certain Extension activities had been overlooked or discounted and thus made to seem insignificant when compared to vocational work.[17]

Outraged Extension faculty prepared a vigorous reply to the survey, issuing it over their own names. Extension was still a pioneering educational agency, they pointed out, but despite its youth was aware of many of its shortcomings. Those which the Allen investigators had dwelt upon had already been noted and discussed; the hopes raised early in the survey that new ground would be broken had been dashed. Worse yet was the report's neglect of certain Extension strong points: the 17,961 registrations in correspondence courses between 1906 and 1915, the 3,741 package libraries sent to 405 communities in the years 1913-14, the community service programs and visual instruction aids provided schools throughout the state.[18] In the confusion of charges and counter-charges, the effect for which McCarthy had hoped perished. Extension was not wholly committed to a program of cash-value courses or those requiring the lowest levels of sophistication. Policy makers within the Division were not stripped of the power to chart their own courses. Vocational education would remain an important

part of the Extension program, but not to the exclusion of
all else. Extension was left with the possibilities of quickly
developing several types of services should the need
arise.

The Division's need for continuous enrollments prompted
advertising tactics not always consonant with the expressed
ideals of Extension staff members. Extension was not
troubled by doubts about its role in society or by the doubts
which some schoolmen still entertained about the ethics of
advertising educational opportunities. The question facing
the Division was not whether to seek to shape the lives of
its constituents, but in what manner; not whether to advertise, but how to do so most effectively. The answers provide
one means of watching the activities of policy makers as
they faced a changing situation.

It was to be expected that privately operated correspondence schools, with their necessary stress upon profits,
would base their appeals upon promises of economic gain.
But what of the normal schools, the colleges, the universities and their extension services? While they were not as
dependent upon student fees as their commercial rivals,
their ultimate success as educational institutions was no
less dependent upon making the public aware of and desirous
for the opportunities they offered. American university public relations services had developed the technique of wrap-
ping school advertising in informational packages, of letting
the public know that the institution which had just made an
important contribution to the field of higher mathematics,
medicine, or history was also enrolling freshmen. Some
extensions, however, had resorted to less refined techniques, and one Wisconsin faculty member expressed disgust with Columbia extension's blanket assurance that
correspondence study under its supervision was certain to
lead to success. The promise was unethical because it did
not consider differences in student backgrounds or capaci-
ties to learn and profit by learning. This seemed to be competing with the shoddiest of the commercial schools on their
own level.[19]

From the beginning of his long period of service in Wisconsin's Extension Division, Lighty appreciated the necessity of informing the public of the educational opportunities
at hand. Ignoring residence faculty rules, he placed a sign
proclaiming the existence of correspondence study in the
window of his Main Hall office. Petty bickering led to its
forced removal, but no such standards of decorum were ob-

served regarding much of the printed material which the
Division came to circulate.

In contrast to the closely worded Extension advertise-
ments posted in factories, school buildings and libraries,
and to the neat, factual bulletins outlining correspondence
course offerings, were series of announcements proclaiming correspondence study as the key to material success.
High school seniors planning to come to the University
were warned that many entering freshmen failed the University English examination. The preventive measure was a
correspondence course to prepare for the test. Bank
cashiers were invited to enroll in a money and banking
course designed "especially for the man who wants facts
and principles compactly and clearly presented, and who
has not time to waste on useless theories. This course
should appeal particularly to the growing young man."
School teachers were invited to enroll in courses designed
to improve their classroom techniques, broaden their
"scholarship," and to help prepare them for "more responsible positions" and advanced certification. University Extension advised engineers, "You can make your own opportunities." If advancement seemed slow, three hours study
per night added up to 156 hours per year and increased
chances for promotion. A single course was advertised as
beneficial to road laborers desiring foremanship, foremen,
inspectors, highway commissioners, engineers, government
officials and materials salesmen alike. "No previous training is required. The only thing necessary is the ability to
read simple everyday English," these men were assured.
On a still broader level, Extension ads described Abe
Lincoln, Tom Edison, and Henry Ford as examples of men
who had succeeded via the home study route. Ford's career
especially revealed how genius plus "persistant, consecutive
study" could raise the man in overalls to untold heights.
And now by correspondence, one could "study the principles
underlying Ford's success."[20]

This optimism was not entirely unrealistic. Better trained
teachers were in demand; the age of the electrical appliance
and the automobile was dawning. Training was needed, and
the state through the Extension Division announced its readi-
ness to prepare individuals for the demands of the new era.
The potential economic advantages inherent in successful
completion of correspondence courses constituted a major
emphasis in Extension's search for enrollments. Dean
Reber actively solicited testimonials from satisfied students

and made such letters available to field representatives and prospective students. To some, these letters indicated that the Extension Division was "doing a real service of great value."[21]

In thus stressing material advantages, Extension revealed the level of its major offerings, the audiences to which it hoped to appeal, and its need to complete with private schools. As more and more students enrolled in courses carrying University credit, however, a new advertising policy became possible. In 1926, Lighty was able to speak out strongly for the "revitalization of the humanities in the minds of young men and women who go to college." He urged field representatives to avoid alienating prospective students by a "commercial" approach which would seem to place Extension's offering of "genuine education" on the "paper grading" level of its private rivals. Two years later, he sounded the real challenge. It was easy to sell courses having "pay-envelope results," he noted, but to fulfill its higher function, Extension must acknowledge and act upon President Van Hise's view that "the least commendable purpose of acquiring knowledge is to apply it to our own advancement." From this point of view, Extension was obligated to instill into its students the desire and ability to benefit mankind.[22] Extension would try to meet that challenge in many ways, yet never without considering the matters of self-perpetuation and expansion.

Courses with "pay-envelope results" versus education for the elevation of mankind—herein simmered a controversy within Extension which is even yet not forgotten. It is reflected in the tape recordings made by Lighty near mid-century, and in the memorial volume published by Reber's friends after his death in 1948. It is the record of conflicting ideas as to the purpose of education—education as a means to achieving a full life, or as a means to achieving personal ambition.

Lighty had come to Wisconsin with a vision of "service" which squared with Van Hise's pronouncements about the University. He liked to cite the 1904 Inaugural Address as the basis for the Extension Division, without always recalling the circumstances which made the address the cornerstone he felt it to be. Lighty also seems never to have been entirely mindful of McCarthy's discontent with Extension work in the spring of 1907, and the manner in which this led to the hiring of Reber.

After Reber's death, Lighty feared that his former

superior was being given undue credit for various developments within the Division. During his deanship, Reber had
officially credited Lighty with the successful organization
of correspondence study work and importance in shaping
the entire Division. Those who after Reber's passing gave
him credit perhaps due Lighty may have acted from un-
awareness of the situation or, in some cases, from malice
born of a conflict which spanned three different deanships.
Lighty was certain that thwarted personal ambition was the
basis for much of the feeling against him. By this same
token, however, he never achieved the position for which he
thought he was being brought to Wisconsin.

Lighty charged that Reber was unable to appreciate the
"Wisconsin Idea" of which Extension was a manifestation,
that he was an opportunist and lacking in the ideals which
distinguished Extension correspondence study from that of
the private schools.[23] In these terms, however, the actions
of neither man were sufficiently consistent to warrant unqualified generalizations. If, as Lighty charged, Reber over-
stressed education for material gain, Lighty cannot shed
responsibility for Extension advertising which played up
similar ends prior to Reber's coming. It would be unfair to
judge Reber without considering that as dean he was publicly responsible for his actions, while his critics had the im-
munity traditionally allowed to the minority opposition. On
the other hand, it would be unfair to cite Lighty's failure to
promote correspondence study work for soldiers while he
held the position of acting dean during World War I as con-
clusive evidence in support of the charges that he was an
incompetent administrator. In a sense, Lighty himself later
buttressed the findings of the regents that while Reber's
personality made life within the Division difficult for some,
it had not affected the success of the work as a whole. In a
letter to Reber written in 1936 after Reber's successor had
been ousted by the regents, Lighty observed,

> Well, that's that. Ten wasted years and worse. The hope
> now is that the University, in so far as its outreach
> function is concerned, may be put back on the track
> upon which it was put by those who in the dark decade
> were all clearly discredited.
>   I trust this latter gleam of hope for a better day may
> be heartening to you, dismal and depressing as have
> been the intervening years."[24]

Extension as Teacher

I would have no mute inglorious Milton in this state; I would have everybody who has a talent have an opportunity to find his way so far as his talent will carry him, and that is possible through university extension, supplementing the schools and colleges.

—Charles R. Van Hise, May, 1908

i don't care if it cost me 200 dollars ill stick to you if you stay by me because ill make it up in the long run.

—Extension Student, 1916

~~~~~~~~~~~~~~~~~~~~~~~~~~~~~~~~~~~~~~~

The combined services of the Extension Division cast the University of Wisconsin in an important role in the everyday lives of countless people not only in the state, but throughout the world. Extension's correspondence courses, aids to schools, and community development, enlightenment and entertainment programs made Madison synonymous with nonresidence education. Portions of the Wisconsin campus were baled and ready for shipment at a moment's notice. In thus trying to meet the various needs of the thousands who turned to it for guidance, the Division was forced to grow, to adapt, to alter constantly its methods of operation and instruction.

On the eve of the First World War, over 300 different occupations were listed by correspondence students—medicine, preaching, teaching, business, factory and technical work, housekeeping, occupations ranging from the "learned professions" to the "most humble forms of service."[1] Many educators and future educators were attracted by this still novel method of guided study. Among them were Paul H. Neystrom of Superior, the first person to enroll under the program administered by William H. Lighty, and K. L. Hatch, later a member of the Agricultural College faculty. The head of an economics department of an eastern college took a course under John R. Commons in order to observe his approach to the topic of labor. And there were men like the principal of Glidden High School who completed seven extension courses before coming to Madison for residence work. Many school teachers, both public and parochial, took several courses, and suggested that others be added to the list of offerings. At the same time, study by correspondence

attracted many laborers, who worked out their lessons after
physically fatiguing days in ill-lighted factories, geologists
in Asia, a paper maker in the U.S.S.R., an advertising
manager in Sweden, the daughter of an American official in
the Philippines. To Extension's foreign language teachers
came Americans planning to travel abroad; to the teachers
of English came immigrants and foreign students. The
average age of those taking correspondence courses was in
the mid-twenties, but there were some like the boy whose
father had opposed his attending school, a fifty year old
"schoolboy wrestling with . . . a simple problem"; and a
woman of advanced age who found in correspondence
courses something to which to cling. Housewives who refused to allow their minds to stagnate or who were unpre-
pared for the problems and tasks of homemaking and
motherhood also turned for aid to the correspondence study
department. So, too, did university and college students
seeking to accumulate credits, and prisoners in state penal
institutions helping to work out their own rehabilitation.
The list was legion. Lessons worked out in quiet studies
and crowded flats, on kitchen tables, in prison cells, tropi-
cal huts and in the mess halls of Alaskan mining camps
were mailed to the Extension Division of the University of
Wisconsin. The geographical spread of this instruction was
as great as the extent of mail service.[2]

What did these correspondence students seek? "i dont
care if it cost me 200 dollars ill stick to you if you stay by
me because ill make it up in the long run," wrote a stationary engineer. Milwaukee industrialist, Thomas J. Neacy,
grumbled that his apprentices who attended Extension classes returned to the shop "so cocky and expectant of great
consideration" that he considered firing the lot. The motive
of material gain was a major one, and Extension students
spread the good word when lessons proved profitable. "My
course in the automobile engine has paid for itself many
times," wrote an enthusiastic mechanic, "and I wish to finance one for my brother." Several companies used the Extension work of their employees as criteria for promotion.
This was material for the popular press, proof of the money-
making value of correspondence study. The Division explo-
ited the case of "Number 19, a farm lad, [who] took a course
of twenty lessons, and after six weeks in the Engineering
Summer School received a position as traction engineer."
And there were more, like the student who became shop
foreman after two years of study; and another who rose

from foreman to superintendent via the correspondence
route.[3]

Early in the history of Extension, elementary level vocational students outnumbered the other correspondence
registrants. As the state vocational schools absorbed this
group, business and commercial courses proved the most
attractive. By 1920, however, it was evident that school
teachers would comprise a major portion of the Division's
students. By 1925, they constituted almost seventy per cent
of those enrolled in the evening classes developed by the
Division.[4] There is little need to probe the reason for enrollment in business courses designed for "practical and
applied ends." Office workers and merchants found study of
the effective use of English and retail and store management profitable, and happily documented their promotions
and increased sales of apples, sugar, and woolen blankets.
But courses in music, art, and literature often had their
cash value, too. Taken by teachers seeking advanced degrees and certification, they were often of as great utility
as were plumbing and steam fitting to laborers. There were,
undoubtedly, those who worked out their lessons for the
sheer joy of it, but existing Extension files contain only
occasional hints of such motivation. Working and professional men and women were primarily interested in greater
financial security, and they found Extension a willing ally.

In 1910, Dr. Charles McCarthy had feared that America's
jobless might resort to revolutions reminiscent of the 1848
violence in Europe. His belief that rural prosperity and
conservatism were causally related encouraged his attempts
to promote economic well-being among the urban masses.
Assuming that possession of industrial skills was a guaran-
tee of steady employment, McCarthy promoted publicly
supported industrial education courses. Tax money set
aside to provide workers something that gave them an interest in the status quo seemed well spent.[5] But was there not
also an American tradition of providing at least equal opportunity for all? If so, University Extension was assuring
Americans of their heritage.

Almost two decades later, Lighty observed that the recent
general strike in England had not degenerated into revolution because of the mental discipline which that country's
adult education program had given labor leaders and union
members.[6] The implication regarding this side of the
Atlantic was clear. The McCarthy and Lighty views revealed a common goal and a shared belief that the goal

could be reached through education. At the same time, their
opinions spelled out the opposed philosophies that affected
so much of life within the division. To McCarthy, social
safety lay in higher living standards. To Lighty, Extension's
great contribution was the dissemination of "authentic" information. Here in microcosm was the conflict between the
economic determinist and the view that man does not live by
bread alone.

In retrospect, it is hard to visualize Extension as standing between the social fabric and revolution, but this is born
of hindsight. The restless, unskilled masses of unemployed
envisioned by McCarthy did not become numerically threatening for several decades. Even the vocational schools soon
lost much of their early character. For a number of years
they served as institutions for students expelled from other
schools, and as centers for night classes in handicraft and
hobby work, while their directors sought statistical devices
with which to pad their real worth. The nature of industry
had changed, and for a time formal worker training seemed
superfluous. Soon wartime conditions created a manpower
shortage which Extension helped to alleviate by its emergency instruction for substitute workers, women and boys
as well as men. The prosperity of the 1920's followed
shortly. The immediate threat to national stability, then,
lay less with the jobless wage worker, than with the short-
sightedness of the educated business and government group.

In academic work, Extension instructors helped convert
a scattering of self-styled revolutionists and socialists to
more orthodox frames of reference,[7] providing evidence
from the students themselves that open and full discussions
are more convincing than one-sided haranguing. But Extension students studying social and economic theory were in
the minority. By July 1, 1922 — the eve of the boom — business
courses had attracted the largest number of students,
25,771, with engineering courses running a close second.
During the same period, 3,127 students had taken work in
political economy, but 5,784 had enrolled in mathematics,
including the various shop or "practical" courses. The
number of home economics students was more than double
the 1,099 who had registered for history.[8] However much
Extension champions intellectualized their efforts at leadership, the Division's role was largely determined for it by
the desires of its clients or current public opinion. Extension offered the aspiring a chance to increase their command of their chosen fields; but the aspiring had already

determined in large part the nature of Extension. By finding
and filling the gaps in the state educational system, the
Division made itself useful and thus retainable.

Defining education broadly, the Division carried its instruction beyond that needed for the better fulfillment of
daily tasks. Evening lecture series, an important aspect of
Extension in the 1890's, were still regarded as potentially
a major phase of the revived work. From an administrative
point of view, a lecture service was an especially flexible
medium which could be altered quickly and with but minimal
inconvenience. Public lectures still had great mass appeal,
partly because entertainment and enlightenment could be
blended in them and audiences enjoyed social as well as
intellectual rewards. It was not until 1909, however, that
Extension was ready to actively push such work. In that
year J. J. Pettijohn, former teacher, school principal,
county superintendent and lyceum agent, became acting
head of the department of Instruction by Lectures. The
diversity of his earlier experience quickly became evident.
To the usual offerings he added "desirable entertainments"
in art, literature, and music—all in the name of service to
the people of the state. His efforts proved temporarily
popular. Through his contact with the program committees
of clubs, civic groups, and schools, an estimated 46,000
persons were reached during the first year of the reorganized lecture service's existence.[9]

The department's selection of programs was a difficult
task. On the one hand, there was the necessity of maintaining the dignity of the University; on the other, the problem
of satisfying public taste. One answer was to quickly remove from the list of offerings individuals who attained any
kind of notoriety. Another consisted of dividing the offerings into University and non-University series. Critics
called the latter—sometimes unjustly—"The Flea Circus."
In 1914, forty University men and groups, and a similar
number of outside speakers and performers were at the
disposal of Wisconsin audiences. On the University list,
Professor Arthur Beatty considered the contemporary English novel, and Professors F. L. Paxson, Carl Russell Fish
and Wayland Chase, aspects of United States history.
Stephen W. Gilman, professor of business administration
discussed "Friend Making," Michael F. Guyer, "Race
Betterment and Heredity," Joseph Jastrow, "The Lanuage
of the Face," William H. Kiekhofer, "Government by Public
Opinion," and E. A. Ross, "Subsurface Tendencies of Amer-

ican Society." From the non-University list, interested
groups could secure Mohammed Ali, who brought the fruits
of his education at Lahore, India, to Wisconsin audiences in
his lecture series on the Far East; Balmer's Kaffir Boys'
Chorus, a presentation of singing, tales of witchcraft and
"amusing" wedding practices; Silas Evans, president of
Ripon College, speaking on "The Battle of Ideas—Militarism versus Peace," and "Jesus and Social Reform"; Dr.
William Sadler discussing "The Cause and Cure of Worry,
or How to Banish the Blues"; Thatcher's Metropolitan
Orchestra with a repertoire including the "Barcarolle" from
Tales of Hoffman, Overture to William Tell, Rubenstein's
Melody in F, Rigoletto Fantasia, and the Blue Danube Waltz.[10]

The communities in which these and related programs
appeared were generally small, ranging in population from
Fond du Lac (18,789) to Luck (383), Glidden (100), and
Allenville (54). In a day before broadcasting and the family
automobile, the programs brought at least some enrichment
to the cultural lives of many—a need Lighty had detected in
his early travels in outlying Wisconsin areas. The Milwaukee Journal termed the service a "great work."
Through it, audiences in Weyauwega heard the Illinois Glee
Club, the Chicago Concert Company, an impersonator, and
an assortment of lecturers. Waldemar von Geltch, violinist
of the University Music Department, shared the stage of
the Neillsville Opera House with a reader from the Expression Department of the University of Kansas, the Chicago
Operatic Company, and economics Professor William
Kiekhofer. Behind the scenes, Extension fieldmen competed
with private booking agencies, trying to convince prospective patrons that Extension's at-cost productions were of
the same calibre as the higher-priced offerings of its rivals.
It was estimated that in a single biennium, the department
saved Wisconsin communities $90,000 over what they would
have had to pay for the "same talent" sponsored privately.
Even so, the fees collected by Extension made the service
self-supporting.[11]

Lighty hoped for something more than the brand of culture
brought to the state by the lecture service. Valuable as it
was, it did not meet the standards of its initiators and was
not comparable to such programs as the Lowell Lectures in
Boston. Lighty felt a surge of hope when in 1920, Extension
and the City Club of Milwaukee assumed joint responsibility
for a series of lectures. Ideally, the entire winter season
was devoted to a consideration of a single broad problem.

Distinguished University men like Carl Russell Fish lectured on recent world problems in a manner deemed "popular and illuminating as well as authoritative." But the early
popularity of the series faded. By 1925, the audiences,
drawn largely from the City Club members, their guests
and Milwaukee Extension students, were so small that
Lighty correctly foresaw the end of a "worthy and promising enterprise."[12] Similar efforts were subsequently revived, but never successfully. Extension offered a variety
of bills of fare to people in quest of an evening's enjoyment
and edification. But serious speakers as well as chanting,
stomping Kaffir boys were unacceptable as a steady diet;
they could not compete for attention with the motion picture
and the radio. The experience indicated once again Extension's need for flexibility.

The vast educational work of the Division necessitated
employment of a huge permanent staff. Of the various departments, each with its bureaus staffed by administrators
and clerical force, correspondence study was both the
pioneer and the largest. From Lighty and his assistant,
Miss Julia Flisch, who organized the work in 1906, the department was expanded to ten instructors by 1909, although
twenty-three others from residence departments still
handled correspondence lessons. Together, these teachers
taught 206 different courses. In 1914, thirty-four full-time,
thirty part-time, and eighteen fee basis teachers and textbook writers were on the Division's staff, which was now
quite distinct from that of the University. Despite the increase in academic as opposed to vocational course enrollments, increased efficiency and budgeting problems resulted in a faculty decrease. In the biennium 1925-26, correspondence-study listed twenty-six full- and four part-time
teachers. In 1914, there had been 4,000 new enrollments
and 10,000 active students; in 1924, these numbers had increased to 10,000 and 26,000.[13]

Creation of a separate and specialized correspondence
study faculty was necessary from both student and faculty
points of view, both of which sometimes seemed lost amidst
the din of academic and state politics. Extension students
were entitled to better study guidance than they had received in the 1890's. Continuity of instruction and dispatch
in handling lessons could be assured only if Extension
could select and supervise its own teachers. At the same
time, it was both unfair and unwise to cajole residence instructors into adding correspondence teaching to already

full schedules. Many had been persuaded or made to feel
obligated to do so, only to neglect the responsibilities they
assumed. One conscientious volunteer concluded that given
the complexity of his Extension duties, his remuneration
was but from six to seven cents per hour. Aside from time
and monetary considerations, Reber and Lighty felt that
successful correspondence teaching demanded faculty
members with the "proper viewpoint." In his 1912 report
to the dean, Lighty noted:

> Extra-mural teaching presupposes a broad democratic
> concept of education on the part of the teachers; it as-
> sumes far-reaching social insight and sympathy. Not
> only are elasticity, flexibility, and adjustability primary
> requirements to this manner of teaching, so far as the
> student is concerned, but a similar condition exists in
> reference to the correlation of accumulated knowledge
> and... culture with the modern requirements of life and
> livelihood.[14]

One of the first threats to successful correspondence
teaching stemmed from the widespread campus attitude that
extension work was of secondary importance and hence conducted by second-raters. An extensionist sharing even
distantly in that point of view courted feelings of inferiority,
burning resentment, or pretended indifference to the work
at hand. In any case, he emerged less effective as a teacher.
In addition, there were problems of dealing at long range
with students of diverse backgrounds and preconceptions,
and the ever-present realization that in popularizing there
is constant danger of vulgarizing. Extension teaching, then,
required much of the spirit of the missionary and the
pioneer. There was work to be done which many considered
undistinguished; horizons were still indistinct, the way yet
uncharted.

Many teachers quickly abandoned the work, and the rapid
turnover of personnel presented a constant problem to the
administration and students. Smooth operation depended
upon a regular and dedicated faculty familiar with routine
which is much more tedious and also more important than
it is in regular classroom teaching. Many of the instructional staff did remain for long periods, however, contribut-
ing their accumulated professional experience to the development of correspondence education: Ben Elliot, C. M.
Jansky, G. A. Hool, and H. E. Pulver in Engineering; Annie
M. Pitman in Latin and Greek; Arthur Beatty, Leila Bascom,

Mrs. Bernice D. Kuney and Frank Crane in English; Harriet
Holt in Mathematics; Miss A. B. Ernst in German; E. B.
Schlatter in Romance Languages.

But what was the actual status of this staff; was it a co-
equal part of the University faculty, an inferior branch, or
the vanguard of a separate institution? Extension's pioneers
themselves were not always clear whether they wished to
spearhead creation of an extra-mural university or insist
upon the Division's acceptance as a legitimate organ of
Van Hise's "third function" of the existing institution.[15] In
the main, however, they favored the latter. From the beginning, Lighty insisted upon integrating the names of his
teachers with those of the residence faculty, and upon a
"room in the sun" when he moved his office from the Free
Library Commission to Main Hall on the campus. Location
of the division's quarters next to the president's office
placed it at the heart of University activities and, Lighty
hoped, clothed it with needed prestige. This invasion of the
hill was not without its skirmishes. Unfriendly residence
men forced and won the Battle of the Window Sign, but
failed in an attempt to relegate Extension to the agricultural
campus. There were those, however, who would always consider Extension a poor relation at best, and one unfit to
share in the "sifting and winnowing by which alone the truth
can be found."

In various ways, members of the Extension Division staff
came to feel isolated from the residence faculty. Until 1922,
Extension teachers assumed that they, like other University
professors, were included in the retirement pension program of the Carnegie Foundation. This assumption was
strengthened by statements attributed to Dean Reber. A
minor crisis developed when discussions about the new
state teacher retirement system revealed that the Foundation's philanthropy did not extend to those teaching on a
subuniversity level, and hence excluded Extension. An error attributable in part to Lighty's insistence that his
faculty be listed with residence men had resulted in Extensionists' names being included in the Carnegie lists.
Teachers hired after 1912 were not so listed, but the con-
tradiction remained publicly undetected for several years.
When it was made known, some faculty members, heaping
blame upon Reber, appealed to the Foundation for recon-
sideration. The indomitable Miss Bascom viewed the
situation differently. In a statement reflecting her interest
in the current question of the Foundation's effect upon

academic freedom, she described herself as a "conscientious objector" against Carnegie money and in favor of
membership in the state system.[16] She and her colleagues
ultimately had no choice. The Foundation rejected their appeal, and the members of Extension's instructional and
field staffs were placed under the state plan. This in itself
made the Extension staff and resident faculty seem distinct.

Even as the Carnegie question was being thrashed out,
Division members began active protests against the "poor
relation" treatment they believed accorded them. The slowness of pay increases and promotions inspired complaints
that the University's advancement policy obviously did not
apply to Extension. By 1926, however, Reber's statistically
backed arguments and Lighty's insistence that Extension
teachers rendered a "similar quality of service" as their
residence colleagues had proved effective. If one considers
the requirements for appointment, the pay scales were not
disparate. The matter of faculty rank was another matter.
Recommended promotions did not receive favorable action,
and the apparent discrimination, especially against women,
drew the ire of Regent Zona Gale. President E. A. Birge
replied simply that the nature of much Extension work did
not qualify those who handled it for the highest faculty
status.[17]

President Birge's position was not untenable. However
widespread and successful its work, Extension was in many
respects a subordinate branch of the University. Indeed,
much of its position and popularity rested upon the prestige
of the parent institution. Wherever University credit courses
were involved, moreover, the residence departments exercised a strong hand in both hiring and supervising the extensionists. Dean Reber's attempts to overcome this depend-
ency ended in his defeat. So, too, was it with the graduate
study offered for a time by correspondence. As for credit
work, then, Extension's staff followed rather than made the
policy. From another point of view, the level of their
courses generally prevented Extension teachers from
meeting one of the most important traditional requirements
for academic promotion. While a few supervised some advanced work, they were more fully occupied with instrucion
of less than university level. The teaching load itself prevented the faculty from meeting another of the requirements
for promotion: productive research. It was not unusual for
Extension teachers to handle such a multiplicity of courses
as to be completely immersed in their preparation and

presentation. At one time, Miss Pitman taught twenty-three
different courses, C. M. Jansky, twenty-two, and Miss
Bascom, six. When Miss Pitman's courses dropped to
eighteen, she reported that increased demands for "administrative coöperation" occupied 20 per cent of her time,
although she was not permitted to record this in her work
reports.[18] Clearly, Extension was primarily a teaching
institution.

As a teaching institution, Extension's accomplishments
and contributions were often of high order. Use of traveling
instructors to augment the early shop courses was but one
of the Division's worthy innovations. More far-reaching
were those in the realm of correspondence study techniques
in which personal contact was not a factor. Frederick
Jackson Turner's early correspondence courses had been
built around a standard set of lesson sheets sent to credit
and noncredit students alike. The former were expected to
make greater use of the attached bibliographies, to submit
topical reports, and to answer the questions with greater
fullness, but the difference was quantitative rather than
qualitative.

Since most correspondence students enrolled for reasons
other than the accumulation of University credit, individual-
ized instruction was in order. Botany courses were constantly revised to reflect the season and the area in which
the student lived. English and education courses were likewise personalized. All students were sent the same instructions and lessons in the early phases of the work, and then
when their individual needs were defined, given specialized
supervision. Language instructors offered their students
not only conventional guidance, but, to those who were
teachers, advice in solving problems of classroom presentation and text book selection.[19]

The members of the regular correspondence study staff
took pride in the fact that they spent more time with the
work of each student than did any residence instructor, and
in the teacher-student rapport that this made possible.
Correspondence teachers like Miss Martha Edwards of the
History Department insisted upon the instructor's right to
deal independently with students, a right that included the
acceptance or refusal of students, reference to another
course or school, teaching, grading, and even dropping them.
In this way a confidential teacher-pupil relationship could
be established, the student's confidence and respect gained,
and an ideal form of tutorial work instituted. The teacher's

rewards were many: establishment of pleasant intellectual
friendships even though by mail, and knowledge that men
who were in a position to judge rated the best correspondence students equal if not superior to those in residence.
There was the pleasure of knowing, too, that some students
had been encouraged to come to the campus, where they
acquitted themselves well.

Along with the congenial and inspiring atmosphere of
these relationships went a hard core of directed study.
Though the Division developed its own textbook series for
its lower level vocational courses in shop mathematics,
concrete making, and banking, standard texts were the general rule in academic work. Reference materials not available in the student's local library could be obtained through
the Wisconsin State Library Commission, the University
Library, or Extension's own department of Debating and
Public Information. With the reading went the advice and
direction of the instructors. History students were led to
think along the lines of the most recent concepts. "Avoid
becoming involved in conflicting doctrinal beliefs in your
study of the Reformation," wrote Miss Edwards, "and look
for the pertinent political, economic and social developments."[20] German language students were obliged to tran-
scribe texts phonetically and then in the several tenses.
Study at home under Extension direction was not of the
carpet slipper and easy chair variety advertised by some
of the commercial schools. In many respects, it was more
challenging than residence study, because each student was
required to master all phases of the work undertaken.
There was no chance of slipping through a class session
without being called upon. Each student was a class by
himself.

The personal letters from students which have survived
in Extension's files reveal respect both for their teachers
and for the courses. While some complained that the paper
and format used in the direction sheets were cheap and
poorly set up, and that lesson correction was slipshod,
praise and gratitude were more often the rule. "I wish I
could teach as enthusiastically close up as you can at long
distance," wrote a public school teacher to Miss Pitman.
More concrete evidence of Extension's increasingly effective teaching methods was revealed by the steadily increasing number of lessons submitted per number of active
students. By 1922, 45.7 per cent of correspondence study
registrants had completed their courses. Three years later,

Lighty put the figure at 55 per cent, contrasting it with the
40 per cent of high school and University students who completed their four-year programs. The comparison was justified, Lighty maintained, by the greater difficulties under
which correspondence students studied and recited.[21] They
were not full-time students living in the atmosphere of the
schoolroom or library, were not spurred on by the stimulus
of competition with others. They tackled their lessons after
full days of work in factory, office, store, or home, drawing
upon their own resources and the carefully considered aid
of their Extension instructors.

There remains another index to the effectiveness of Extension's correspondence study work, namely its recognition
by institutions of higher learning. Aware of the calibre of
the Extension Division's credit work, the University of
Wisconsin approved it as fulfilling part of the requirements
for graduation. It was not a case of blindly accepting evidence of correspondence course completion, for similar
recognition was given the work of other university extensions only after they had demonstrated the qualifications of
their faculties. Purdue University accepted the correspondence credits approved by the University of Wisconsin.
Michigan Central Normal School respected Wisconsin correspondence credits as early as 1911, and several years
later, the faculty of the University of Michigan, moving
with the national trend, voted to accredit such studies pur-
sued through the Universities of Chicago and Wisconsin.[22]

But what about the masses whose needs, however simple,
Extension's pioneers had promised to serve? Public service had been one of the driving forces behind the 1906 reorganization. But there had also been the matter of extending University influence in the face of the competition of its
rivals. Both promises required the securing of large
audiences; neither proved easy to fulfill. Even after two
decades of extension experience, Lighty observed, "As a
rule, there is no army of our populace ready-made with a
hunger and thirst for knowledge. They are not sufficiently
informed to know what to secure and how to ask for it. This
is, no doubt, a part of the function of an educational institution."[23] To enable people of the state to realize the benefits available to them through Extension required that
public interest be aroused. This was the task for which the
Division's field service was organized.

Though such a state-wide force had been anticipated prior
to his coming, it remained for Dean Reber formally to block

out and inaugurate the work. In line with the early focus
upon the Milwaukee area, it was here that the first Extension district was established in 1908. The following year,
the second was centered about Oshkosh. The advantages
realized in the arrangement met expectations. Debating and
public discussion work showed a marked increase within
the organized areas, and home study students were given
personal advice and encouragement. Significant, regarding
future developments in Extension work, were the correspondence study classes which were quickly organized in
elementary and engineering subjects. Patterned after the
earlier aid accorded factory workers, classes were soon
meeting in public libraries, manufacturing plants and stores
in the cities surrounding the district headquarters. By the
mid-twenties, when Extension districts had been established
throughout Wisconsin, it was estimated that the division
was giving help of some sort to almost 3 million people.
Extension's popularity in some areas was reflected in the
vigorous though belated fight waged by the city of Oshkosh
to hold the headquarters of the Lake Winnebago District
when plans for moving it were made known, and by the
equally spirited and successful fight waged by Appleton to
secure them.[24]

The work of Extension field representatives was diversified—push the various services offered by the Division,
enroll, advise, teach, and seek out lax students. The routine
duties went still further, for fieldmen also gave advice regarding the strategy of releasing new courses, reported on
state political developments, and served as Extension representatives in meetings with college and normal school
presidents and teachers, high school audiences, industrialists, and worker groups. Sometimes field work involved
intense competition with the agents of privately operated
correspondence schools and entertainers' agencies. Benno
W. Meyer, a pioneer fieldman had to redouble his efforts in
La Crosse when his International Correspondence School
competitors mechanized their operations by acquiring an
automobile. In 1920, Mary Farrell, one of the Division's
few women field organizers, demonstrated her ingenuity by
becoming one of the first of her colleagues to purchase a
car in order to increase her contacts.

Within the field service as elsewhere in the Division,
idealism and reality were not always comfortable bed-
fellows. In his official report of 1910, Dean Reber approv-
ingly quoted a fieldman's appraisal of the Division.

"University Extension work is not a trade and not a business, but it is a high grade of professional social service.... The professional attitude required includes enthusiasm, sympathy for real men and women, willingness to work hard.... and willingness to study how to make the work more effective.... You are really working for the people of the state.... Your success is to be measured by <u>what</u> <u>good</u> you do for <u>them</u>."[25]

But how could one measure "good"? Field representative Marshall Graff argued that the matter had to be reduced to statistics: "... service can accurately be measured by the number of student registrations taken and the amount of money collected, because the finest educational institution in the world could not teach if it had no students.... This cannot be done unless the field force registers them," he concluded.[26]

The Graff approach had its merits. It could produce graphs, charts, enrollment lists and ledger books understandable to the most dollar-and-cents minded. It armed Extension administrators with a method for quickly evaluating their fieldmen, and the legislature with the means of quickly evaluating the Division. On the other hand, it encouraged some fieldmen to exchange glowing promises for names signed on the dotted line of Extension enrollment blanks. Indeed, one fieldman found a group of public school teachers approachable only after they had been assured University credit for a minimum of effort. Then came the blow. As Division teachers made known their demands, the disillusioned protested to Madison that they had been assured that the courses would involve no reading or written reports, and at most token final examinations. This was an abuse that was all too likely to occur when service was reduced to numbers. One field representative himself complained to his enrollment-graph conscious superior that "there have been too many loose promises ... about credits."[27] The field force produced students —any students; the rest was up to the teachers.

With the development of its field service, the Extension Division boasted a state-wide educational empire. Its centrally controlled organization contained possibilities of rendering the University the greatest of service, or at the same time, disservice. The fieldmen were the University's representatives, their personalities and work often constituting the criteria by which the people living far from

Madison judged the institution. At the same time, the very
complexity of the Division contained the possibility of its
carving an individual existence for itself, of becoming an
institution in its own right and a competitor instead of an
adjunct of the University.

A challenge to University unity was already developing
outside of the institution. Despite Extension's introduction
in Milwaukee of classes for teachers and work in home
economics, there were those who felt that the University
was not paying sufficient attention to the educational problems and needs of the largest city in the state. In 1909, the
feeling crystallized into a demand for a Milwaukee branch
of the University which would offer a curriculum similar to
that available in Madison. Optimistic city school officials
made plans to provide a centrally located building for the
project. Conferences with University officials, however,
led to suspension of the branch plan. President Van Hise
explained that branches would but weaken the parent body,
while the students who attended them would be deprived of
the library and laboratory facilities of the Madison campus.[28]
Thus blocked, the city school board appointed a committee
to meet with University representatives to consider plans
for increasing the efficiency of correspondence study activities. The movement to inaugurate university-grade work
in Milwaukee was not dead; two years later it again appeared, this time briefly before the state legislature.

Extension gradually entered the field from which the
University had shied. Even before the drive for a branch
university had been blunted, Dean Reber was attempting to
demonstrate the need for an evening law school in Milwaukee, and actively increasing the number of Extension
instructors aiding correspondence students and conducting
actual classroom work in engineering and business in that
city. His explanation was logical: it was more efficient and
economical to have the instructional staff permanently
located where it taught, rather than sending it out from
Madison.[29] Within this line of development, however, lay
the seeds of a large and permanent Milwaukee branch of
the Extension Division.

Following general Extension policy, the Milwaukee
District under the supervision of Kenneth G. Smith had
staved off, by altering the nature of its courses, the loss of
students threatened as a result of the creation of the vocational school system. Elementary work was de-emphasized
in favor of "higher engineering subjects," Spanish, public

speaking, literature and medical courses. Most of these
were offered in night school, but in 1919, an educational
emergency made possible the addition of regular daytime
classes. This expansion of the Extension program was
based upon the group of students created by government
educational subsidies for veterans. Dean Reber convinced
the regents of the students' need for day classes, and of
the feasibility of Extension satisfying the need. The new
undertaking necessitated additions to the Milwaukee faculty
until by 1922, fifteen regular instructors were meeting day
classes, and seventeen those scheduled for evenings. In
that same year, over half of Extension's 6,647 classroom
students were in Milwaukee.[30] In line with its boasted flexibility, the Extension Division recognized and met a sudden
opportunity to render educational service, and in so doing,
not only further justified its existence but added to its
growing prestige and organization.

The impetus provided Extension activity by the enrollment of veterans was but a temporary one. By 1922, these
students had exhausted the courses offered or had completed their training. To meet this threat to its Milwaukee
program, the Division opened its day classes to all wishing
to do university-grade work, and in the fall of 1923, offered
a full-time freshman and sophomore program.[31] Teaching
methods and examination schedules were coördinated with
those of the Madison campus, but in other ways the Milwaukee work tended to become autonomous. By 1924, only
two professors were teaching both in Madison and in Milwaukee, the remainder of the city staff being permanently
located there. Extension District Superintendent, John W.
Powell, who was immediately responsible for the Milwaukee
project, insisted that all Extension work carried on in the
area be handled through his offices. Duplicates of the
records of district students were transferred from Madison
to Milwaukee.

It was not a case of the Milwaukee organization working
at cross purposes with those responsible for Extension
policy decisions. Dean Reber and members of his field staff
worked diligently to secure the legislative appropriation for
the new building which the expanded work required, a building which became the symbol of the permanence of the new
development in Extension work.

The building proposal provoked the concerted opposition
of those whose positions it threatened. Dean Edward A.
Fitzpatrick of Milwaukee's Marquette University tried in

vain to block this extension of the state University on
grounds of incompatibility with the state constitution, and
in so doing asked several pertinent questions. What were
the University's intentions? Did it plan to use the wedge
made possible by the veterans' bonus law to establish a
permanent branch of the University? If so, was it necessary; were not Marquette and other educational institutions
adequately meeting Milwaukee's needs?[32] Other protests
came from the editor of the Madison Capital Times who
asked, "Detaching ... the University from Madison by
piecemeal?"[33] President Van Hise had seen the dangers of
such a move in 1909 and had blocked it. The less far-sighted
President Birge seemed not to grasp the significance of
the development, or was incapable of countering the desires
of those legislators who favored this program for their
area. Well might he have heeded Dean Fitzpatrick's warning, "The history in other states of branch educational institutions is not conducive to educational harmony even
within the institution itself."[34] The warning proved also
prophecy, but for the moment the University and its Extension Division were undeterred. Champions of the move
foresaw a great future for the work, envisioning the railroad network radiating from Milwaukee carrying Extension
representatives up and down the lakeshore, and students to
the Milwaukee Extension Center.[35]

Extension as Humanitarian

The establishment of the University Extension Division
and its development as an extra-mural college represents a social invention. This is a method against which
the conservative instincts and impulses of human nature
and society set themselves. These instincts and impulses operate powerfully in favor of self-preservation
in a state of nature, but retard with equal power those
enlightened industrial, commercial, agricultural, and
social advances which are based upon discovered and
ordered knowledge.

—William H. Lighty, 1912

University Extension was an integral a part of Progressivism as were the Social Gospel, the American Economics
Association, the Underwood Tariff, and the Anti-Tuberculosis Association. With them, it attempted to be of service
to every citizen by breaking up the monopolies enjoyed by
the few in selling, the money market, education, and medical care. The goal: a good life for all who could profit from
being shown the way. The Division's work in education has
already been considered, but William H. Lighty, especially,
realized that a trained worker in poor health was of little
value to himself or to society, and that jobs are not plenti-
ful amidst community strife. Extension approached these
problems in characteristic fashion, by taking portions of
the University to the people. After seven years of service,
Dean Louis E. Reber commented that the Division's community programs for health and education were but "new
forms . . . and signs of normal growth," that the ideals to
which Extension was dedicated were unchanged.[1]

Not all men possessed the background, inclination, or
time to pursue the good life through correspondence study.
Lighty viewed this as a challenge. Since Extension—and
hence the state—was obligated to search out and aid all
within its power, and since home study opportunities were
an inadequate vehicle, existing opportunities had to be supplemented.[2] If posters, exhibits, institutes and community
festivals could do the job, their employment was fully warranted. This continuing academic unorthodoxy provided Extension with further claims to existence and the right to

grow. The problem of coördinating these complex services
was now a major one. It fell in large part to Professor John
Gillin, Extension sociologist, and his Committee to Avoid
Duplication of Effort.

The developing Extension program elicited both criticism
and praise. Many residence faculty who could approve of
correspondence courses questioned the value, validity, and
finally the dignity of the rest of the Division's efforts. To
their hostility was added that of men outside the University
who denounced all social amelioration programs as interference with natural laws—or often their own economic and
political aspirations. But along with condemnation came
evidences of support—support from the people who turned
repeatedly to the Division for aid, and from members of
the legislature who approved requests for appropriations.
The spirit of one group of backers was reflected in W. D.
P. Bliss's hearty exclamation to Lighty, "Well, well! This
is what Josiah Strong wanted the churches to do. Now the
universities are going to do it!"[3]

Generations of intellectuals had debated the problem of
the individual versus the community as the proper starting
point for reform movements. Wisconsin extensionists did
not exhaust themselves in such Brook Farm discussions,
but directed their efforts at both. Since the age of Emerson,
life had become no less real, but more complex, and a sense
of urgency spurred on those who sought solutions to problems bred of human interaction. How could each individual
be made to contribute productively to the integrated activity
of community life? How could the advantages of community
life best be tendered each individual? Extension tried to
show the way. Assured of its beneficence, it devoted a
major portion of its administrative and instructional staff
to the development of better individuals, hence better communities, hence better individuals.

One definition of "better" appeared in the underlying
philosophy of the Ethical Movement. Ideally, this international, religious, but nondenominational organization was
founded upon respect for the "spirit of truthfulness" rather
than any "particular formation of truth," and strove to produce a world marked by "fellowship of difference in unity."
In practice, the men and women who belonged to chapters
of the American Ethical Union discussed the elimination of
"chicanery from commerce," the establishment of "economic justice between employer and employee," educational problems, and aesthetics. The resulting messages were

handed on to the poor and immigrants by social workers
and through settlement house activities.[4]

In 1908, Lighty, who was a Union member, helped bring
its School of Ethics and its dynamic director, Anna Garlin
Spencer, to Madison. This was part of an effort to rid the
group of domination by its New York members, and to locate its headquarters centrally. Madison had much that
made it attractive: scenery, library research facilities, a
university dedicated to serving the public welfare, and the
Extension Division with its techniques for distributing that
service. The friendly reception extended Union leaders
whom Lighty escorted to meet University and state officials
seemed to promise a happy future.

The School of Ethics met four summers in conjunction
with the University Summer School. Felix Adler, Jenkin
Lloyd Jones, Jane Addams, David S. Muzzey and Wisconsin's President Charles Van Hise formed part of the corps
of lecturers who discussed problems in philosophy and
religion, the law, family living, and militarism. One
hundred and forty-nine persons enrolled the first summer.
Then the number dwindled to too few to warrant continuation of the work.[5] The impact which the Ethical Movement
had on the state was at best indirect. It is impossible to
measure the effect, for example, of the appearances of
F. J. Gould of the Moral Instruction League of England.
Extension helped publicize his doctrine of public school
"moral and civil training" as a means of character development, but there analysis must stop. It is clear, however,
that quantitatively, the Ethical Movement never progressed
beyond the planning stage. The teachers, judges, and clergy-
men who attended the sessions were but a handful of even a
small segment of society. The Ethical Movement in the
state suffered from two major weaknesses, namely relative
inaccessibility of its program and narrowness of appeal
reminiscent of the Extension work of the 1890's.

Extension based its welfare program upon mass appeal.
Dr. Charles McCarthy's meat-and-potatoes philosophy was
readily understandable to the least sophisticated; skills
assured greater employment opportunities, and these, increased economic security and resulting social and political
stability. The Division presented its program in terms as
stark. Dr. Gillin, reflecting the reformist attitude of his
generation of sociologists, set the scene in an address to an
Oshkosh audience. Poverty was an obvious evil. What
caused it, who was responsible, and how could it be elim-

inated? Gillin allocated the blame to both society and individuals. The former bore the responsibility for technological unemployment, industrial accidents, and in large measure, illness. Individuals were accountable for poverty
stemming from intemperate use of alcohol (25 per cent of
poverty was attributable to liquor, he maintained), sexual
misconduct, and thriftlessness. Whatever the cause, these
conditions sapped the vitality of the individual and society.
Their elimination, therefore, was of primary importance
and could be accomplished by the spread of knowledge and
the development of coöperative action. Extension assumed
responsibility both for the distribution of the necessary
information and for its organization into effective reforms.
Reflecting upon this ambitious expériment in state-supported
advancement of the general welfare, Dean Reber concluded
that an "infinite variety of civilizing activities has grown
out of the widening of the scope of the traditional
university."[6]

Extension's concern for popular well-being extended from
cradle to grave. It included improvement of individual and
community health, and betterment of human relations. In
developing its health-for-all program, the Division employed
correspondence courses, newspaper columns, booklets,
posters and charts, mobile demonstrations and package
libraries. In 1913, the work was coördinated in a special
Health Bureau headed by Dr. Hoyt Dearholt of the Wisconsin
Anti-Tuberculosis Association. From it flowed advice on
prenatal care, maternal and child health, and related subjects. In coöperation with the Federal Children's Bureau,
Extension staged Better Baby Weeks. Home nursing courses
were developed for housewives, courses in the teaching of
physical education for teachers. Information about com-
municable diseases and quarantine regulations was distributed to schools throughout the state.

Extension was not content merely to help assure the
young a healthy start. It endeavored to give them inspiration and, through its vocational courses, tried to fit those
who did not go on to school for employment or promotions.
But since life consisted of more than securing and
holding jobs, there were courses in income management
and home repair and decoration. Homemakers were encouraged to enroll for dressmaking instruction, an effort which both the Division and its students came to
regret. While steam engine manuals could be used year
after year without revision, women's clothing design

instructions could not. The angry denunciations of women
who learned that the dresses they had so carefully cut out
and sewed were out of style became especially discom-
fiting when accompanied by doubts as to the validity of
the work of the entire Division.

Extension was particularly active in the fields of industrial and public health. Employers and workers were sent
information on the prevention of industrial accidents.
Extension offered courses to untrained health officers,
bringing them information about water supplies, sewage
disposal and vital statistics. When state law required that
each county maintain a nurse, Extension quickly announced
a course for nurses entering the field of public health.[7]
Only when their imaginations became sterile would Extensionists fail to justify their position of existence through
service.

It should have occasioned no surprise when the Division
undertook an industrial smoke control program; what was
unusual was that for a time Extension pondered the legiti-
macy of such action. Industrial development caused many
cities to consider the problem of smoke pollution. Even in
Madison, McCarthy battled the management of a smoke-
belching brewery near his home, finally suggesting that the
University Engineering School be consulted. "That's what
they're there for," he assured the brewers. When Fond du
Lac residents registered similar complaints with their city
government, it asked Extension for aid. But could such help
be extended within the legitimate scope of Division work,
its administrators wondered. Recalling Extension's dedi-
cation to advancing the general welfare, they gave their
approval. After a series of firing tests, Engineering Professor Ben G. Elliott delivered a program of lectures to
interested heating engineers and janitors. The highlight of
the series was to be a practical demonstration revealing
the superiority of enlightened over unenlightened firing
methods. But the one method proved as smoky as the other.
The city's mayor, however, absolved Elliott of all blame,
and reported that after the course, complaints about smoke
decreased sharply. The only ones still heard concerned
those plants which had not coöperated in the class sessions.
The long-run success of Professor Elliott's work is revealed by the requests for repeat performances in such
cities as Eau Claire and Madison. At the same time that
Extension was clearing the air, it was as a corollary pro-

moting the more efficient use of fuels.[8] As with the
Farmers' Institutes, an important share of the cost of the
Division to the taxpayer was written off in terms of con-
crete economic gain.

Extension's boundless concern for the general welfare
led it into the fight for pure milk and sanitary bakeries,
and against tuberculosis. Coöperating with private financial
backers and the Milwaukee School Board, the Division
sponsored exhibits for school children and adults, who were
shown the food value of milk and, conversely, its potential-
ity as a disease carrier. In 1908, Extension accepted the
request of state bakers to coördinate the activities of food
chemists, the U.S. Department of Agriculture, the Food and
Drug Commission experts and "practical bakers." The
success of the first year's Bakers' Institute led to a second
such program. Here again is an illustration of the direct
and indirect benefits provided by Extension. While the Institute was certainly of value to bakers, the consuming public also gained from the discussions of food values, adulter-
ation, and vermin control.

So, too, was it with the anti-tuberculosis campaign to
which Extension contributed its teaching and information-
distributing techniques. Besides personal and family suffer-
ing, the White Plague had cost employers tremendously in
terms of lost manpower, and society had suffered the loss
of productive effort and goods. Researchers, doctors, enlightened employer organizations, labor unions, and insur-
ance companies coöperated in the fight, and early in the
century, Dr. Dearholt could announce that the problem had
been reduced to one of administrative control, had become
a "problem for sociology rather than medicine." The prevention and cure seemed to have been discovered; what remained was to make this knowledge effective. This necessitated spreading information not only among workers and
their families, but among employers. Sometimes the latter
proved difficult pupils. Dr. Edward F. Mc Sweeney, Chairman of the Boston Consumptives Hospital, was prevented
from speaking in Milwaukee, despite an invitation from
Mayor Emil Seidel. Men who generously contributed to the
support of sanatoriums opposed the public discussion of
preventive measures. They saw only too clearly that mention of an adequate, healthful diet, ample fresh air and rest
might be translated into demands for higher wages and
more healthful working conditions. Professor John R.

Commons determined the strategy for work with this group:
they cannot be forced, he reported, they must be slowly
educated.[9]

Extension assumed the role of educator. Frank A.
Hutchins, Extension architect and field organizer spoke
tirelessly for the cause. Working with the Milwaukee Merchants' and Manufacturers' Association, the Division carried the antituberculosis crusade throughout the state.
Besides sponsoring platform speakers and mobile displays,
it provided correspondence courses for the students of the
Wisconsin Anti-Tuberculosis Association Apprentice School.
Thus did private philanthropic organizations, the State of
Wisconsin, and the purchasers of Christmas Seals show
common cause against a common enemy, although not without some question being raised about the propriety of spending tax money for the purpose.

However intense man's preoccupation with his immediate
physical welfare, he usually possesses some interest in his
environment and his relation to it. Many extensionists realized that the McCarthy program stopped short of providing
for this need, and they attempted to fill the gap. The initial
efforts proved fruitless because of their makeshift character.
The intellectually curious workingman was offered a correspondence course called "Labor Movements and Socialism,"
whose historical and theoretical approach to wages, unions,
and employers' organizations was likely to prove unintel-
ligible to him. This course, like many others deemed of
special interest to him, was based upon college economics
and history texts. Its authors failed to consider that the
worker's background and experience did not prepare him
for an academic approach to a subject. What he could not
understand, he disdained or suspected. The worker wanted
the guidance of those who could speak his language and who
exhibited at least some personal understanding of his
problems.[10]

This was no indication that workers were interested
solely in wages. In 1907, coöperating English labor and university representatives outlined a study program for working men and women. History, sociology, political and physical science were prominent among the subjects listed.
British extensionist Alfred Zimmern explained to Wisconsin audiences that the major aim of the program was not to
win wage increases, and that workers were aware of the
fact. The goal was a widening of the worker's interest and
outlook, enabling him to see his problems in relation to

others. In the United States, labor organizations themselves
were establishing special schools. Through the Boston
Trade Union College, the International Ladies' Garment
Workers University, and classes sponsored by the Chicago
Federation of Labor and the Women's Trade Union, working
people received instruction in history, law, English, story
writing, physiology, and health. In Wisconsin, the Milwaukee
Workers' College offered courses in public speaking, par-
liamentary law, and economics. However cultural the programs might sound, they were designed to equip workers
to meet employers and the latter's public information
services on at least equal grounds. Between 1919 and 1922,
the American Federation of Labor launched a nationwide
program of worker education. The effort was to be wholly
union-oriented and to be presented by men experienced with
trade unionism as well as with the academic disciplines.

To outsiders, this seemed to threaten community integration and welfare, and many colleges and universities volun-
teered to offer to workers courses designed to overcome
their growing group-consciousness. Amherst, Bryn Mawr,
the extension divisions of the Universities of California and
Wisconsin tried to enroll working girls in the hope of giving
them "new ideas about the universe and their relation to it."
At Wisconsin, summer school scholarships were offered
them, entrance requirements waived, and special tutors
hired to help them with their studies. The movement failed.
Labor leaders who were influential even outside their unions
correctly surmized the motives behind the program and
refused to sanction it.

Gradually the Extension Division of the University of
Wisconsin wooed the confidence of forces which regarded
the University with suspicion. The division coöperated with
the Milwaukee Labor College in helping young labor leaders
conduct discussions of specific problems — not unemployment in general, but in the case of building trades workers,
seasonal unemployment. This captured and held the attention
of the union officers and members, and helped them to see
themselves as integral parts of their community rather
than as isolated segments. To the optimistic, this pointed
the way to the decline of the old time union boss with his
reliance upon force and bluff, and to the rise of trained
negotiators bargaining from wide knowledge and understanding.[11] It was while reports on this work were crossing
his desk that Lighty pointedly observed that worker education in England—a counterpart of University Extension in

America—had minimized the danger of violence in labor-
management relations.[12] This was in line with his interest
in the welfare of the community as a whole and provided a
latter-day statement of the Ethical Union's stress upon
"fellowship of difference in unity."

Industrial workers formed but a portion of the community
in which they lived, and were nonexistent in many Wisconsin
areas. Merchants, clerks, real estate agents, and salesmen,
however, were familiar figures in the village as well as the
city. To these, too, Extension tried to speak in terms of
the general welfare.

Business courses appeared among the earliest correspondence study offerings. In 1910, R. Starr Butler, former
high school teacher and general agent for Proctor and
Gamble was retained to administer the work. McCarthy
attempted to use the Allen Survey to force increased stress
upon elementary business subjects, but extensionists successfully defended offering relatively advanced courses.

> ... the value of the average unit of educational produc-
> tion among the advanced students is likely to be much
> greater than the value of the average unit results ob-
> tained in the case of beginners. One employer set on the
> right track by means of a correspondence course may
> be of far more economic and social value to the com-
> munity than a hundred minor employees whose effici-
> ency is increased by the same means.[13]

A major Extension goal in working with the upper level
student was to enable him to see beyond details, to see his
business as "part of a great whole."

In actual practice, however, most business courses were
designed for "immediate application." It was well enough to
muse that the salesman sold both goods and service, but in
fact he was primarily interested in the former, and Extension realistically appealed to him in that vein. In anticipation of New Freedom financial legislation, the Division
prepared courses in money and banking to which the data on
the Federal Reserve System could be added as soon as it
became available. To enable businessmen to cope with the
new income tax law, a course—which subsequently was not
always kept up to date—was offered in that field. French
and Spanish language instruction was presented with an eye
to enabling businessmen to capture and hold foreign markets.
Store owners were urged to register their salesclerks for
courses that would prepare them to use "personality" and

"psychology" to overcome consumer resistance.[14]

In its other direct aids to business, Extension tried to come closer to stressing community advancement. The lectures it offered through Chambers of Commerce, Rotary Clubs, and businessmen's associations contained both a dollars-and-cents appeal and due emphasis upon service. So, too, did the "Industrial Relations Bulletin" and the "Retail Bulletin" which informed subscribing businessmen about employment cycles, job analysis, absenteeism, wages, industrial housing, selling techniques and bookkeeping methods. But when representatives of the business world commented on these services, it was upon their cash value. The statement of the Oshkosh Chamber of Commerce representative that Extension's supporters were repaid dollar-for-dollar was a counterpart of that of the young clerk who happily announced that thanks to a correspondence course, he had been promoted from "heavy work and boys shoes to men's, children's and Misses' stock."[15]

Working piecemeal with groups which the Division hoped to convert to enlightened self-interest was but one phase of the campaign for individual advancement combined with social unity. Of more dramatic nature were community-wide efforts of which the already cited public health program is an example. Attempts to provide social centers, means of improving city governments, large-scale organized recreation programs, coördinated charities, and finally community integration were further manifestations of this Extension activity.

Considered individually, the various parts of the program contained little that was new or unique. The settlement house was a common sight in most cities of the Western world. Through planned social activities and sometimes ambitious educational programs they brought hope and something beyond the drabness of daily existence into the lives of those they served. The skeptic might jeer that this work added up to the cultivation of approved escapes, but this is to overlook the spirit in which much of it was carried on. Hull House workers pledged themselves to prevent strikes from becoming class warfare; Jane Addams deeply believed in the superiority of the spiritual over the material.

In 1906, the year of the revival of extension in Wisconsin, Lester Ward coined the term "intellectual egalitarianism" to articulate denials of the innate inferiority of the "lower" classes. He charged that to deprive them of educational opportunities led to great social waste. Three years later,

Herbert Croly concluded that contrary to the hopes of the
nation's founders, Americans had become divided into
groups, each with its own manner of life, way of thinking
and outlook. The problem facing the nation was that of finding a "social ideal" to make heterogeneity synonomous with
strength and unity rather than with weakness and disunity,
to inspire "consistency" in the midst of desirable differences. In Germany, men were talking of the individual and
social benefits of organized play, concepts brought into
America by the Turnverein, and given a rationale by John
Dewey. And there was still awe and fear of the city. Josiah
Strong, who regarded individuals as the cells of society and
could argue, therefore, that individual selfishness dis-
ordered the whole, predicted, "The city is to control the
nation: Christianity must control the city; and it will."[16]

Groups throughout the United States were using these
ideas as guides for action. A growing movement was afoot
to convert public school buildings nightly into community
centers where general educational and naturalization classes could be conducted, branch libraries and health centers
maintained, and encouragement given local artists and musi-
cians. Rochester, New York, had worked out an especially
elaborate program administered by Edward J. Ward. In
1910, interested citizens succeeded in bringing him to Milwaukee, where he enjoyed the support of the Social Democratic administration and the powerful Milwaukee Journal.
His way had been prepared, too, by the civic consciousness
inspired by the Extension Division and H. H. Jacobs, crusading head of the University Settlement House.

Ward's stay in Milwaukee was brief. Though the Rochester
program had revealed that the free discussion carried on in
its schoolhouse community centers had resulted in a modi-
fication rather than an intensification of opinions, the Democratic and Republican old guard feared the political conse-
quences of such a program. When the Social Democrats
were temporarily dislodged from power, Ward's position
became insecure.

Dean Reber saw a use for Ward in Extension, and found
a place for him among the writers of fireless cooker and
garbage disposal bulletins in the department of General
Information and Welfare. Ward's job was to promote "neigh-
borhood democracy" through the schoolhouse program, to
develop the New England town meeting in Wisconsin. In
1911, the state's last Progressive legislature approved of
schools being used for such purposes. Using the law and

Extension as a wedge, Ward established some forty-five
centers in Milwaukee, La Crosse, Oshkosh, Portage, Appleton, and Stoughton. Three cities employed full-time directors, and a number of school boards hired principals only
after they agreed to act as directors. But the program
quickly stagnated, and within two years was dead.[17] Ward
revealed deficiencies as an administrator, but the causes
lay deeper. The centers were too scattered to attract partisan political support. Still more important, people did not
feel the need to participate in such activity. Living in increasingly disciplined employment situations, they preferred to manage their leisure time personally.

Extension tried the civic center program, found it unpopular in the state's comparatively small cities, and
abandoned it. There was other related work that could be
stressed. Lighty, and then Gillin, administered the affairs
of the State Conference on Charities and Correction, which
the former had salvaged out of the breakup of Anna Garlin
Spencer's Social Service Institute in Milwaukee. The Conference attempted to coördinate the activities of the many
charitable organizations operating in Wisconsin, to help the
Big Sisters, juvenile protective and ministerial associations,
ladies' aid societies, and poor departments avoid overlapping of service. In 1920, the Wisconsin Conference on Social
Work was established as a state agency, and Extension
bowed out of the picture, its tour of duty in this area
completed.[18]

Still, the nature of local governments made them ready
recipients of authoritative advice and aid. The Extension
Division's assumption of the responsibility for aid was a
development of the work once handled personally by Professor Richard T. Ely and by the League of Wisconsin
Municipalities and the Legislative Reference Library. All
too often, local officials lacked formal training or adequate
experience for the positions to which they were elected.
Their errors proved expensive to the entire community. In
an era of increasing urbanization and resulting weakening
of old social controls, this cost could be measured not only
in wasted tax dollars, but in community disorganization.
The Division made itself a clearing house for information
on local government, standing prepared to aid in whatever
way it could.

How did London solve a century-old sewage problem? How
did Rome solve its chronic housing shortage? The answers
could be obtained from the Municipal Reference Bureau by

return mail. Closer to home, the Bureau's circulating collection of ordinances and related documents enabled officials to see how others had approached certain problems, and with what results. The Bureau staff also conducted questionnaire surveys and tabulated their findings on waste disposal, salary schedules, traffic routing, smoke control, milk distribution, and—of special importance after the World War and the increasing popularity of the automobile —dance hall regulations.

Model ordinances and even model police forces (available to any community through the help of correspondence study and lecture courses for law officers) were not complete substitutes for the rural social controls which sociologists felt were disintegrating in the urban environment. The national proportions of this problem were revealed by the sessions of the Civic and Social Conference held in Madison in 1911. Delegates heard Governor Woodrow Wilson urge maintenance of a fluid society so as to bring more Lincolns to the top. Wisconsin's Dr. McCarthy pointed to the need for voter education lest crude laws be shaped by crude hands. The major emphasis, however, was upon the need for community centers functioning as sources of information, inspiration, and directed recreation. No one challenged the speaker who traced the presence of hooligans, streetwalkers, grafters and dishonest politicians to improper childhood training, to the fact that their communities had not seen to it that "all . . . boys and girls played the proper games . . . in the proper way."[19]

Here was something along the lines Wisconsin extensionists had been following, and the Division hastened to supply the people of the state with a program of organized recreation. In so doing, it laid the basis for one of its most lasting accomplishments. The Bureau of Community Music and Drama, directed by tireless Edgar B. Gordon, set out to remedy and prevent social problems. There was a challenge in the finding that most crimes were committed between the hours of 6:00 and midnight, when men and women freed from the discipline of their jobs were left to their own devices. Given the assumption that the community was responsible for the conduct of its individual members, it was also obligated to teach them social coöperation, and the means were "Play as education."[20]

The Bureau program encouraged the development of community and school music, drama festivals and folk dancing. Ready coöperation was found among the many state national-

ity groups which still remembered and encouraged the folk
arts. The sympathy of the legislature for such activities
was demonstrated by its authorization in 1913 of city, town
and village band concerts. But the matter of social reform
was never distant. Margaret Wilson, daughter of the President of the United States, spoke for many when she told
Wisconsin audiences that the "hope of democracy" was
music descriptive of neighborliness and good will. Professor Gordon saw in community music a means of unleashing
"immense social power." Through it, diverse people could
be united, and as groups induced to listen or create while
as individuals men were often unapproachable in these
areas. The aesthetic side of mass creative activity was not
overlooked, but its advocates usually placed greater emphasis upon its other potentialities.

Professor Gordon and his staff made their influence felt
through aids extended to school, civic and recreational
groups, establishment of institutes for music and drama
teachers, and personal appearances before education and
parent associations. Local leaders for folk dancing and
community singing programs were trained by the Bureau,
and dramatic presentations fostered. The great emphasis
upon the drama was based upon the thesis that it was particularly suited to developing a spirit of coöperation. Baton
and grease paint became symbols for one of Extension's
answers to the challenge of how to make leisure hours constructive ones, promote community-mindedness, and finally
to heighten mass appreciation for artistic expression.

Extension's most ambitious welfare effort was in combining many of its services into compact programs called
Community Institutes. With characteristic enthusiasm, the
Division prodded the old New England "public spirit of helpfulness and coöperation" among Yankees, Germans and
Scandinavians alike. Its goals were ambitious, namely to
locate and repair "weak spots in the fabric of government,"
to encourage "harmonious community organization," and to
offer communities a "new lease on life."[21]

As with most of its other work, Extension launched the
Community Institutes as answers to concrete problems.
Major concern was developing over the deterioration of
rural-urban relations. This problem had occasioned consideration during the days of the early Farmers' Institutes,
but more recently, men like Professor Charles Galpin,
rural sociologist with the College of Agriculture, were encouraging rural-urban understanding as a prelude to "Better

farming, better business, better living." Businessmen, too,
were coming to understand that the prosperity of town and
country were interwoven. The Wisconsin Bankers' Association and Milwaukee Chamber of Commerce coöperated
with the College of Agriculture in sponsoring a special
grain demonstration train. Local merchants were beginning
to feel the competition of the great mail order houses with
their special appeal to farm and small town folk. Paid newspaper propaganda against the distant firms was a start, but
more positive measures seemed necessary to keep money
within the community.[22] Small towns were beginning to
notice, too, the problem long confronting their farm neighbors: the steady drain of local youth and talent into the
cities.

The mechanics of the Community Institute were patterned
after those of the Farmers' Institutes. There was the effort
to make them seem locally-sponsored and geared to local
needs. In an attempt to assure the latter, Extension men
met with local groups before coming into a community, and
in that way sometimes became special pleaders rather than
objective reformers. Having canvassed a local situation,
Extension launched a publicity campaign, displaying supposedly discussion-provoking books in local store windows,
hoisting street banners, putting up posters, inspiring newspaper articles, and writing to influential townsmen. Local
committees stockpiled food for out-of-town guests, and made
hall, nursery, and restroom arrangements. Leaders generally found the community coöperative. Not only were there
material benefits to be gained, but the spirit of boosterism
was being fostered by businessmen anxious to attract new
capital while encouraging the spending of wages and salaries
within the community. "Remember, there is no place like
home," one small town newspaper editor constantly reminded his readers. When domestic science girls of
Kaukauna High School served Institute businessmen apple
pie and ice cream, they sang "On Kaukauna" to the not un-
likely tune of "On Wisconsin."

The programs were pitched to appeal to as wide a cross
section of the surrounding population as possible. Farmers
were attracted with promises of free meals, special prices,
marketing advice and discussions of the "proper relation"
between town and country. There is no such thing as isolated prosperity, both farmers and merchants were admonished; the town must prosper if the country is to prosper;
the country must be progressive if the town is to be success-

ful. Merchants and farmers must learn to respect one
another, to appreciate each other's contributions and needs.
The better roads urged by Institute speakers had both economic and symbolic significance.[23]

Also in line with the goal of community integration were
the attempts made in De Pere and Kaukauna to heal the
religious and civic breaches which were disrupting the
school system. In De Pere, too, the Institute's bridge engineer entered the conflict over the best type of structure to
span the Fox River. In both cases Extension advice was ignored. Even the friendly expressed disappointment at the
clichés the University's education expert confused with
practical advice. While the Institute suggestion that a steel
bridge be built was probably sounder than the advice of the
salesman trying to sell the community one of concrete, the
Extensionite misjudged and alienated his audience.[24] Many
"men from Madison" had yet to learn that such audiences
were not only entitled to consideration and respect, but
rated special treatment if their traditional suspicion of the
University was to be overcome. They had yet to learn, too,
that the nature of a community could not be discovered in
a few hours, and that a series of lectures, even when accompanied by community singing was no antidote for attitudes rooted in generations. With but an occasional excep-
tion, communities did not invite the Institutes to return.

Waning interest in the Institutes coincided with increasing
friction among the University's extension services. Charges
and denials of overlapping were hurled back and forth between the general Extension Division and the College of
Agriculture. Accusations of interference with each other's
Institutes were also exchanged. Although these clashes were
to leave personal scars, they were but incidental to the decline of the Division's community programs.[25]

International developments temporarily gave the people
of the United States the "social ideal" for which Croly had
hoped. America's entrance into the war against Germany
helped unite a nation and helped Extension to find another
raison d'etre. The Division marched to war by remaining
the Extension Division. Quickly it placed its popularizing
and distributing techniques at the disposal of government
officials. From its presses came correspondence courses
and bulletins on home nursing and industrial techniques for
women workers, reprints of official proclamations, and
advice on gardening, efficient use of fuel and the utilization
of garbage. For those who wondered about the causes of the

war, special package libraries were quickly assembled and distributed. Division field men who had been aiding correspondence students to understand slide rules and ledger books proved equally adept at demonstrating techniques of bandaging and splint application.

The excitement and enthusiasm of the war years were followed by the sobering effect of the postwar depression. Extension failed to gain the state appropriations it felt necessary, and in 1922, Dean Reber warned that in the continued absence of legislative relief, fee-producing activities would have to be stressed at the expense of other forms of Extension service. Since correspondence study produced the greatest income, it seemed the logical line of work to develop. Division administrators eliminated those services which were unprofitable, among them some which had rendered a real service. Few people missed the Community Institutes, but discontinuation of the Bureau of Industrial Relations and courses in business administration provoked newspaper criticism of the legislature. If a stratagem was involved, it did not produce the appropriations desired. Financial stringency plus decreased public interest in non-academic programs forced the Division to change its appearance.[26]

Extension could not escape its times. Its medical and community programs were carried on within a social and political milieu which made them appropriate as to time and place. This thesis is reiterated in the matter of the contrasting tenors of the Division-sponsored National Newspaper Conference of 1912, and the Division's contribution to the war effort. In 1912, the topic under consideration was, "Are newspaper and magazine writers free to tell the truth?"[27] Five years later, the Division offered its services in the distribution of war propaganda. This is not to condemn; it is to indicate that in general, Division policy was made for it by the community in which it existed.

Problems in Communication

If I were a voice, a persuasive voice
That could travel the wide world through
I'd fly on the wings of the morning light
And speak to men with gentle might,
And tell them to be true!
I'd fly o'er land and sea,
Wherever a human heart might be
Telling a tale, or singing a song,
In praise of the right, in blame of the wrong!
                    —Charles Kingsley; a favorite
                    quotation of W. H. Lighty.

The Extension Division's contributions to the field of nonresidence and adult education included the development of
techniques for reaching its diverse and far-flung audiences.
Since its students could not come to it, it had to go out to
its students. The creation of "traveling professors" to
supplement correspondence study work was probably an
innovation. In other instances, Extension tried to improve
upon methods already demonstrated feasible. Correspondence study, lectures, institutes, and community development
projects generally fall into this category. So, too, does the
Division's textbook publishing venture. The International
Correspondence School's shop-level textbooks made Extension's original mimeographed study guides and aids seem
comparatively shabby. On the other hand, when the Division
underwrote its own publication venture, it won immediate
renown. Although the development of the radio as an educational device held much promise as a means of making the
boundaries of the University synonomous with those of the
state, the Division per se did not try to exploit its possibilities. Members of the Extension staff, however, did give
their energies tirelessly to the matter, and William H.
Lighty, especially, came to be regarded as an elder statesman in the field.
    Extension's early shop and technical correspondence
study courses were given in fields and under conditions
which required the preparation of special guides and textbooks. Ordinary duplicating methods proved inadequate, and
Dean Louis E. Reber sought a commercial publisher for

Extension materials. His final choice was McGraw-Hill Book Company, which was widely respected for its technical and engineering volumes. In answer to the question of the legality of having University work done by other than the state printer, the attorney general found that the proposed Division texts were not state printing in the sense intended by the legislature when it circumscribed such work. No legal barrier, therefore, existed. McGraw-Hill anticipated the profits from a general sale of the books; Extension envisioned more attractive texts, little financial risk on those that proved unpopular, the advantages of the company's advertising outlets, and a steady flow of royalties.[1]

The Division's plans for course promotion in 1911 hinged upon the Board of Regents' ready approval of Reber's actions. Given the fact that Extension enrollments were being threatened by creation of the vocational school system, and that a new group of students had to be sought, haste was important. While the Executive Committee quickly sanctioned the printing measure, the president of the Board, W. D. Hoard, who was an agricultural representative and an outspoken critic of the Division, dissented. He objected, he said, to a private company making "merchantable use" of University property, and the limitation of the school's rights to "its own" books, while it remained financially responsible for their revision. Moreover, the 10 per cent royalty seemed inadequate to him. Hoard contended that the regents could make more advantageous arrangements by controlling the copyright and doing the printing themselves. Dean Reber's subsequent consultations with the University editor and other publishers revealed that McGraw-Hill's estimates of printing costs were advantageously low.[2] For a time, however, no one in authority cared to risk the repercussions possible for taking the initiative in sanctioning the proposed contract. The books remained unprinted as the fall school term began.

Extension remained hard-pressed for suitable study guides and materials and the anticipated general market remained untapped. Nearly twenty texts were ready, or almost so, for the printer. In the spring of 1911, however, the regents authorized the contract. The first manuscript sent to New York dealt with structures, and became the pioneer volume of the Engineering Education Series. McGraw-Hill advertised the books as "cornerstones and foundations of vocational education in the country," describing them as sources to which the worker confronted by

everyday problems could turn with ease and assurance.
Reber considered them "simple, direct and vocational."
Subsequently, D. Appleton and Company was awarded a similar contract for Extension business and home economics
texts.[3]

Much of the work of guiding the books through the press
was done by the secretary of the correspondence study
department, himself. Lighty watched sentence structure and
sales promotion with equal vigilance. His occasional enthusiasm for "journalese" and "catchy" titles sometimes
proved embarrassing. He urged that the possible common
and "uninteresting" titles for a text for factory foremen be
dismissed in favor of "The Winning Foremanship." A
McGraw-Hill executive felt such a title would "kill the
book," and yet he could not help being "amused" by its
Horatio Alger tone. Perhaps, he hinted, earlier Extension
texts could be renamed, "Onward and Upward, A Brief
Course in Practical Shop Mathematics"; "Sweeney's Solil-
oquies in Elementary Bookkeeping and Accounting";
"Jansky's Elementary Juice." Lighty agreed to a more
prosaic title.

For a few years, Extension's books enjoyed a wide general sale. Among the schools adopting them were Pennsylvania State College, Brown University, Maryland Agricultural College, Pratt Institute, and the Universities of
Illinois, Minnesota, and Pittsburgh. The text, Shop Arith-
metic, was used in industrial schools at Madison, West
Allis, Pound, and Milwaukee. The United States Navy placed
a large order for Professor C. M. Jansky's books on direct
current machines, elementary magnetism and electricity.
The work as a whole won favorable comment from abroad,
too. The principal of an Ontario technical school was enthusiastic about the text on shop sketching. An expansive
English reviewer of Professor Jansky's text on electric
meters introduced his subject by congratulating Wisconsin
students on being able to study under Richard T. Ely, and
finally went on to applaud the book. He was particularly
impressed by the generosity shown by manufacturers in
supplying the author with information and pictures, and concluded that only the book's failure to include European data
restricted its sale to the United States.[4]

Between 1912 and 1922, thirty-one text books were published by the Extension Division; over 288,604 copies were
sold. Written by Extension faculty members or by authors
under contract to the Division, they became Extension

property. Between 1912 and 1924, royalties totaling $81,990
went to the Division. In 1922, however, authors possessing
Extension status for a specified length of time were allowed
20 per cent of the royalties, up to a maximum of $500.
Arrangements also included possible shares for other
members of the Extension faculty meeting certain service
requirements. Sales of the books, however, had been declining markedly since 1920. By 1932, they were such that
royalty distributions among the faculty members could be
measured in pennies, and the practice ceased. Other writers
and publishers had entered the field, and after 1926, the
Extension administration concentrated upon teaching liberal
arts rather than vocational courses. One of the still salable
books had been so revised that the author refused to have
it published any longer under his name.[5] The text book publishing venture had been a necessary part of the off-campus
education program. Now obsolete, it was readily abandoned,
a further evidence of Extension's policy of service when
needed.

Radio, like the A-bomb, stemmed in large part from the
nation's universities. Among the many university physics
departments whose faculty and students experimented with
radio transmitters and receivers was that at Wisconsin.
Under the direction of Professors Edward Bennett and E.
M. Terry, a wireless sending station, 9XM, had been set up
even before World War I. When wartime regulations forced
the dismantling of many similar stations, that at Madison
received Navy orders to continue its experimenting. In 1922,
it was granted a federal license and the call letters which
still distinguish it: WHA. WHA is unique not only in the
field of technological development, but as the pioneer station
devoted to educational broadcasting.[6]

William H. Lighty was one of the nation's first educators
to see the possibilities of radio as a means of carrying
education to a far-flung audience. The Extension Division
had long struggled with problems of space and time in carrying its messages to the people of the state. Here was a
medium which might transcend both. Lighty observed the
popular interest in the physics department's "wireless"
exhibit at the State Fair, and concluded that radio was here
to stay. He and Professor Terry consulted with Dean Reber,
and in 1922, President Birge appointed Lighty chairman of
a committee on educational broadcasting.[7]

The early broadcasts, which were scheduled for but a few
hours per week and were suspended during University

vacation periods, were a potpourri reminiscent of extension
work in its broadest sense. In coöperation with the state
Department of Agriculture, weather and market reports
were broadcast. The major emphasis, however, was upon
giving the listening public descriptions of University activities. Once the professors could be convinced that broadcasting was not undignified, a great many read papers over
the air.[8] Although copies of their addresses had to be filed
with Lighty and the president's office, University sponsorship of the station saved the speakers the embarrassment
of outside attempts to censor their scripts. The Indiana
University extension division's use of a commercial station
as its outlet proved unsatisfactory when the management
insisted upon deleting speakers' remarks deemed critical
of the government.[9]

University lecturers who were accustomed to addressing
large classroom and auditorium audiences were for a time
unnerved by studio broadcasting. Professor John Guy
Fowlkes was a "trembling aspen" during his first appearance, and most others had similar experiences. Lighty ar-
ranged the broadcasts to be as representative of University
life as possible. Baccalaureate exercises were sent out
along with talks on foreign affairs, bee keeping, and descriptions of students festivals. Professor Herbert Page of the
Law School readily consented to speak on his specialty, but
suddenly turned to Lighty and asked, " . . . what the hell is
the law?" No less colorful, but in another vein, were the
radio appearances of William Ellory Leonard giving his
own "Literary Readings." Athletics-conscious Wisconsin,
however, was generally more receptive to the broadcasts of
varsity basketball and then football games.[10]

In the years, 1924–25, Professor Terry, his assistants,
and student operators improved the transmitter to eliminate
some of the many "dead spots" in the state, and the interference in certain areas of "some screechy woman from
St. Louis." A soundproofed room was set aside in Sterling
Hall for the broadcasts of large musical organizations, and
efforts were made to increase the appearances of members
of the School of Music. In 1924, Lighty and his committee
planned a long-range series of fifteen-minute educational
talks interspersed with musical entertainment.

Many Wisconsin residents were no less interested in
WHA's success than were members of the University faculty. They felt themselves participants in a great experiment
which would lead to the perfection of their own state radio

station. Gathered for social evenings in homes, public libraries, radio stores, state and county institutions, and pool
rooms, they listened to the broadcasts and faithfully sent in
their "Applause Cards." These noted not only details of
reception, but reaction to the content of the programs, and
the relative merits of receiving sets. Many listeners gained
a sense of community solidarity from the group singing
programs. University geology students encamped at Devil's
Lake invited nearby cottagers to share in such broadcasts.
"Someday the whole country will be singing in unison via
Radio," wrote an enthusiastic listener. WHA was the
people's station. A fourteen-year-old boy planning to fish
for mussels asked for a lecture on the subject on a night
convenient for him. Many listeners concluded their fan
letters with the plea, "Please write." Parents of students
on the campus wrote asking whether the speakers knew
their sons and daughters, many of whom had long since left
school and were "married, of course." A Waunakee resident
commented after hearing a broadcast on food and nutrition,
"My wife is taking on flesh quite a good deal ... also have
a Daughter who is much too fleshy, this is why a little advice might be good...."[11]

These, however, were but some of the aspects of educational broadcasting. The Milwaukee Journal quoted Lighty's
enthusiasm about the "great possibilities of etherizing education," and predicted a revolution in educational methods
and institutions. Extension enrollments had surpassed those
of the residence school before the advent of radio, and now
countless thousands more students could be reached by the
Division. Some began to inquire about taking degrees by
radio. Despite his enthusiasm, Lighty counseled caution.
"There is no question but that radio broadcasting has very
great educational possibilities for the future [he noted], but
it is not complete enough to do much in the way of consecutive instruction." His surveys showed that radio audiences
preferred diversion and entertainment to serious matters,
but then did not college students generally exhibit a similar
attitude? The situation was far from hopeless; it was a challenge. In this regard Lighty informed Dean Reber, "The
educational radio broadcast must win the ear of the radio
audience and so organize its broadcasts so as to make as
much as possible of the universal appeal while radio receiving is in this formative period." And yet Lighty char-
acteristically hesitated to exert a major effort during the
crucial period. Explaining that the time was not yet ripe for

large-scale educational work, he spoke of trying to "stimulate a greater interest in scientific and accurate knowledge,
a keen intellectual curiosity and the challenge of the prob-
lem-solving attitude among.... listeners."[12]

The results appeared in 1925 in a course of consecutive
lectures launched on an experimental basis. The subject
matter chosen, food and nutrition as related to personal
health and happiness, was presumably of general interest.
It was conducted by Miss Nellie Kedzie Jones, State Leader
in home economics extension in the College of Agriculture.
Listeners were invited to enroll in a correspondence study
course which complemented the fifteen-minute broadcasts.
While Lighty described the effort as the first of its kind,
Marietta College had attempted similar work a few years
earlier. The results had proved disappointing.[13] Perhaps
the choice of course material prevented the Wisconsin endeavor from also enjoying the success anticipated.

Educational broadcasting was yet young, however, and
perhaps there was still room for exploration. In WHA's first
year, high school principals began to inquire about broadcasts for their students. The University broadcasters saw
the possibilities of encouraging schools to install radio receivers, as once they had encouraged the purchase of stere-
opticons and motion picture equipment, in order to provide
outlets for the services of the Extension's Bureau of
Visual Education.[14]

Lighty's general questioning of school heads in 1924,
however, revealed that a "considerable number" were uninterested in or unaware of the possibilities of the "radio-
cast" as a factor in education. In the spring of 1925, Lighty
again sent out questionnaires. City school authorities manifested marked enthusiasm for radio as a means of supplementing class work. Although a mere 14 per cent of the
county superintendents returned their questionnaires, they
were generally favorable, except for pointing out that the
reception of WHA programs was often poor. Only 4 per cent
of the principals of state elementary schools returned their
question sheets, indicating almost total lack of interest on
their part.[15] The results revealed that the areas which had
the greatest need for outside educational aid desired it
least. In time, the increasing numbers of radios in rural
areas would lead to greater interest, but a promotional,
friend-making venture was also in order. Only gradually,
however, did WHA's program directors relax their opposition to the appearance of non-University groups, however

qualified or however popular. In the mid-twenties, while the
Extension Division was seeking to increase its enrollment
by devoting ever more attention to the plans of high school
graduates, high school bands found WHA happy to arrange
broadcasting appearances for them.[16]

Wisconsin's developments in educational broadcasting
were paralleled by similar work elsewhere. Universities or
their extension divisions in increasing numbers sent out
programs through their own or commercial stations. The
Universities of Oregon, Nebraska, Indiana, and Chicago
were among those employing commercial outlets; the Universities of Colorado, Iowa, North Dakota, and Pennsylvania had their own stations. Reasons for doing no broadcasting whatsoever included skepticism about the educational
value of such activity, lack of money or knowledge of how to
proceed, and the opposition of residence faculties who were
opposed to extension work of all kinds. Many of those in the
field, however, looked to Lighty and the Wisconsin experiments for guidance.[17]

Lighty played a leading role not only in the development
of the content of educational broadcasting, but in its recognition by the Federal Communications Commission and in
related discussions at meetings of the National University
Extension Association. When Glenn Frank succeeded E. A.
Birge as president of the University of Wisconsin, Lighty
counted upon his aid in launching a radio adult education
program. He succeeded in securing the appointment of an
all-University committee for this purpose, only to find the
president suddenly uninterested. Lighty's own role in broadcasting activities was terminated shortly thereafter when
Extension's Dean Chester Snell all but retired him from
active service.[18]

During the 1930's, educational broadcasting took the steps
envisioned in 1925. A University Radio Research Committee
of representatives from the Schools of Education and Music
conducted an extensive experiment in the effectiveness of
radio in teaching music and current events to the pupils of
the sixth, seventh, and eighth grades. Twenty-five Dane
County schools received regular radio instruction. The results, as measured by true-false examinations, were checked
against those obtained from twenty-five control schools. The
committee concluded that radio was of educational value
when no qualified teacher was available, and as such was a
means of supplementing classroom work. Children in outlying districts had come to feel, too, that they were en -
joying advantages similar to those of city school pupils.[19]

The Committee's emphasis upon radio as a supplement to guided classroom study is of major importance in an era when administrators of many educational institutions are considering how to reach the largest number of students with the smallest number of teachers. Radio and television have their possibilities, but the idea of their being used as a substitute for classroom work is as unsound as the prediction so popular in the early 1920's that in short order people would be going to college in carpet slippers, seated comfortably beside their radios instead of in classrooms. There are certain advantages inherent in the classroom situation that cannot be duplicated by the mass media. Of great importance is the element of discipline resulting from student attendance and attention. There are the matters, too, of interaction between teacher and student, and competition among students, and these cannot be achieved outside a personal situation. Given an arbitrary choice between classes of correspondence study alone, or of radio alone, the formers' provision for interaction make them superior. As supplements to classroom or correspondence work, however, radio and television are of decided importance. In one further respect, it would be well to consider the results of televised education upon academic freedom. While it would be possible for students to receive an unprecedented number of different approaches and views, would not the actual tendency be toward the creation of academic Big Brothers similar to the political dictatorship of George Orwell's novel 1984?

By 1931, "The Wisconsin School of the Air," developed through the efforts of Harold E. Engel, who had the coöperation of educators and the University, was presenting schools with extensive programs in civics, music, art appreciation, nature study and health. These proved popular with both teachers and students, despite their creation of classroom problems in scheduling and subsequent discussion. Lectures of a more advanced nature were given by University and Extension teachers, and administrators used WHA facilities to give the listening public a better understanding of University activities. The Extension Center at Milwaukee broadcasted both talks and course work over WTMJ, the Milwaukee Journal station.[20] In 1940, almost 300,000 elementary and high school students were regular listeners to School of the Air broadcasts. In 1939, over 3,000 pupils assembled in Madison for a music festival growing out of Professor Gordon's radio work with them.[21]

The state station's existence raises two major objections

which will not be silenced in the foreseeable future: monopoly of wave lengths desired by private groups and the use of tax money to finance the work. During the early 1930's, a group of commercial broadcasters sought transfer of WHA's two frequencies to private control. The director of the state station, H. R. McCarty, kept them from gaining a complete victory by pointing out the weaknesses in some of their arguments. To their suggestion that the University be given broadcasting outlets through private stations by means of wire hookups, McCarty retorted that scheduling problems would be resolved to the disadvantage of the school. He cited as an example the fact that WHA had constantly offered its programs to private stations. Only one had taken advantage of the offer, and it had cancelled the arrangement as soon as it found a sponsor to pay for using the time.[22] If the type of educational and cultural programs which distinguish WHA from the other stations on the air are to be continued, it will have to be under state auspices. But should the tax-payer be obliged to support programs in which he as an individual might have no immediate interest? A suggested answer is best framed as a question: does not the consumer pay daily in the costs of items he purchases for the support of the commercial programs in which he may have no interest? In the one case, the taxes are levied by the elected representatives of the people; in the other, by groups whose responsibility is in the main to stockholders. WHA has gone a long way toward carrying out the "third function" assigned to the University by President Van Hise early in the century. The entire history of the effort is studded with criticism, much of it justified, much of it constructive. Whatever their nature, however, the attacks have helped the station remain vital and have prevented its sponsors from relying too heavily upon tradition or "fine sentiment."

Competition and Transition

While the university extension movement was actuated
... by no other purpose than to perform a larger service to the state of Wisconsin, we have found that it was
wise simply from our own point of view.
—President C. R. Van Hise, 1913

The war years proved a dividing mark in the emphasis Extension placed upon its work. The break was not sharply
defined, but during the first half of the postwar decade, the
Division drifted away from the forms of activity which had
distinguished it earlier. The changes were more pronounced
in some areas than in others. Citizenship training became
more formalized; work with the underprivileged came to
mean a greater emphasis upon helping in the rehabilitation
of inmates of state penal institutions. The professional
training of teachers was given more attention; the old community health program was replaced in large part by postgraduate seminars for physicians. Even more important
during these final years of Louis E. Reber's deanship was
the increased amount of University credit work sponsored
by the Division, and especially the development of freshman
and sophomore classroom offerings in Milwaukee. These
changes were the products both of opportunities seized and
of financial necessity. They resulted in increased Extension
competition with established educational institutions as it
tried to maintain a place for itself in the life of the state.

Postwar government subsidies created a new group of
students. Federal and state agencies designed to help in the
rehabilitation and readjustment of former servicemen and
women were prepared to finance the instruction of certified
veterans. It was already traditional for Extension to rise to
such situations. This opportunity to be of service was made
the more attractive by the curtailed appropriations of the
postwar depression years. These factors made necessary
not only the search for new fields of activity, but for those
of a fee-producing nature. The Division had four hundred
courses available, and a variety of means for presenting
them. Correspondence teaching was supplemented by the
establishment of local classes wherever a minimum of fifteen petitioners so requested; regular engineering and

business classes were formed in Milwaukee. A few veterans
even received personal instruction on the Wisconsin campus
from members of the Extension staff. Most of the work done
by veterans was of a vocational nature; the relatively few
University-credit courses were taken by correspondence by
residence students during their summer vacations.[1] As recorded earlier, the Milwaukee classes provided the Division
with a wedge for establishing a two-year college course in
that city. This development opened a new era of Extension
activity, and brought the Division into active competition
for students with not only the Milwaukee Normal School and
Marquette University, but the parent body itself.

The program for rehabilitation reflected community interest in the relationship between its individual members'
welfare and their value to society. In an important sense,
Professors Frederick Jackson Turner and Richard T. Ely
had pondered this general problem in the 1890's, when they
worried about the assimilation of the foreign-born and suggested education as the means of preparing them for useful
citizenship. After 1906, Extension's language, civics, and
shop training courses helped immigrants as well as citizens
by birth find useful places in the community. By offering
information about current and controversial political matters
Extension also aided citizens to discharge their civic duties
more intelligently. This was the work of the department of
Debating and Public Discussion organized by Frank Hutchins
soon after Extension's revival, and developed with the aid
of Miss Almere Scott, who succeeded him as secretary
after his death. Through bulletins and package libraries, the
department made people aware of the complexity of given
political issues. During the first year of its existence, the
department received over three thousand requests for materials from individuals, high schools, women's and farm
groups, and city government officials. In 1922, 17,114
package libraries were loaned. Hutchins characterized the
work as a "potent and fundamental way of educating for
citizenship." The press, pulpit and platform seemed of limited value in training their audiences for the responsibilities
that accompanied the right to vote. Here was a form of education, free from pedagogy, which made the entire elector-
ate a potential class in the area of current events and which
encouraged informed debate and discussion.

While acknowledging the importance of widespread debating, Dean Reber felt that it was impossible to measure
its impact. Perhaps his position constituted a defense

against the charges that the Division had played a vital role
in the earlier defeats of the Republican Stalwarts. Dr.
Charles McCarthy, on the other hand, had no doubt of the
value of using discussion and debate to secure political ends,
and demanded that debating be made a compulsory campus
activity. Many conservatives agreed with the McCarthy
thesis that public discussion was often a prelude to political
effectiveness, and for that very reason opposed it. This
feeling led to the attack upon the School House Community
Center program in Milwaukee, and appeared again when in
1917, Regent G. D. Jones, a politically conservative businessman, opposed use of University buildings by a forum
group on grounds that one of its leaders had a reputation as
a trouble-maker and organizer of a student waiters' union.[2]

The patriotism exhibited by so many Americans during
the years of World War I emerged from the conflict as a
feeling that conservatism was inherently respectable. A
wartime issue of the Wisconsin Journal of Education reflected confusion bordering on hysteria in its account of a
mass teachers' loyalty oath at the State Convention followed
by a pledge to build both American and world citizenship.
The Journal demonstrated its own patriotism by reprinting
an editorial condemning teachers "lukewarm" in patriotism,
"doubtful" of American ideals, "befuddled with half-baked
Socialism and afflicted with a sneaking admiration for other
forms of government and other national ideals."[3] Within a
few years, while a group of University men were losing a
fight against passage of a state Pure History Law, others
were defending the school's action in barring the speaking
appearance of Scott Nearing. In Milwaukee, Extension
coöperated in classes for trade unionists, which, it was
hoped, would lead to peaceful and informed bargaining re-
placing strikes and violence as labor's way of obtaining its
ends. At the same time, an Extension representative shied
away from a forum group because it seemed dominated by
women of the trade union movement and Extension participation would lead to unfortunate identification with the movement. Extension leaders had once openly allied themselves
with the Progressives. They had responded willingly to the
call for help from the Social Democratic administration in
Milwaukee. Now, in 1927, during the "Prosperity Decade"
of Republican rule, a Division representative feared becoming entangled with a reputed socialist. Before the war,
Extensionists had helped promote the cause of state political
and educational leadership; now they stressed the American

home and home town as the bases for American ideals.[4]
Current ideological conflicts were reflected within the Division, to be sure, but the conservative theme was dominant.
Extension was at peace with the times, but no more so than
when it had coöperated with the Progressives during their
domination of the state scene; no more so than when the
Division's foundations had been made firm by its coöperation with Wisconsin manufacturers.

Extension's postwar citizenship-training effort went beyond the supposed mass appeal of package libraries, by
offering aid to specific organizations. For a time, much
interest was focused upon a large group which but recently
had acquired full citizenship: women. Having won its long
struggle to secure the Nineteenth Amendment, the National
Woman's Suffrage Association became the National League
of Women Voters. Women "had" the vote; now they were to
be instructed in its effective use. In July, 1920, the Extension Division coöperated with the Wisconsin League of
Women Voters in sponsoring a School of Citizenship. University President Birge and residence and Extension faculty
were prominent among the speakers who addressed the
meetings in the State Capitol. The men comprising the University part of the program gave it a prewar Progressive
ring. Extension sociologist, John Gillin and Professor M. V.
O'Shea of the School of Education, an extensionist with experience dating back to the Ely era, spoke on "Social Welfare Through Education" and "Social Welfare Through Legislation." History Professor Frederic L. Paxson defined
America's great problem as that of changing a government
of negation into one of action, of "getting results in spite of
checks." He cautioned, however, that development should be
in a "line of continuity" and "without destruction." These
were echoes of yesterday. The non-University speaker who
concluded, "I believe in America because of her ideals
worked out in institutions that are just,"[5] proved in harmony
with the times; in November, America's newly enfranchised
women helped elect the administration which promised a
return to normalcy.

Extension also worked with those whom society had deprived of freedom and citizenship, the inmates of prisons.
Among the prominent experiments in the history of American penology was that begun in 1871 at Elmira State Reformatory in New York. Prisoners of the fifteen- to thirty-year
age group were sentenced for indeterminate periods and
released when, after a period of education, they seemed

ready to resume their roles in society. Richard T. Ely's participation in the Elmira program convinced him that the study of political economy developed the "ethical nature" by its directing of attention "to the general welfare in the ordinary and habitual concerns of life." He felt such study formed the basis for a "practical every-day religion." Many states, however, found it profitable to use prisoners in industry and road construction. Wisconsin was among them, and the advantages and disadvantages of the program were the topics of widespread discussion. While strong industrial lobbies fought the practice of making binder twine at the state prison, the conservative editor of the Oshkosh Daily Northwestern applauded the use of convict road laborers who were doing something "morally encouraging" without competing with honest folk.[6] Organized labor did not take kindly to this brand of reform, but the largeness of Milwaukee audiences attending Jacob Riis' lectures on penology revealed the general popular interest in prison matters and in "doing something" for the prisoners.

In 1907, the chaplain of the State Penitentiary at Waupun began to encourage the inmates to take University correspondence courses. The following year, Extension sought the coöperation of the State Board of Control in offering a program of "useful courses of instruction in state institutions such as prisons, reformatories, etc." Lighty hoped the legislature would incorporate the courses into the state's rehabilitation program, thereby assuming their cost. Such was not the case. While the Division was encouraged to offer work in the State Prison, the Girls' Industrial Home and the State Reformatory, financing was left to the students. Professor Gillin's sociology classes in Milwaukee established a scholarship fund for deserving Waupun inmates, who were asked to repay the money later but were not pressured into doing so. The selection of men to receive the loans was the responsibility of the warden and Chester Allen, Oshkosh District Representative of the Extension Division.[7]

Allen made a careful study of inmate education levels and aspirations, and in scheduled conferences helped prisoners select correspondence courses best fitted to their needs. The aim was to reform the individual by interesting him in his own rehabilitation, teaching him habits of study, and giving him a chance to develop ambitions and skills which would later be of use to him and to society. The students were impressed with their future importance to their communities and were made to see that they were personally

responsible for achieving these goals. The study program
was regarded as a privilege which could be withdrawn for
misbehavior. Some of the prisoner-students came to regard
themselves as superior to their fellows who passed their
time brooding or were caught up in a craze, common among
inmates, to develop a perpetual motion machine. One of the
most talented and publicized of these students delighted his
teachers by confirming their assumptions about social devi-
ation in almost their own terms. Poverty and lack of family
life had led to his ignorance and drifting, and hence to his
life of crime, he wrote. Somehow he had retained two major
virtues: he neither drank nor smoked. Training for a job
was the answer to his problem—and the Extension Division
was offering that.[8]

Allen, and later other instructors, were allowed inside
the prison evenings, after the gates had been closed, in
order to help and encourage students with the lessons being
prepared for correction in Madison. Most of the work undertaken was of a job-training nature: courses about gasoline
engines, electric meters, store management, bookkeeping,
show card writing. A few students, however, studied English,
psychology, and history. There was hope here—what seemed
a new chance. The ambitious could develop technical skills;
the illiterate could learn to read, thereby attaining the
means of greater communication with society. In many
cases, the statements of prisoners revealed a childlike faith
that their courses contained a miraculous ingredient assuring them a more secure, happier future. While inconclusive,
there are indications that the hopes of the organizers of the
work were at least partially realized. Discipline problems
were proportionately fewer among students than nonstudents,
and the recidivation rate, lower. In 1922, 192 prisoners
were registered for Extension work; in 1924, 145; and in
1938/39, 43. Fifty-two per cent of those who began correspondence courses completed them. Despite unusual study
conditions and in some cases course interruptions caused
by release from prison, this figure was almost on a par
with the 55 per cent completion Lighty reported for all correspondence study in 1925.[9] Once again, the Division
served where there was work to be done, and stepped aside
when general approval of what it had attempted led to the
creation of more specialized services.

Extension's most consistent appeal was to school teachers
and administrators. Not only were its courses on methods
and on specific subjects of value to them, but so, too, was

its service as a clearing house for teaching materials of
such specialized nature that they were beyond the financial
reach of many schools. Teachers, in turn, became a major
source of support for Extension work. True in the 1890's,
it was again the case with the program launched in 1906.
Professor Turner pointed out the at least three-fold advantage inherent in Extension-teacher coöperation: it resulted
in better-prepared and more competent teachers, and as a
result, a better quality of student doing work beyond the
high school level, and it increased the prestige and influence
of the University.

The University had continued its teacher-education program even after the establishment of the state normal
schools. Between 1866 and 1896, seven normals, each with
its own president but all under a single Board of Regents,
had been created. Instead of relaxing its work in the field,
the University increased it. During the Van Hise administration, a model high school was built in order to end the de-
pendence of University practice teachers upon the city
schools and the various residence departments. The reinsti-
tution of correspondence courses increased the University's
role in teacher preparation. Teachers unable to attend
campus classes were urged to undertake home study courses
designed to help qualify them for certification, improve
their classroom performances, broaden their "scholarship,"
and ready them for "more responsible positions."

For a time, Extension and the normals coexisted peace-
fully. As Turner had suggested, the Division occasionally
employed normal school men to teach its courses. Professor
Theron B. Pray of Milwaukee Normal, for example, taught
Extension classes for teachers. The president of Platteville
Normal School kept Madison newspapers and copies of The
Badger, the University yearbook, available for his students.
Extension fieldmen paid numerous goodwill visits to normal
school administrators and faculty, and helped in the working
out of a program which facilitated the transfer of students
from normal schools to the University during the Junior
year.[10] Continuation of such harmony would certainly have
benefited the entire state system of education, but soon the
normals openly regarded Extension as a competitor.

Extension's coöperation with other institutions in the state
educational system included supplying important services.
For a few years after public schools began to assume responsibility for training students for industry, Extension
instructors of manual training visited schools unable to

maintain full-time teachers. The quality of the instruction
can be partially gauged by the many prizes won by the students at the State Fair. More far-reaching was the program
of the Bureau of Visual Education, headed for many years
by William H. Dudley, formerly of Platteville Normal. The
Bureau added thousands of motion picture reels and slides
to the nucleus of the slide collection of the Wisconsin Latin
Teachers' Association. Early development was patterned
after that of the work of the University of the State of New
York. To make maximum use of its loan material, the Division encouraged local schools to purchase projection equipment. A scandal was averted by Dean Reber's assurances
that Mr. Dudley had disposed of stock in a company that
would have benefitted from such sales before assuming his
position with the Division. The use of visual aids gained
respectability from the endorsement of Harvard's President
Charles W. Eliot and the label of efficiency from an experiment carried out in the Racine schools. The latter indicated
that the employment of such classroom devices reduced the
number of student failures, and thereby the cost of instruction. The Division's slides and motion pictures widened not
only the mental horizons of countless public school pupils,
but those of the adult members of numerous civic groups.
Residents of Neillsville borrowed materials depicting
"Historic Boston," "The Landing of the Pilgrims," and
activities of the United States Army, loggers, and polar ex-
plorers. In 1924, a Division artist traveled abroad coloring
slides of art masterpieces, a project that must have caused
some to wince. But Extension was addressing the many, just
as it did in the numerous slides it produced and distributed
for community singing.[11] This general, unsophisticated approach was in line with the Division's original ideals and
goals. Not until it could narrow its field of activity could
the Bureau of Visual Education become effective as an
agency of formal education.

Extension's search for students brought it into increasing
contact with high school graduates. "Equip yourself for success. Higher education will give you your best chance,"
high school seniors were advised by bulletin board posters
supplied by the Division. Those who could not go to the University at once were encouraged to accumulate University
credits by correspondence study. Those who did plan to go
immediately to the campus were warned that great numbers
of freshmen failed the English placement examination. Extension had the proper preventative in the form of a correspond-

ence course. There is no doubt that those who enrolled in it
did well on the test, but in 1916, a high school principal
raised the question of the reason for the examination failures. He suggested that the University and the high schools
had drifted too far apart. To this provocative statement
were added an increasing number of requests from high
school principals that correspondence courses be provided
students unable to take classroom work. Partially at the
insistence of Miss Leila Bascom, the Division began to push
regular high school courses during the mid–1920's.

There were administrative reasons, too, for the new emphasis. Both the University and Extension were experiencing
a stiffening of the competition for new students. Beloit College had made arrangements with many state high schools
to facilitate entrance of their graduates. Ripon College was
thought to be planning a similar program. There was a warning, too, in developments in Michigan. Schools in Benton
Harbor had been experimenting with the regular use of
International Correspondence School courses. K. G. Smith,
Michigan State Supervisor of Industrial Education and former head of the Extension program in Milwaukee, described
the program as a "refined form of the same plan we used
to use ... for evening and other special classes." Dean
Reber instructed Mr. Allen to inform Wisconsin school administrators that the Extension Divison could provide similar , but superior service. The beginnings then made
resulted in hundreds of enrollments, and proved of unex-
pected value during the depression years which lurked such
a short time away.[12]

The relations between the University and the state's public schools were reflected in the former's role in the Wisconsin Teachers' Association. "Pop" Gordon's group singing
programs became a traditional part of the state meetings.
In 1914, University President Van Hise was elected to the
presidency of the Association in a demonstration against
the school consolidation program of Governor Philipp. Until
1923, Professor O'Shea's articles on aspects of University
policy and activity enjoyed a prominent place in the Wisconsin Journal of Education. In the latter year, however,
Association elections resulted in a lessening of University
influence. E. G. Doudna, the new secretary, reorganized the
Journal to emphasize technical matters for teachers in the
lower grades. Lighty urged his Extension staff to join the
Association and to vote at all elections in order to bolster
University influence.[13]

These developments stemmed from the undercurrent of competition that had long existed between the normal schools and the University. The eruption of the 1890's had been stilled, but only temporarily. The University continued to make itself felt in matters which the normals considered within their province. The normals, on the other hand, were not content to remain specialized teacher training centers. Through faculty lectures and later formal extension work, they developed their own spheres of influence. In 1911, they secured legislative authorization to offer two years of college work. Two years later, however, they failed to win the right to present a four-year college program. Some observers thought the effort an attempt to drive out the private colleges. Others saw in it an opportunity for young people to achieve college degrees inexpensively and without leaving parental control. The problem to which the normals hesitated to fully address themselves was that of how to fill the state's growing need for an adequate number of effective teachers.

Few would dispute State Superintendent C. J. Cary's statement in 1908 that Wisconsin needed "many more good teachers." The State Teachers' Association struck at existing low professional standards by sponsoring legislation making a minimum of six-weeks teacher training a prerequisite for a certification examination. C. S. Rice, State Supervisor of School Libraries, charged that most teachers failed to keep abreast of advances in their professions; Professor O'Shea suggested that they be encouraged to attend the University Summer School. From another point of view, Superintendent Cary deplored the lack of men in the field, and the resulting "feminization" of education. Wages were such, however, that few men saw in teaching a desirable career. This situation was made the more acute by the wartime decrease in male enrollments in the normal schools. The growing teacher shortage posed special problems in areas heavily populated by the foreign born, whose children required special attention in the schools. [14]

Coupled with the problems of the numbers and quality of teachers was that of the most desirable curriculum for high school students. The University's Dean Edward Birge held that they be given a general background based upon an "enriched" program of studies. This led to the charge that the University was ignoring local needs and fastening an antiquated course of studies upon the high schools. Professor W. H. Cheever of Milwaukee Normal argued for less Latin

and more science, for preparation for "life." Away with the
tacit domination of the University over the state's educational system, he urged, and let the normals maintain their
rightful supervision of education in Wisconsin. While the
University and the normals battled over influence and competed for enrollees, the people of the state learned that a
Russell Sage Foundation survey ranked Wisconsin twenty-
eighth in educational "efficiency." By 1920, it had fallen to
thirty-third. In 1921, the Wisconsin Teachers' Association
announced that seven hundred of the state's teachers lacked
minimum requirements in professional or scholastic
training.[15]

By this time, Extension's correspondence and class work
for teachers was well established. Besides the regular
academic offerings, there were special teachers' review
courses and courses designed to fill sudden professional
requirements. When state law required that those in charge
of school libraries have specific training, Extension
launched a vocational course for acting high school librar-
ians. The first year, over two hundred teachers registered
for instruction, but subsequent enrollments dropped as the
normals began to offer such work. Normal offerings in
school management also caused Extension to abandon its
course in that field. When the legislature required that
physical education be added to the school curriculum, Professor Gordon and his assistants helped meet the sudden
need for specialized training with correspondence courses
and demonstrations before teacher groups. Some normal
school men felt that the correspondence method was imprac-
ticable for this work, and indeed, the course was open to
criticism. The Division offered aid to school superintendents, too. Many who led faculty discussions admitted their
unpreparedness for the work. Consultations with Extension
led to the development of ready-made programs for the
schools. University men addressed some of the meetings;
papers and reports by teachers were featured at others.
Besides aiding both superintendents and teachers, Extension
had found a means of extending its influence into many
small schools hitherto beyond its reach.[16]

In other ways, too, Extension's education of teachers
proved of mutual benefit. On the basis of a study of certification examinations, and conferences with several county
superintendents, the Division offered a special series of
correspondence courses for applicants for teachers' certificates. Ostensibly since the courses did not parallel those

offered by the normals, no effort was made to gain their
coöperation. In 1917, the Manitowoc and Sheboygan County
superintendents began to accept Extension grades in these
courses in lieu of qualifying examinations. Rural school
teachers, especially, enrolled in increasing numbers in
Division courses. Though the legality of this means of
awarding teaching certificates was questionable, the practice continued. State legislation defining the professional
training of teachers did not specifically include the Extension Division as an accredited institution, and county superintendents were in no position to judge schools beyond the
high school level. In the autumn of 1923, however, State
Superintendent John Callahan approved Extension and the
acceptance of its grades, and authorized the Division to
publish his decision. Subsequent University bulletins
noted that state and county superintendents recognized
certain Extension courses as being on a par with those
in the University School of Education and the normal
schools.[17]

The state's postwar educational crisis provided Extension
with more opportunities to enhance its influence. The work
undertaken was not essentially new, but consisted of a combining of already established techniques. Through consulta-
tion with state and county normal school representatives,
"coöperative schedules" were drawn up, listing the correspondence study courses counting toward graduation in the
respective institutions. The schedules varied with the
coöperating schools. Not all courses acceptable for normal
school credits were of University grade. The Executive Committee of the State Normal School at La Crosse insisted
upon courses commensurate with the normal school regents'
decision to stress teachers' courses instead of college
work.[18]

Much of the initiative and responsiblity for the necessary
negotiations lay with Extension fieldmen. Their work was
facilitated by Extension offers of aid to the normal schools.
The Division could not ignore the off-campus service and
spheres of influence the schools had developed. It seemed
logical to participate in this work if at the same time
the advertising of correspondence courses could be promoted. Extension fieldmen informally advertised normal
schools and forwarded the names of prospective students
to them. Lighty summed up the situation with a touch of
irony:

The very fact that those who are headed for some of
these other institutions learn that the Extension Division
extends opportunities which appeal to them because, for
example, they need additional preparation or perhaps
must work and earn money for a year or two, has a
tendency to proselyte in favor of the University, although
this is never in the minds of any of the University representatives.... [Extension is], therefore, eager to arrange cooperative schedules and secure the cooperation
of the executives and faculties of the above named institutions so that the field organization of the Division may
intelligently and helpfully serve many who will never
attend the University of Wisconsin.[19]

Extension and the University School of Education also
exerted influence locally through one-and two-day schools
for teachers. This program had the approval of the director
of the School of Education and relied upon the residence
faculty for its teaching staff. It was regarded, however, as
Extension work. The term "school" was selected instead of
"institute" in order to lend dignity and professional appeal
to the meetings. Such popular professors from the School of
Education as H. L. Miller and Arvil S. Barr conducted programs of lectures, round-table discussions, and when possible, demonstrations. The immediate success of the school
at Marshfield helped fieldmen sell the work elsewhere —
Spooner, Rice Lake, Shawano, Ashland, Medford, Manitowoc,
La Crosse. As usual, opinions on the value of the work
varied, ranging from unqualified approval to the conclusion
that the visiting professor was vastly overrated. On the
other hand, the presentations were beyond the grasp of at
least some of the attending teachers.[20]
Typically, the Extension administration was not solely
concerned with carrying enlightenment into the far corners
of the state. " ... there are excellent reasons why I should
have Professor Miller in my territory, and these are in
addition to the direct benefits of the day's teaching," wrote
one fieldman. These reasons boiled down to promoting Division activities. Lighty saw in the schools an excellent means
of advertising correspondence study courses, especially
among rural teachers who "are very frequently inaccessible
... to our influence and solicitations." Marshall Graff, who
had been instrumental in launching the sessions, viewed
them as a "big boom to every type of Extension work."[21]

More enduring in the Extension teachers' training program were the seminars and classes conducted by faculty
members of the School of Education. Unlike the one-day
schools, the work was of University grade and for University credit. Though popular with teachers, the effort led to
further complications with the normal schools. Far from
the early normal-school–Extension coöperation in the case
of Professor Pray, the Division now operated in conjunction
with the growing University School of Education. When
normal school men sought to teach Extension classes, the
Division tactfully discouraged them. The resulting shortage
of instructors, especially in normal school areas, cost the
Division many students. Extension found it difficult to explain its refusal of the proferred services of normal school
faculty. While excuses were phrased in terms of unfamiliar-
ity with University procedure, they had other bases. They
included the fear of having ultimately to discriminate among
normal school faculty members, and the fact that residence
departments would not recognize all of the work done under
such instructors.[22]

The normals and such colleges as Lawrence developed
extension programs of their own. Superior Normal recruited
a class in direct competition with Extension fieldmen, and
refused to accept University correspondence study credits
on grounds that the University refused to accept theirs.
When University Extension recruiting cost Milwaukee
Normal an estimated one hundred and fifty students, the
latter sent an agent to Sheboygan to develop classes in competition with the Division. It also sponsored an advertising
campaign in the Wisconsin Journal of Education. To Lighty,
the situation began to appear as though the "two ends are
making a drive upon the middle." But Extension influence
had become entrenched. In the five year period ending in
1932, 15,627 Wisconsin teachers had registered for correspondence courses. In 1931, one-eighth of all teachers in
the state were sending in correspondence lessons.[23]

Extension's work with students and teachers was based
upon undeniable needs. At the same time, the Division was
doing more than supplementing the work of existing state
institutions. It was actively competing with them in its own
behalf and that of the University. This activity marked a
movement away from the ideal of spontaneous service and
toward the institutionalization of work.

Other events, too, revealed the changing nature of the
Division. Before the war, Extension had promoted a state-

wide program of popularized health education. Concomitantly, it had prepared a course for lay health officers and offered Milwaukee doctors lectures on immunization. In 1916, the House of Delegates of the State Medical Society asked the Division to develop an extensive program of postgraduate medical instruction. A committee met with the regents, and in 1917, the legislature voted an appropriation of five thousand dollars per year for the work. While not in line with the Division's aim of popularizing knowledge, the effort dovetailed with other professional training work offered since 1906.

Although the legislature intended the program as a war emergency measure, the appropriations and instruction continued after the Armistice. Dean Reber charged that the Medical Society and the University Medical School were using them to advance themselves and to build up a supporting group of county medical societies. Reber's protests were to no avail. In 1921 and 1922, 185 obstetrics and gynecology clinics and lectures (25 with films), were held in 28 Wisconsin cities. By 1924, this type of program had been largely supplanted by the sending of lecturers to the meetings of county medical societies. Reber fumed that the films on human reproduction being shown audiences of women and girls were of greater value to the state than the physicians' program, and hoped for a revival of the "ideal of Medical Extension."[24] Certainly it would have been more in keeping with the spirit of the work of the early part of his administration. What he ignored was the question of the desirability of reviving the prewar program. Not only had new media of information become available to the public, but the Extension Division itself had so changed that some, with perhaps a degree of chronological license, now look back upon the period of 1907 and 1926 as the "Golden Age" of Extension in Wisconsin.

Extension in
Prosperity and Disillusionment

The great adventure of adult life is infinitely more en-
grossing, more baffling, more implicated with the possibilities of pleasure and pain, of success and failure than
is any world cruise. You may not be captain of the social
craft in which you journey, but you can be captain of
your own inner life, and of the expression you give it.
—University Bulletin, 1936

In 1926, after nearly two decades of directing the activities
of the Extension Division of the University of Wisconsin,
Dean Louis E. Reber retired. His unending struggle to blend
the ideal and the expedient into a workable program merit-
ing the support of the people of the state and the legislature
had been fruitful. Extension had become known and respected not only throughout Wisconsin, but throughout the
world. Its success had done much to remove the stigma
from correspondence study, and to establish standards for
state contributions to the general welfare. Reber had placed
an indelible stamp upon the Extension Division, and the
Division, upon American education.

Reber's choice for his successor was Chester D. Snell,
Director of the Extension Division of the University of North
Carolina. Negotiations with him were begun in February,
1925, and were concluded in the spring of 1926 after Snell
had met several times with Glenn Frank, recently appointed
president of the University of Wisconsin.[1] Frank and Snell
saw in each other much to be admired, and within the Division there was an atmosphere of happy expectancy. This
was the era of the economic boom, of the assured future.
But under the new deanship, Extension, like the society of
which it was a part, was to go from prosperity to want, from
optimism to disillusionment.

Snell was a graduate of Springfield College, had done
some graduate work at Columbia, and been active in the
Interchurch World Movement and the YMCA. Soon after
leaving college, he had been given charge of the Extension
Division at Chapel Hill and aided in its marked expansion.
" ... young, tall and broad, with a ready smile and just a

shade of [southern] accent," he was an ardent camper and
fisherman. An administrator rather than scholar or teacher,
Snell was intensely aware of those of his qualities which
seemed to point toward and symbolize success. "There is a
side to me which perhaps you have not seen," he wrote
Reber, "—when running in high gear I am quite an autocrat
and a driver—you know it takes that to build an efficient
organization in a short space of time."[2]

Efficiency was a word commanding respect in all fields
including education. Schoolmen were proudly emulating the
tenets of the time-study experts. An editorial in the Wisconsin Journal of Education asserted, "Letters of the alphabet
after a name are meaningless unless followed by the magic
letters of efficiency—o.k." Reflecting this spirit, Dean Snell
announced that his first major objective was to make the
Division's routine more efficient and his office the nerve
center of all its activities. Administrative, bookkeeping, and
student record procedures were streamlined to the point
that Snell's critics charged him with "Fordizing." On the
other hand, veteran extensionist Leila Bascom noted that as
a result of Snell's bringing the Milwaukee Center once again
under the close supervision of his office, red tape had been
cut, instructional materials suddenly made available, and
that a new spirit of helpfulness was to be observed among
members of the clerical staff. Dean Snell offered quantitative but inconclusive proof of the value of his accomplishments. The average number of correspondence lessons received yearly per registration increased from 3.3 in the
biennium 1924–25 to 4.1 in 1927–28. This upward trend,
however, had been in evidence since 1920, years before
Snell's coming to Wisconsin.[3]

Dean Snell's efforts at centralization were well-organized
continuations of the work of his predecessor. The reorganization of the field staff was foreshadowed by Reber's belated
attempt to channel all official contacts between Madison and
field organizers through his office. Dean Snell, who made
greater use of lieutenants, created the special office of
Director of Field Organization and named Chester Allen to
the post. This agency not only controlled headquarters-field
relations, but served as a training school for new field men.
Although the Milwaukee Extension Center had previously
grown into a semi-independent unit, Snell's regular visits
and administrative reorganization tied it more tightly to the
parent institution.

Changes in routine are generally expected of a new ad-

ministration. Of more significance were the dean's plans
for the future and their effect upon his relations with the
administrative assistants and faculty members carried over
from the Reber period. Prior to coming to Wisconsin, Snell
requested briefings from Dean Reber and Correspondence
Study Department chairman, William H. Lighty. Lighty replied in terms of Extension's early ideals, selecting President Charles Van Hise's address, "The Idea of Service" as
a key document. Reber wrote in terms of budget and personnel problems, of his building plans and specific hopes
for the revival of medical, music, and dramatic extension
along the North Carolina lines which paralleled the early
Wisconsin efforts.[4] Reber's written legacy was to loom
large in Snell's administration.

Snell's early requests in matters of staff appointments
were immediately and understandably respected. Teaching
vacancies were filled as he indicated, and other changes
effected. Field representative Chester Allen, whose service in the Division went back to before the war years, was
promoted to assistant professor. The office of assistant
dean was created, and R. E. Ellingwood of the department
of Business Administration named to it. Ellingwood's responsibility for the handling of routine left his superior free
to concentrate on policy making. It was here, however, that
Snell's manifestations of youthful self-assurance were overshadowed by his feelings of insecurity and resulting depend-
ence upon two major sources: President Frank and the
Reber manuscript.

The dean and the president agreed that the people of the
state had little need for extension work of vocational and
high school levels. What was now called for was an educational program to enable adults to adjust themselves to the
rapid economic and social changes of the age. Although
announced with fanfare, this desire to integrate the activities of the Division more closely with the life of the state
was but a restatement of earlier Extension policy. Snell's
critics testified that he admitted possessing no concrete
goals of his own, that he acted in accordance with the wishes
of the president and influential University faculty members.
Certainly in his early years in Madison, the dean hesitated
to move without specific presidential sanction and support.
Taken aback by the University regents' statement of their
inability to find "positive results" in his administration, he
asked President Frank for a statement in writing about his
plans for Extension services, the Milwaukee classes and

their "new approach to the problem of adult education." On other occasions, when presidential wishes left him in doubt, Snell turned for suggestions to members of the Board of Regents.[5]

The Reber memorandum left little room for interpretation. It contained Reber's hopes that a new wing be added to Extension's Madison headquarters, suggestions for additional financing of the Milwaukee building project and the disposition of personnel problems. Lighty was mentioned specifically. His years of meritorious service and excellent advice seemed overshadowed by his lack of executive ability. Administrative readjustments were in order, if possible without injuring the veteran department head whose tenure dated to the very beginning of Extension's revival.[6]

As had Reber, Snell inherited a staff and policies not of his making. Reber had found it necessary to keep the men who had been with Extension from its inception. Snell had no such compunctions and rid himself of those he deemed inefficient or uncoöperative. Within a few years, six out of fourteen major administrators were replaced. Snell admitted that his firing had been rapid, but explained that he was well acquainted with the Division even before he formally assumed his post. "I admit that a rather complete 'wrecking' job was done," he wrote President Frank, "but I do not think there are many people who will say this interfered with the regular program; in fact, I think conditions began to improve from the start."[7] Dean Snell underestimated the cumulative effect of wholesale removals upon those who remained and were vulnerable to his personal decisions of worth. When faculty protests eventually reached threatening proportions, he maintained that his program had enjoyed the sanction of President Frank.

It was inevitable that Snell, the ambitious newcomer, and Lighty, the elder statesman, would come into conflict. The dean had Reber's estimate of the man, was so constituted personally that he could brook no opposition, and had quickly shown his disregard for tenure. While Lighty, on the other hand, disclaimed any rancor at being bypassed a second time for the deanship, his bitterness toward Snell proved long-lasting and beyond professional contempt. In 1929, he and Snell clashed over the Division's advertising methods which Lighty characterized as making "friends with the mammon of unrighteousness." The dean dismissed Lighty's views as "bunk—theoretical bunk." Subsequent disagreements over the liberal education program sponsored

at the Milwaukee Center resulted in charges that Lighty was
failing to coöperate with both the field and instructional
forces. Not caring to risk a furor by forcing Lighty's removal, Snell stripped him of his authority. Malcolm G.
Little, a Chapel Hill extension veteran and assistant director of the Milwaukee Center, was brought to Madison as
assistant dean and given Lighty's duties. Lighty retained
his old title, but was relegated to making full-time studies
in the field of adult education. The correspondence and field
services were now virtually in Snell's own office.[8]

Dean Snell's attempt to bring the Milwaukee Center within his purview, however, ended in disaster. He had quickly
made himself unpopular with both its students and its faculty. Dismissal of a popular member of the English Department led to student charges that he had been "framed" because of his frank criticism of the teaching and administrative staffs. Not being primarily concerned with the
Division's constant battle of the budget, the students further
resented the requirement that they pay five dollars per
credit, the regular Extension charge, which placed their
total fees above those charged for residence work in
Madison. Milwaukee administrators, however, were able to
manipulate protest rallies into ineffectiveness, and turned
one major effort into what seemed to them an "enjoyable
farce."

Faculty discontent, which more than matched that of the
students, had several bases: Dean Snell's efforts to deprive
the Center of its customary autonomy, his related stress
upon teaching as opposed to scholarship as a criterion for
promotion, his refusal of money for research, his firing
policy, and his reappointments of assistant professors on
yearly rather than the usual three-year basis. While Snell
explained that depression exigencies dictated that he not
commit Extension financially far in advance, it seemed
clear to the men affected that he was using the system as a
club over the heads of those who did not agree with his policy and plans for the Center. An element of punishment was
also suspected. A psychologist, Dr. L. E. Drake, who had
most consistently asked for and had been refused research
funds, was also the secretary of the Executive Committee of
Local 253, American Federation of Teachers, which had
become an anti-Snell bastion.

The matter came to a head in the late spring of 1934 with
the dean's refusal to reappoint Assistant Professor Donald
C. Broughton, who had been on leave to conduct biological

research. Dean Snell explained that as a research man,
Broughton would find the emphasis upon teaching within the
Center uncongenial. In an open letter to his colleagues,
Broughton replied that the move dramatized Snell's disre-
spect for research, leaves and tenure, and predicted a shat-
tering of faculty morale.[9]

The Broughton letter was but part of a concerted move
against the dean. Four days later, the Milwaukee County
Federation of Teachers petitioned President Frank to investigate Extension. In reply, Milwaukee Center department
heads asserted that the attacks were not representative of
faculty feeling, and deplored the publicizing of the tenure
situation. The lines of conflict were now becoming clear,
save for the positions of the regents and President Frank.
Their attitudes were made known shortly.

President Frank did not formally present the matter to
the regents until the October meeting, when, as anticipated,
absences left the session in the hands of anti-Snell men.
Dean Snell later maintained that this move and the accompanying recommendation for an investigation of his administration were at the time unknown to him.[10] The results
came quickly. A regent committee held secret hearings in
Milwaukee and Madison, compiling over a thousand pages of
testimony bursting with pent up antagonism against the dean.
The records are still closed, but a partial transcript exists
in the Lighty manuscript collection: Snell had been foisted
upon an unsuspecting Reber by men anxious to be rid of
him; Snell was unfitted by education for his position, a
frightened man who could not make his own policies; Snell
was dictatorial with his subordinates whom he kept in line
by unethical methods; Snell was guilty of poor sportsman-
ship in his personal relations. However justified were some
of the charges, elements of personal bitterness were too
numerous and strong to remain concealed.

Their hearings concluded, the regents asked Snell for his
resignation, and President Frank suggested he comply. The
dean refused on grounds that he had never acted without
having consulted the president, and he then attempted to
throw the situation into a new framework by charging that
the attack against him had resulted from his refusal to
countenance "subversive activities, improper conduct and
immorality on the part of a small group."[11] Given an opportunity to document his statements, Snell offered in evidence his correspondence with the president, and an affida-
vit charging certain of his accusers with immoral conduct

aboard a private yacht sailing Lake Michigan. Counter affi-
davits were quickly introduced into the record.[12] This was
material for the yellow press. Obscured for the moment was
the University of Wisconsin of Presidents Bascom,
Chamberlin and Van Hise, of Professors Babcock and
Turner, of the regents' resolution dedicating the institution
to the sifting and winnowing for truth. In its place rose a
nightmare of pettiness, half truths, chicanery, politics and
immorality.

The regents reaffirmed their decision regarding the dean,
but this time gave him no opportunity to resign. President
Frank attempted to shed all but a minimum of responsibility
for Snell's appointment and actions. He praised his qualities
as a successful organizer of routine and as a financial
manager. He granted, too, that Dean Snell had improved the
quality of the Madison staff, but deplored his "personal
qualities" and "administrative methods" which had destroyed morale, promoted factionalism, and disrupted the
entire University. To Lighty, however, the real tragedy lay
in the fact that during Snell's administration there had been
no genuine effort to recast the Division's goals beyond those
formulated by his predecessor.[13] The task before Snell's
successor was to be a difficult one from any angle. The position fell to Frank O. Holt, widely known leader in state
educational circles and currently University registrar.

Lighty's major indictment of the Snell administration
might have been leveled at University President Glenn Frank
as well. The dean and the president repeatedly issued statements about their new departures in education, but, with
changed dates and proper names, they were but echoes of
the optimism of the earlier years of the Reber administration.

In 1907, the dominant educational philosophy of the Extension Division had emphasized the practical defined as
money-making. Counter to that theme ran another based
upon the need for intellectual discipline and the strengthen-
ing of character. These views and their relationship to one
another were a part of the social milieu of the era. During
the succeeding years, which were ones of relative prosperity, educators felt it more important to emphasize subjects
assumed to help students interpret the world and aid them
in solving the problems of everyday life. The champions of
the "new education" hailed it as a development important as
the industrial revolution. Education was to be no longer
"formal and verbal," but designed to translate new concepts
into man-on-the-street terms. The "new" approach was to

mold teachers and students into a great team in search of
truth, which when discovered would result in "social control,
not individual control." The schools would stand between
"civilization and chaos."[14] To many Wisconsin extensionists,
however, these were but cleverly restated commonplaces.

President Frank tried to commit the University to a program designed to extend to people of all ages opportunities
for economic betterment and intellectual and spiritual enrichment. Given the early rapport between the president and
Dean Snell, this vague policy seemed to promise Extension's
return to the institute and community activities whose
abandonment Dean Reber had regretted. In 1928, Snell announced with journalistic fanfare the launching of a new and
enlarged program of Extension service. But what was new
in the offerings? Surely not the aids extended small businessmen hard pressed by competition from the chain stores,
nor the course in electric meters, nor coöperation with the
Milwaukee Labor College, correspondence study for prisoners, or even the community dramatics program directed
by Miss Ethel Rockwell, a Wisconsin student who had returned to Madison via Chapel Hill. There was refurbishing,
to be sure. The Division's original slide collection was re-
viewed and in large part discarded, and Extension produced
a number of educational motion pictures. A film entitled,
"Wisconsin, Its Government at Work," rightfully earned the
praises of the regents and the state legislature. But this
was largely a matter of adapting a popular technology to a
policy of long standing. Medical Extension was revived, but
along the lines into which it had fallen during Reber's deanship. Postgraduate courses rather than community health
programs formed its backbone.

While helping Extension to promote specialization because
such was temporarily expedient, President Frank decried
the overspecialization of the average school's program,
which, he charged, led to "scrappiness of culture." Schools
had "begun as tools and ended as tyrants of the spirit of
man," he declared. They had become overorganized, factory-
like, and far removed from the ideal of a great teacher sur-
rounded by eager students. "Oh, Lord of Learning and
Learners [Frank entoned], we are at best but blunderers in
the God-like business of teaching.... We have been content
to be the merchants of dead yesterdays, when we should
have been guides to unborn tomorrows.... May we know
how to relate the coal scuttle to the universe.... May we
be shepherds of the spirit as well as masters of the mind."[15]

This philosophy was given form on the Madison campus in the University Experimental School directed by Professor Alexander Meikeljohn. In Extension, it grew into the adult education program in liberal arts conducted at the Milwaukee Center. Agreeing that the era called for adult education, Frank and Snell, working with Division and residence men, sought to develop a program similar to that of the Danish folk colleges with their noncredit courses designed to encourage self-education. The effort was made easier by administrative necessity. Correspondence study enrollments had been steadily decreasing while those in classroom courses had been growing. In addition, Milwaukee librarian, Matthew Dudgeon, reported that in 1927, 1,723 people were doing "some systematic and serious reading" along lines prescribed by the American Library Association and his own staff.[16] Classroom work, perhaps even that of a cultural nature, seemed a promising popular outlet for the Division's offer of service.

The University and Extension men with whom Snell consulted in mapping the Milwaukee program spoke in terms of inspiring in adults an outlook in which "fairness and beauty" would outweigh emphasis upon material possessions and numbers. This could be achieved, it was assumed, by popularizing knowledge of the "fundamental motives and purposes and beliefs ... which underlie all human experience and bind it together." Thus would men be liberated from superstition and religious intolerance, and enabled to find esthetic enjoyment even in buying stockings and hanging wallpaper. Enabled by whom? President Frank knew the answer: by teachers who held themselves "in virginal aloofness from the formalizing taint." It would be well, however, cautioned an Extension man who had just spoken of cultivating the esthetic tastes, to offer some courses in diet, exercise, clothing, and ventilation.[17]

The liberal arts program was launched in connection with the opening of Extension's new Milwaukee building. The odor of fresh plaster may have convinced some that they were participants in a great innovation, but the curriculum reads otherwise. There is no question of the quality of most of the offerings: University of Chicago men lecturing on "The World and Man, A Survey of Natural Science," Max Otto's "Philosophers from Plato to the Present Day," and courses in social problems, the Bible as literature, art, nutrition, home decoration, health, and business. There were no entrance requirements for students, however; their voluntary

attendance was accepted as evidence of their sincerity and
willingness to study and learn. The liberal arts enthusiasts
had stumbled into the same pit that had claimed nineteenth
century University Extension. They found that they could
attract audiences, but making them into students was another
matter. It was this which led Lighty to grumble that the program was highlighted by handing people pieces of paper
stating that they were educated. Who were the approximately
seven hundred people who registered annually for the Milwaukee Center special night classes between 1928 and 1931?
Why did they come? As with University Extension during
the 1890's, the majority were women. When ranked by occupation, teachers, housewives, and stenographers headed the
list. This strongly suggests that many of the registrants
were more interested in filling the coal scuttle than in finding its relation to the universe. Of the 3,300 adults registered in all Extension evening classes in 1931, 80 per cent
were seeking vocational or professional advancement.[18]
Frank and Snell had accomplished little toward answering
the challenge contained in President Van Hise's inaugural
address, namely that the University give the lie to those
who dismissed America as a nation of "money grubbers."

The depression, signaled by the stockmarket crash of
October, 1929, taxed the administrative and teaching talents
of the entire Extension Division. Policy makers had been
pondering the problem of successfully adapting people to an
era of increasing leisure and preventing society from disintegrating before the forces of sloth born of surfeit. Now
Extension looked out upon the widespread enforced leisure
of unemployment and a society with many desperate and de-
moralized men. At the same time, it faced the task of guaranteeing its own survival. The legislature had to be convinced of the need for adequate appropriations, and people
of the state, of the value of registering for Extension work.
Service and survival—to an urgently new degree were these
concepts inextricably intertwined. The flexibility of which
the Division had proved capable served it well. Its broad
view of service enabled its leaders to adapt it to meet their
definition of the needs of the era.

With unemployment figures ever rising, a guidance program directed by Malcolm S. MacLean, former newspaper-
man and faculty member of the University of Minnesota, was
established at the Milwaukee Center. MacLean approached
the problem before him as one on mental hygiene. Idle men
lacking necessary physical and mental outlets tended to

stagnate, brood, develop feelings of inferiority, and become
burdens to themselves and the community. The guidance program
gram was designed to help these men analyze themselves,
to recognize their own weaknesses and strengths. This approach to unemployment as an individual problem was
adopted by the vocational schools as well. It appeared significant that in the early months of the depression, few of
the jobless who haunted employment agencies had had vocational school experience.[19] Perhaps, as Dr. McCarthy had
argued decades earlier, there was always a place for trained
men. It followed, then, that men without jobs would do well
to obtain technical and shop training so as to be immediately
employable when economic conditions improved.

An informal counterbalance to the stress upon individual
deficiencies appeared in the Extension dramatics program.
Miss Ethel Rockwell, who directed the work, had a flair for
civic pageants in which members of the community rubbed
buckskin-clad shoulders in combatting Indians and pioneer
hardships and, before the last cue, had fought their ways to
peace and well-being. Such programs, clearly anticipated
before the war, were given profundity by the times. Miss
Rockwell was convinced that civilizations were made or
broken by the manner in which their people spent their
leisure time. Coöperative work in the drama, which involved
all the arts and encouraged individualism within a group set-
ting, was bound to produce an "alert intellect and wholesome
spiritual adjustment to the world about us and to our fellow
beings." Forced to view the matter from an accountant's
point of view, Dean Snell ordered a cessation of the "financial fliers" in pageantry and increased concentration upon
such "prosaic activities" as small productions and aid to
little theater groups.[20]

In his effort to secure work to compensate for the loss of
a private constituency unable to meet Extension fees, Dean
Snell offered the legislature the Division's services in any
state-sponsored program for rehabilitating the jobless. Legislative aid soon appeared in an appropriation of $30,000 to be
used for Extension courses for the unemployed. Expenditure
of the money was administered by the State Industrial Commission, which also controlled a subsequent $12,000 loan
fund created to help students at the Milwaukee Center. Immediately Extension's public relations services urged the
people of the state to take advantage of these grants. "The
use of spare time is the best investment, especially during
the widespread unemployment," one bulletin advised. "A new

world is in the making," stated another, "Important changes
in operation and management are forecast. It is inevitable
that those who are best prepared will be given the places of
responsibility." After all, was not prosperity still just
around the corner, and the only real thing to be feared, fear
itself?

Extension's efforts to enroll teachers, a group with relatively steady incomes, were increased. In the years 1933–34,
almost one-half million pieces of literature were mailed to
them in addition to the materials distributed personally by
fieldmen. Hopes for developing formal coöperation with the
Civil Conservation Corps were partially dashed when the
Department of the Interior announced its own plan for as-
signing educational directors to the camps. The Division
then sent these men correspondence study bulletins for general distribution. "Are you making the best use of your
leisure time in camp?" one asked; "Will the way you are
using it prepare you for advancement in business, industry,
a vocation or the professions?" Coöperative book-rentals
and study plans were suggested, and all CCC students were
charged the state residence fee of five dollars per credit
rather than the out-of-state fee of eight dollars. Requests by
camp educational directors that correspondence courses be
turned over to them were refused by the Division. It preferred to keep the teaching and resulting fees within its own
control.

Despite these efforts and the revision of correspondence
courses under the supervision of Assistant Dean Little,
home study enrollments continued to decrease. In the biennium 1931–32, registrations taken by the field staff had
dropped between 750 and 800 below those of the preceding
biennium, a loss of about $11,000 to the Division. Fieldmen
were urged to step up their campaigns, and a new source of
enrollments was opened. Earlier in his deanship, Snell had
deliberately turned his back upon courses of high school
level. Faculty members, too, had often hesitated to accept
high school students because of their academic immaturity.
Suddenly Extension offered them a cordial hand. Correspondence courses of high school grade were quickly written, and
school officials were assured that the Division meant to
complement, not compete with their offerings. Extension–
high school coöperation led to a program reminiscent of the
factory and shop work of 1907. Students prepared their
lessons under the supervision of local teachers, but actual
instruction and paper correction remained in the hands of

the Extension staff. By the fall of 1932, within a few months
of the inauguration of the program, 145 high school students
were enrolled in 169 different courses.[21]

The high school program helped check the downward trend
in correspondence enrollments. The additions of state-
financed unemployed students gradually boosted correspondence study figures to a new high. By 1934, they had surpassed the temporarily more popular class registrations
7,645 to 7,120. Interestingly, while the courses were generally taken for immediately practical ends, men students
barely outnumbered women, an indication that economic responsibility was not as determined by sex as at an earlier
period. Between the bienniums of 1930–31 and 1934–35, the
Extension budget, including appropriations and fees, was
cut from $573,075 to $411,000. The strain on the Division's
general financial situation was somewhat alleviated, however,
by salary cuts and waivers, part-time employment and releasing of some personnel, and the adaptability of its administrators and faculty in time of crisis.[22]

Widespread unemployment and the inability of many high
school graduates to go on to college focused increasing attention upon a problem which had been simmering within the
University and its Extension Division, namely the development of junior colleges. In 1932, Wisconsin high schools
graduated 23,000 students. Before the depression, 40 per
cent of these young people would have continued their formal
education in some way, while many others would have been
absorbed into business and industry. Now a growing number
in both groups found the doors to the future closed. Worried
local school officials attacked the problems of trying to
maintain the morale of these youths while keeping them out
of the job market. Postgraduate study seemed the answer.
Racine experimented with a "leisure time college," which
attracted few students but won the favorable attention and
offers of aid from University faculty members.

School officials and educators decided on concerted efforts
to solve the "youth problem." In the spring of 1932, representatives of these groups met with State Superintendent
John Callahan. Dr. W. W. Kelly, president of the Green Bay
School Board, spoke for many when he asserted that community responsibility for young people did not cease with
high school. Something more would have to be undertaken to
head off their depression-bred demoralization and delin-
quency, to check the "rapidly approaching chaos." The first

measure taken was passage of a resolution recommending
that city school boards cooperate with the Extension Division
and vocational schools in presenting high school graduates
with opportunities for advanced study. Extension–vocational
school coöperation was not only a feasible means of offering
the broadest of curricula, but also a legal one. The law
which Dr. Charles McCarthy, aided by President Van Hise
and Dean Reber, had written in 1911 creating the vocational
schools had also empowered the latter to contract for Extension instructors. Dusted off, it seemed to offer the Division a new field of endeavor. Beyond the letter of the law,
however, lay the question of the University administration's
approval and coöperation.

The resolution suggesting this new Extension activity was
no sudden development. Dean Snell's early abandonment of
lower-level work had led to increasingly cordial relations
between the Division and the State Board of Industrial Education. In the absence of competition for students, there was
room for coöperation. Fieldmen were instructed to cement
the relationship, which had immense possibilities for both.
Wherever possible, Extension classes and other activities
were carried on within vocational school buildings.[23]

At the same time, Dean Snell was becoming increasingly
interested in the possibilities of sponsoring junior college
work, and was discussing the matter with prominent men
outside the University. In 1929, during a legislative investigation to determine the feasibility of again integrating the
entire state educational system, the possibility of building
junior colleges around the state teachers' colleges or the
Extension Division had been suggested. President Frank,
enamored of noncredit adult education, testified that junior
colleges would offer no economic advantage. Dean Snell,
however, pointed to the work along these lines at the University of California, and warned the president that "sooner
or later," Wisconsin, too, would have to take serious cogni-
zance of the matter.[24]

The depression hastened that time, and the break between
President Frank and Dean Snell. Both vocational school and
Extension administrators favored the linking of their facilities. George P. Hambrecht, Director of the State Board of
Vocational Education, reported that the unemployed were
entering his schools in ever increasing numbers, and that
his staffs were unable to meet their divergent educational
needs. A two-year college credit program taught by Exten-

sion and locally administered by vocational schools seemed in order. It was even possible that such emergency measures would merit permanency.[25]

Support for and opposition to the move induced coöperation among people with varied motives. In favor of the development were those who desired an expansion of the work under their control. At their sides stood those who feared the excesses of idle youths, and parents who saw the possibilities of less expensive education for their children. Backing also came from those who envisioned civic development touched off by the presence of higher level educational institutions in their cities. In opposition stood President Frank and some University faculty members whose reasons included fear of a decentralized University, hope for some supposedly superior program, and doubt about maintaining academic standards in the wilds north of Lake Mendota.

President Frank's unfavorable attitude temporarily prevented the full development of Extension–vocational school plans. Dean Snell and Director Hambrecht, however, planned to go as far as possible without technically opposing the president.[26] At the request of local administrators, Extension classes were integrated into the programs of county normal schools at Mayville, Wausau and Wisconsin Rapids. Individual Extension classes were developed as fully as possible in cities throughout the state. In the 1923–35 biennium, over one thousand students were enrolled in such work in Antigo, Fond du Lac, Kenosha, Madison, Mayville, Racine, Rhinelander, Sheboygan, Wausau, and Wisconsin Rapids. This still did not constitute even a full freshman program, but it provided both a start and an indication of the popularity of such an undertaking.

President Frank remained unconvinced. In the spring of 1934, he informed the faculty that such offerings had outlived their usefulness, that what was needed was a "freshly conceived" program of University services to meet the demands of changing times. But he had nothing fresh to offer.[27] On the other hand, despite his many shortcomings, and his vacillation during the controversy, Dean Snell had helped launch a major phase of Extension work. Its full development, however, awaited the efforts of other administrations.

Extension in War and Peace

The Extension Division of the University of Wisconsin is
a part of the public educational system of the state and
it is eager to make its services available to any citizen
of the state who may desire to benefit from such services.

—F. O. Holt, 1940

In our educational system, more than in any other
agency, the mechanical and automatic destroy the essential spirit. The spirit of our educational system—the
spirit that makes inspired leadership for our youth, that
hunts down the diseases of our race, that, in brief, is
found in the everlasting pursuit of illusive truth—that
spirit is always smothered by mechanical and automatic
valuations.

—Governor Phil La Follette, 1931

The 1930's heralded a reintensification of the perennial conflict between critics of the social and economic order and
those to whom the suppression of such criticism seemed a
duty. As in earlier critical eras, the conflict was shifted to
the level of morality versus immorality. Hence, to many,
there seemed no middle ground. This was the Era of the
Job. Millions of Americans constantly wrestled with the
problem of securing or holding one. Government aid and the
organization of workers seemed to offer the best immediate
solutions, but did they not flout principles that had made
America great? Traditionalists professed to detect overtones of Bolshevism in the measures, a threat of revolution.
At that, however, the material demands of labor unions and
bonus marchers were understandable. As long as they were
advanced openly, they could be answered by neatly turned
phrases, and if need be, night sticks. A matter of greater
consternation were the American youths who questioned the
assumption that all was right with their world and who
flocked into social studies classes with skepticism and
penetrating questions. Conveniently ignoring the facts of unemployment and widespread want, some traditionalists held
the schools responsible for these attitudes. There developed
a steady demand that the lower grades again use the McGuffy
Readers, which taught patriotism instead of criticism. The
American Legion launched its extensive and expensive attack

153

upon the Rugg Social Science Series, and drugstore magnate,
Charles R. Walgreen, withdrew his niece from the University of Chicago in order to remove her from the influence
of supposed radicals.

The position of American universities during this era of
depression and suspicion was an awkward one. Declining
revenue made direct and indirect federal and state subsidies
vital, and many schools, including the University of Wisconsin and its Extension Division, came to lean heavily upon
them. But was there a price tag attached to this aid? Now
more than ever were the schools dependent upon the good
will of articulate minorities whose voices filled legislative
halls and whose threats to boycott a campus could not be
dismissed lightly. To placate them could mean that research
and instruction be oriented to serve their purposes. Even
in a period of few jobs, however, there were those in academic life who exercised their obligations of insisting upon
freedom in research and teaching. Some who fought for
the principle did so without always realizing that responsibility and probity are necessary concomitants of freedom.
But this was true, too, among those who sought to make the
schools mirrors of their prejudices by attempting to silence
those with views contrary to their own.

Between the general public and the pressure groups within it on the one hand, and the University research and instructional staffs on the other, stood the school administrators. The nature of their problems necessitated that
possibly far-reaching decisions be made quickly. It is not
surprising, therefore, that in retrospect, some of their
actions appear to have been based upon little more than expediency. Monetary matters and enrollments necessarily
loomed large in their considerations. They were obliged,
moreover, to view their responsibilities from the angle of
taxpayers and parents of students, as well as of custodians
of Western academic traditions.

The years of Frank O. Holt's deanship were ones of rapid
change, which added to the complexities of Extension administration. During the thirties and forties, depression, war
and peace gave the Division's struggle for existence-through-
service an ever-changing complexion. Finances were a matter of concern to the entire University, and special defi-
ciency appropriations proved necessary. The Extension
Division, which relied heavily upon its fee income, suffered
when the presumed passing of the economic crisis led to
the discontinuation of legislative appropriations for courses

for the unemployed. War in Europe, too, had its effect as
expansion of our armed services further decreased the
numbers of actual and potential Extension students. Certain
Division costs remained relatively fixed, however. High
quality correspondence teaching called for maintenance of
an adequately compensated, top-flight staff. Chester Allen
argued logically that since correspondence registrations
depended in large part on his field service, the service
should be not only maintained but expanded.

Extension's depression measures included the discontinuation of unprofitable programs and the development of those
promising profit. The Bureau of Dramatic Activities was
finally closed. Staff members were transferred from services which produced no fees, and given teaching assignments.
Traveling teachers were urged to keep their expense ac-
counts to the minimum commensurate with the dignity of
their positions. But the developing international situation
ended to nullify such efforts. In the fall of 1941, Dean Holt
announced, "Every day and in every way I get madder and
madder at Hitler. And we have reason to be concerned because our budget is so adversely affected." Though by dropping much of its work the Division had reached a new degree of self-support—$66\frac{1}{2}$ per cent—its largely self-supporting classes were seriously threatened by the decreasing
enrollments, caused by America's prewar military prepara-
tions. The situation indicated the exertion of concentrated
efforts to develop popular outlets for Extension services.[1]

The high school correspondence courses developed during
the previous deanship were advertised with renewed vigor.
New teaching techniques were tried, and the coöperation of
local school authorities encouraged. Dean Holt actively supported passage of a state law legalizing payment of correspondence fees by local school districts and operating
boards. He elaborated the usual Extension contacts with the
high schools into a University and College Day, on which
the representatives of educational institutions met with
interested students. This provided a means of emphasizing
in the presence of competing colleges the relative inexpen-
siveness of enrolling in Extension courses. In 1936, Dean
Holt succeeded in making legislative scholarships, origin-
ally intended for students enrolling in the University, appli-
cable to Extension Centers as well. During the war years,
plans were made to enable those whose high school education had been interrupted by military service to continue
their studies by correspondence.[2] Service to the people of

the state continued to be both an end and a means for the
Extension Division of the University of Wisconsin.

During the depression years, freshman center class work,
begun under Dean Snell, became a substantial part of the
state's educational system. The obstruction of its development by University President Frank ended when he was replaced by Clarence Dykstra. The success of experimental
efforts in Antigo and Rhinelander led to a meeting between
representatives of the Extension Division and local school
authorities. Orvil E. Olson, Director of the Antigo Vocational School, and author of the "Antigo Plan" under which
students, the community, and the State Board of Vocational
Education shared the costs of a freshman program, described the success of the work in his community. A representative from Rhinelander buttressed his remarks with
an account of community-Extension coöperation in his city.
Lakeshore educators pointed out that if Extension did not
expand its center program, other schools would meet the
demands of Wisconsin students. The University of Chicago
was already developing plans for Racine, and at Sheboygan,
Mission House was carrying on an extensive public relations
program in the high schools. A survey conducted among
Marinette High School students revealed a decided interest
in a state junior college. Certainly there was impressive
evidence of substantial interest in the development of local
two-year college programs.[3] As in 1906, Extension had to
meet its competition quickly.

The conference touched off the long-delayed state-wide
Extension day-school program. Medieval and modern history, Spanish, algebra, and geography were among the offerings of the Division's circuit-riding instructors teaching in
Racine, Manitowoc, Green Bay, and Wausau. Long-estab-
lished understanding governed the selection of these
teachers. While the Division reserved the right to employ
whom it would, instructors were engaged only with the con-
sent of, or nomination by, the concerned residence departments. The History Department was especially active in
defining the conditions under which credit instruction was
offered. Inspection tours of center classes by residence
men led to strong recommendations regarding hours of instruction, scheduling of classes, and improvement of local
library facilities. The time spent by instructors traveling
between centers posed a particularly thorny problem, and
Professor Paul Knaplund recommended that work in isolated and distant places be conducted by correspondence

only. In 1937, an inspection of Extension Centers by Professors W. B. Hesseltine and R. L. Reynolds led to their recommendations —which became a fixed policy—that history instructors be limited to a maximum of three years with the Division. Rather than permanent positions, the posts were to be regarded as "post-doctoral teaching internship[s]." Instructors had reported that in their relatively isolated teaching assignments they missed the academic shop talk and exchange of ideas which constitute a major part of campus life. The positions seemed to offer little to increase an instructor's morale; even his pay was less than that of men in the county normals. There seemed real danger, therefore, that prolonged work of this sort would lead to disgust or to a lapse into dull routine.[4]

On the other hand, there was need for able and experienced teachers in the center programs. These instructors were responsible for helping students who but a few months earlier had enjoyed the life peculiar to the public high school adjust to higher levels of scholastic work. The freshman often needed the guidance and encouragement of mature teachers as he was forced to develop increasing independence, was shown new areas of knowledge, and given the opportunity to seek a field on which to concentrate. The freshman year was one in which weak students could be spotted and directed into other channels of endeavor. These were matters to which the scholar did not always give the fullest attention. It is understandable, therefore, that other departments did not follow that of History in limiting faculty tenure.

Center students often faced problems less likely to affect those doing residence work—such problems as home interference with their study, and, in some cases, an unsatisfactory school plant. While the facilities offered by the new Manitowoc Vocational School were adequate, the second floor quarters at the Merrill City Hall were not, and the county normal school at Wausau was overcrowded. Center students were also deprived of the stimulating campus contacts with young people from many places and of many persuasions. Extension attempted to overcome such disadvantages with a guidance and counseling program. To make the eventual shift of many Extension students to the state University less confusing, a residence student committee organized an orientation program similar to that given entering freshmen.

Under plans similar to that pioneered in Antigo, Extension

center work became popular throughout the state. In the
school year 1936/37, thirteen Extension centers, excluding
Milwaukee, boasted a roster of 304 students. In addition,
132 others were enrolled in Extension work conducted in
three county normals. But the improving economic conditions which accompanied Europe's march to war decreased
public interest in Extension offerings. Enrollments in the
first semester of the 1937–38 biennium dropped to 258, and
normal school registrations to 44. The financial loss to the
Division was approximately $13,000. In answer, Division
policy was altered to stress concentration upon the development of a few centers, rather than on spreading efforts over
a large area. But further difficulties arose. State aid to
vocational schools offering Extension classes was stopped
as the result of criticism that such money should be used
for genuine vocational courses. In Antigo, for example, this
meant that the Division had to seek at least $1,000 per year
from local sources. Then America's active participation in
the global struggle severely dented male enrollments. In
1942, Fieldman Marshall Graff viewed the Freshman Center
program as "almost a thing of the past." It had been a boon
to youths whose futures were threatened by the depression,
had increased University prestige, and recruited students
for residence work. The fees collected had made the program virtually self-supporting. Now the early hopes for increasing success seemed dashed. Pessimism in the usually
ebullient Graff was an ominous sign. The Extension Center
program which had been born in one crisis seemed doomed
by another.[5]

In its wartime search for service outlets, Extension
moved into a field which Professor William H. Lighty and
Dr. Charles McCarthy had considered over thirty years
earlier: an integrated correspondence study program for
members of the armed services. In 1910, Norman Hapgood's
revelation of widespread illiteracy among navy enlisted
men provoked questions of his patriotism, but also led to an
attempt at YMCA-Extension coöperation in encouraging
correspondence study on shipboard. Though the public support of President Taft was secured despite his reluctance
to intefere in Senator La Follette's bailiwick, and the University regents were finally persuaded of the efficacy of the
work, the opposition of a YMCA administrator killed the
efforts. During World War I, Lighty's initial enthusiasm
for developing an integrated study program in army camps
gave way to hesitancy and then opposition. Unpredictable

wartime conditions seemed to threaten the success of any
such program. Many individual members of the armed services, however, did study under Division supervision. During
the postwar era, the Army conducted its own specialized
military correspondence study work for officers. In an attempt to stimulate cultural courses among them, University
of Wisconsin correspondence study catalogues were distributed by the teaching staff.[6]

The pre-Pearl Harbor military draft and activation of
National Guard units placed an ever growing number of
young men in army camps. Most intended to return to civilian life as soon as possible, many to resume interrupted
educations. Among these were Wisconsin youths, ordered
to a camp in Louisiana, who investigated the possibilities
of correspondence study. Dean Holt saw in their interest a
means of inducing the federal government to subsidize such
work. The Army Chief of Staff, however, decided that military training was in itself a full-time job. If an individual
soldier wished to study in his off-duty hours, that was his
personal responsibility. Meanwhile, commercial correspondence schools began erecting signs near army camps,
urging enrollment in preparation for desirable civilian employment. The University Extension Division found it un-
necessary to compete on these terms, however. The state
legislature authorized and financed correspondence courses
for Wisconsin citizens in the armed services. The program
received free advertising in the Army and Navy Journal,
camp newspapers, and by Wisconsin draft boards.[7]

Dean Holt attempted to expand this work on the basis of
Lt. General Ben Lear's statement that troops needed an
education in current events. The army, however, was preparing its own orientation program, although it was willing
to partially finance courses taken by personnel enrolling in
approved correspondence schools. The University of Wisconsin Extension Division was one of those so designated.
Following the attack on Pearl Harbor and the United States'
declaration of war, the Army announced a still more extensive correspondence study program. On December 24, 1941,
plans for a correspondence school to be called the Army
Institute, located wherever the Secretary of War would
direct, were revealed. In February, a contract was completed between the government and the regents of the University of Wisconsin, providing for this instruction. Professor C. M. Jansky, Extension pioneer who had proved an
excellent program organizer, built an instructional staff

from the existing University force. By March, 1943, 639
servicemen were actively enrolled. A United States Armed
Forces Institute survey of the work reported 80 per cent of
the instruction as "excellent." One of the main problems
encountered in the remaining area was that of inexperienced
correspondence teachers who found it difficult to convert
the marking of papers into a teaching technique.[8] Besides
the instructional service, USAFI also purchased courses
from the University Extension Division and prepared paper
bound editions of standard textbooks for use by its correspondence students. In every theater of the war, USAFI
came to stand for home and hope for the future.

The cessation of hostilities and return to civilian life of
millions eligible for the "G. I. Bill" revived the Extension
Center program. Field reports submitted to Madison during
the summer of 1945 indicated the possibility of full freshman programs at Manitowoc, Sheboygan, Racine, Kenosha,
Green Bay, Wausau, Spooner, Ladysmith, and Ironwood,
Michigan. No longer was the problem one of finding enough
students to justify the effort, but rather one of finding sufficient instructors.[9] In 1945, too, Extension Center fees
were brought into line with those charged for University
residence study. The change marked the culmination of a
long-standing demand on the part of Extension students. It
also ended the pretext that center work was not really University work. The Extension Division was now truly an extension of the University. As after World War I, the sudden
increase in the numbers of students presented Extension
with an opportunity for service which it was quick to seize.

The center program helped relieve the strain placed upon
the University by the sudden influx of veterans. University
President E. B. Fred optimistically predicted that the
swollen enrollments were not temporary, and suggested that
plans be made for handling a steadily increasing number of
students. The Milwaukee Journal editorialized in favor of
making extension centers which were the most favorably
located into full-scale junior colleges with real campus at-
mospheres.[10] The Milwaukee Center became an example of
the degree to which a well-located center could be developed.
At the same time, however, it continued to provide University officials with the touchy problem of defining its place
in the Extension Division. In addition to its downtown
campus, it operated four suburban centers and administered
Extension work in the entire county. Instructors in other
centers were responsible to Extension department heads;

Milwaukee's departmental chairmen reported directly to the
residence departments. Influential groups demanded graduate work in the city, though residence men felt that available offerings and faculties did not meet necessary
requirements.

Extension leaders envisioned a state educational network
which, with the normals and other colleges, would bring a
college within fifty miles of every Wisconsin home. From
the standpoint of service to the people of the state, the hope
was highly commendable. In view of the decentralized state
education system, however, it anticipated a rivalry not only
for students, but for funds and faculty. The University faced
the problem of competing with a branch upon which it had
once depended to extend its influence.

The Extension Division center program presented its
administrators with complex public relations problems. It
seemed well that in addition to his duties with the Division,
Dean Holt headed the University Committee on Public Relations. Aided by such groups as the Extension Field Service,
the Committee attempted to give the public a better understanding of the University. Too often were discussions about
it clouded by controversial issues; too often did the press
point up the dramatic and bizarre in its unfolding story.
Along with constructive critics were always those whose
major aim was to embarrass the school or to achieve personal publicity. The University had never lacked friendly
newspaper and magazine outlets, but these were generally
impersonal. Holt, a well-known educator even before he
came to the University, enjoyed the personal confidence of
a state-wide audience. It was a position which was to be
sorely tested during his tenure.

The University meant many things to as many observers.
Governor Phil La Follette saw in it a means of aiding the
state's small businessmen. Madison restaurant owners, on
the other hand, were much concerned about the loss of trade
caused by the operation of University eating facilities, and
demanded an end to the use of tax money for such purposes.
President Glenn Frank described the University as an integral part of the life of the state, a beneficient people's
institution devoted to the public welfare. At the same time,
the editor of the Capital Times scoffed at the stereotype of
the impecunious, devoted savant, revealing that some professors were actually "go-getting businessmen" who supplemented their salaries handsomely by doing research for
private organizations.

Was the University a radical or a conservative institution? The principal of the Kewaunee High School, incensed when the instructor asked him to cease attending meetings in his school classes conducted by the University's School for Workers in Industry suspected the former. He condemned E. N. Schwartztrauber, director of the school, as "ultra-progressive" and hence unfit for his post. The "things that were being taught in those classes," he charged, harmed the reputation of the entire school. On the other hand, abandonment of the University's rule against accepting money from private sources caused Progressive Lieutenant Governor Henry Huber to lament, "The god of the dollar is at the helm." Freedom of research and publication were being threatened, he maintained, and added that Old Bob La Follette would never have approved taking money of the "Rockefeller sort." Huber suggested that the legislature might be compelled to intervene in University affairs. At the same time, E. F. Brunette, well-known conservative legislator from Green Bay also threatened legislative intervention in the University to prevent what he deemed useless expansion of Extension activities.

The personal actions of members of the student body and the faculty also inspired criticism. Reflecting an aspect of the intellectual life of the 1920's, a student group at the dormitories established the "Circle of the Godless," which seemed the more sinister because of the announcement that coeds were to be admitted. During the next decade, newspapers printed photographs, branded as fakes by the Women's Self Government Association, supposedly revealing coeds drinking beer in the dormitories. Parents of a Milwaukee Center student protested that girls were smoking and playing cards in the building. More perturbing yet, were evidences of faculty and student leftist activity. Professor E. A. Ross openly organized student tours to Russia. Several members of the Milwaukee Center faculty planned similar summer trips, upon which they hoped to build popular courses for the fall semester. Former University of Wisconsin students who appeared before a Chicago judge regarding possession of Communist propaganda were told that the school had poisoned their minds with "theoretic socialism" while they were too young to resist.

Men in political life were quick to capitalize upon those matters. Representative Hamilton Fish of New York found campaign material in them, as did John Chapple of Ashland, Wisconsin, who prefaced an unsuccessful senatorial

campaign with an attack upon the University. However, not
only institutions of higher learning had become suspect.
From Wausau came charges of the existence of communist
tendencies among high school students who had taken social
science courses. People associated with the schools were
thinking and acting in a manner which some regarded as
threatening to the established order. Events within the Extension Division buttressed this suspicion.

Dean Snell's decision to fight his dismissal by the regents
in 1935 touched off an episode which ultimately revealed the
political interests of some who investigated the matter. The
depression era wave of bank robberies, rural unrest, the
flowering of unionism, renewal of interest in Russia, and
growing opposition to the New Deal, lent urgency to Snell's
charges that subversives and libertines had plotted his
ouster. When President Frank was subpoenaed to appear
with documents related to the case, it was supposedly to
throw light on communism and similar irregularities within
the University. A legislative investigation was conducted
under the chairmanship of Senator E. F. Brunette, Green
Bay Democrat. The senator's predisposition can be at least
partially gauged by his applause of the strongarm tactics
against alleged student radicals by a group of University
lettermen calling itself the Silvershirts. Newspaper headlines reveal the way the Snell situation was publicized:
"Hunt for Campus Reds Turns to Search for 'Free Lovers'";
"Wisconsin U's Morals Sifted." As sex replaced subversion
as the public's major interest in the case, snickers became
laughter, and the investigation was terminated. The committee's report revealed the political axes which some of the
members hoped to grind. The original document, which was
withdrawn for correction soon after it was handed to re-
porters, contained references to the New Deal as the "Raw
Deal" and condemned attempts to "change or overthrow the
Constitution," a statement which was later reworded to read,
"change by force ... [etc.]." The report, which contained un-
substantiated charges that the University welcomed Com-
munists and encouraged Communist teachings, was accorded
newspaper space for several weeks. The regents replied
that the committee had produced no evidence to support its
conclusion, but this sober statement received far less publicity than did any of the sensational items. This did not
mean, however, that the University had no newspaper backing. At the height of the controversy, the Burlington _Free
Press_ editorially condemned trial by innuendo and insinu-

ation, and maintained that the radicalism of the campus was
the radicalism of Copernicus and Columbus. [11]

Students reacted to the situation in several ways. One
charged that thirty radicals were corrupting the entire campus. Others maintained that undergraduates were too busy
preparing for their futures to be attracted by "romantic and
exciting diversions." A student "Committee of 19" demanded
that witnesses intimately aware of campus conditions be
called before the Brunette Committee, and that those who
had been attacked as radicals be given the "constitutional"
privilege of replying. [12]

A series of episodes following hard upon the Snell case
revealed the determination of state groups to fight publicly
for the principle that views contrary to theirs were not to
be tolerated. It was usually not a matter of proving the dis-
senter in error, but of emphasizing his difference, which in
itself was interpreted as a threat, incompetency, or malice.
To some, the Extension Division's employment of men with
skins other than white or ideas other than "Conservative"
seemed intolerable. This situation, however, gave University and Extension administrators an opportunity to define
the nature of the center program, and to reveal whether off-
campus social studies courses would be shaped by the demands of local pressure groups or by larger considerations.
These questions contained an echo of President Charles Van
Hise's statement during the Stalwart-Progressive struggle
almost two decades earlier: " ... the spirit of the University is in irreconcilable conflict with those who hold that
the present state of affairs is the best possible, who believe
that existing conventions, morals, political and religious
faiths are fixed...." [13]

Growing public awareness of international tension and the
fear of outsiders as competitors for jobs complicated the
Extension Division's finding a satisfactory circuit for Instructor S. I. Hayakawa, a Canadian of Japanese extraction.
There was no doubt of his professional ability; his tendency
to make biting remarks, however, had made him a number
of personal enemies. Division representatives canvassing
local opinion of Hayakawa expressed surprise at the retorts.
A high school principal remarked, " ... he should be teaching in Ethiopia"; a salesman asked, "Just what is the idea
of the University sending a d ... foreigner to teach white
men's kids?" Another respondant asked why "foreigners"
were being brought in while "white" teachers were out of
work. A more informed man expressed his willingness to

have Hayakawa teach at the local center if at the same time
he could explain the critical situation developing in Asia.
Vocational school boards denied any feeling of prejudice
against Hayakawa, but hastily added that their constituents
would never tolerate his presence.[14]

The Division settled the matter by placing Hayakawa in
an area unmarked by outspoken opposition to him. In such
cities as Rhinelander he found among creative writing
groups those who appreciated what he had to offer. The decision was administratively wise. On the other hand, it revealed the Division as a compromiser rather than a leader.
There could be little doubt as to the presence of racism in
the situation.

Elements of local prejudice also figured in the case of
Albert E. Croft, sociology instructor, who had taught Extension classes for the unemployed and had been an early advocate of a full freshman program at Green Bay. During the
Snell administration, Croft's consistently large classes
indicated his popularity as a lecturer. His remarks before
these classes, however, were not always politic. He chose
to paint a particularly unflattering picture of holding companies before a class entertaining employees of the Green
Bay Power and Light Company. In Fond du Lac, his classroom statements about social control and the declining
power of the church enraged a visiting Notre Dame graduate,
who reported the matter to a local priest. In the following
attacks upon Croft, a number of his students, some pointing
to their Roman Catholic backgrounds, rallied to his defense.
His lectures were described as stimulating and challenging,
and if above the sophomore level, were, after all, being attended by adults. A visit by Extension representatives to
the offended churchman resulted in the latter's statement
that he would offer no objection to Croft's remaining in the
Fond du Lac post.

With the Snell episode still fresh in the public mind, Dean
Holt found it expedient to review the case. Croft was charged
with irregularities in Extension routine, inability to get
along with his colleagues, and overloading his class rolls to
the point that the University calibre of his work was questionable. Letters sent by some of his former students contained denials of further charges that Croft had revealed
"unbalanced judgement" in his stress upon social controls
in the changing American economy. Despite a flurry of letters from protesting students, Croft found it best to secure
employment elsewhere.[15] The remarkable aspect of the case

had to do with the criticism of Croft's stress upon social
controls. The field which was pioneered by E. A. Ross of
the residence faculty was considered appropriate for campus work, but not in local communities where it seemed to
threaten the prestige of pressure groups.

More sensational from the standpoint of public interest
was the case of T. Harry Williams, Extension history instructor. On Armistice Day, 1936, Williams repeated an
address at several schools in the cities comprising his
teaching circuit. His talks involved an interpretation of what
lay behind the decisions which had plunged nations into war,
and the manner in which men were encouraged to fight.
Within this framework, Williams listed Abraham Lincoln as
an example of a leader who had been prompted by matters
of political expediency to make decisions leading to war.
J. P. Morgan was cited as an example of a financier whose
involvement with the Allies had been instrumental in the
United States' going to war in 1917. Popular knowledge of
these factors, Williams suggested, could help prevent future
wars.

The address at Wausau touched off a storm of protest.
The findings of the Nye Committee had helped prepare the
public for Williams' statements about Morgan, but although
the version of the Lincoln story was no novelty in history
seminars, it was sufficiently unknown to be disconcerting
to some, and to provide others with ammunition for an attack not only upon Williams, but upon the University and all
higher education. Abraham Lincoln, Civil War President,
the Great Emancipator and a founder of the Republican party—
a warlike image of the national and party hero was intolerable to those who had come to identify war and threats of
war with Democratic administrations, and who were seeking
to revive the Republican party.

At an American Legion Armistice Day dinner in Wausau,
Williams' statement about Lincoln was denounced as a
"damnable lie," and there were dark warnings of commun-
istic borings from within. "When you and I fight 'Red Stuff'
...[we] are fighting for our Maker," commented an editor-
ialist in another city. A seventy-four year old man was reported as anxious to lead a posse to throw Williams into the
lake. A hostile newspaper editor condemned the presumptu-
ousness of a brash young instructor, who seventy-one years
after Appomatox, challenged the views of the war held by
his elders who had read Civil War histories written soon
after the conflict. The Appleton Post-Crescent concluded

that regardless of the circumstances of Williams' address
and its subsequent interpretation, he could not be forgiven
for having spoken in a "wise guy manner," for having made
an uncalled for, muckraking attack upon a national hero.
The deeper nature of the uproar, however, was apparent to
some. A history student, hearing that Williams' position
was to be refilled, submitted his professional qualifications
to Dean Holt, along with assurance that he had a "rather
conservative political outlook."[16]

Without consulting Williams as to what he had actually
said, school authorities in Wausau suspended his classes.
Williams protested that he had been misinterpreted, and
that the remarks which were making headlines had been
torn from context. Several hundred Wausau high school students, charging that Williams was being done an injustice,
prepared a supporting statement. Their petition was confis-
cated by local school authorities, who later explained that
they acted to prevent a student strike. A number of educators who had heard Williams' talk could recall nothing com-
munistic in it, and questioned the way it had been reported
in the newspapers. The original story had been written by
a Wausau reporter who had not heard any of the addresses,
but had used Williams' brief. The Madison Capital Times
cried, "Witch Hunters Over Rib Hill," and found it significant that the attack was launched by "old moss-backed re-
actionaries," while a major portion of his defense came
from people of student age. Some likened the attack on
Williams to the assault on Richard T. Ely; the Wisconsin
Federation of Teachers protested against the violations of
Williams' "constitutional rights" in having his classes suspended without a hearing. Hayakawa saw in the situation an
opportunity for Holt to strike hard at the Wausau Record
Herald, which was turning the Williams affair into a general
Red hunt. Holt's announcement that he would defend Williams
won the applause of the Division's strongest supporters.

The principals in the situation met in the office of Professor Paul Knaplund, Chairman of the University History Department. Professor Knaplund immediately seized the
initiative, challenging the action of the local school officials
in confiscating the student petition and warning of the danger
of allowing small groups to dictate school policy. Holt and
Frank supported this stand. Threats to provide no replace-
ment for Williams, and a consequent credit loss by his
former students, caused the Wausau Vocational School
Board to reconsider its position. Williams was permitted

to resume his teaching. Some in Wausau felt that Professor
Knaplund had been unnecessarily brusque with the local
school men, although one of them assured Holt that he har-
bored no ill will against him, at least. A Two Rivers' newspaper editorial slapped at the manner in which Williams
had been forcibly reinstated. Certainly the University had
asserted its right to appoint and withdraw instructors. The
lines on which the battle was fought, however, did not bring
it to grips with a more important matter, namely that of
any citizen's right to be challenged on the validity of his
actual assertions rather than emotional interpretations of
them, to stand or fall as an individual rather than as a
stereotype. Even so, while Mr. Graff summarized the events
as a "great victory" for the History Department, he hoped
that the eventual price would not be too high.[17] Loss of public favor could mean a loss of students.

Another episode that might have been used to pull the
University beyond the tugs of minority groups ended in ca-
pitulation to forces which had assumed the mantle of guard-
ian of public morality. Despite departmental advice to the
contrary, an English instructor at the Kenosha Center used
Thomas Wolfe's Look Homeward Angel in his freshman
English class. An irate parent, an attorney, protested thus
exposing teenagers to what he deemed immoral literature,
and hinted at a Communist plot to demoralize American
youth. He cited the offending instructor's dubbing the Saturday Evening Post the "Moron's Gazette"; what were the
attitudes toward the New Masses, the New Republic, and the
Nation? The attack was carried on largely, however, as
morality versus immorality. The parent catalogued the
book's allegedly obscene words and episodes, and urged
Dean Holt to see for himself the sort of "filth" with which
young minds were being poisoned. He insisted, however,
that schoolmen had no more ability to judge such matters
than others, and less right than the parents who furnished
not only the taxes, but the students. Were not professors,
after all, well-known practicers of birth control? Of deeper
significance, was the attitude displayed toward the work in
educational institutions. "It is barely just possible that this
instructor . . . has not learned that the classroom is not an
open forum from where he may expound his own views and
theories whether they be pleasing and acceptable to students
or their parents."[18]

The outraged parent enlisted the support of a federal
judge and several civic leaders. At a poorly attended

meeting, the Kenosha Civic Council voted to inform the
regents of its indignation. The local public library had already withdrawn Look Homeward Angel from its shelves,
but a scattering of letters urged Dean Holt not to surrender
in similar fashion. C. W. Thomas, Assistant Professor in
Supervisory Charge of English Work in the Field, conceded
the questionable literary merit of the novel, but denied its
moral unfitness for classroom use. He recommended, however, that offended students be allowed to substitute Giants
in the Earth. Dean Holt concluded that while he had been
informed of the accuracy of Wolfe's portrayal, circumstances dictated his recommendation that the book be removed from the reading list. The Division had proved no
match for an articulate minority group.

On the eve of the great war against totalitarianism, the
Extension Division revealed unwillingness to fight racism
openly, to champion the right of individual expression other
than by a show of force, or to challenge those who claimed
a monopoly upon morality. The Division had yet to announce
clearly that it was a public institution and above pleading
the causes of organized minorities. Extension had assumed
great responsibility in the educating of Wisconsin youth.
Yet if it was to prove that it had something more at stake
than its own well-being, it would have to take a stand beside
those regents who had heard the case against Richard T.
Ely, and the campus administrator who had defended the
teaching rights of Max Otto.

It is true that these were the publicized cases. An element
of chance exists in even their having been called forcibly to
public notice. Numerous instructors with backgrounds similar to those whose work gained such attention were never
involved in such controversies. At the same time, where
issues were made public, the Division administration might
have acquitted itself in better fashion. The author hastens
to add that during his experience as a circuit instructor
under Holt's successor, Dr. Lorenz Adolfson, Center administrators did prevent uninformed but noisy local groups
from interfering in instructor-student relationships.

On a lower educational level, Extension tried to combat
what seemed public apathy toward political life. With characteristic vigor, it inaugurated a program of citizenship
training for youths approaching voting age. Precedents for
such activity dated to the Division's very beginnings. In
later years, the work was usually presented as institutes,
and sponsored in coöperation with women's voters organi-

zations. Such efforts, however, reached comparatively few people, and to a great degree, only those already interested and informed about the matters under discussion. Now Extension and community leaders expressed alarm at widespread civic irresponsibility, apathy, and increasing general willingness to accept the rule of "organized minorities," and popular acceptance of government from the "top, down." A round-table discussion on municipal administration conducted in Manitowoc by Professor R. J. Colbert led to local suggestions for a program designed to impress future voters with a better understanding of their duties and responsibilities, and give them a deeper appreciation of American democracy. There followed a series of weekly discussion meetings attended by young people. The culmination of this "Training for Citizenship" was Citizenship Day, on which the new voters were formally enrolled as citizens.

The effort was widely copied. Other counties followed Manitowoc's lead, and the legislature voted to make such work mandatory throughout the state. A number of states patterned programs after Wisconsin's pioneer effort. The initiators of the movement, however, soon found their efforts fruitless. The state law had no means of enforcement, and more important, the public misunderstood and soon tired of the effort. Colbert had envisioned training local leaders to conduct the programs, but the popular impression developed that the Division would send representatives to meet directly with the future voters. The people who assembled often did so merely to be exhorted and entertained. Locally, too, disproportionate emphasis was placed upon the Citizenship Day festivities rather than the preparation of which they were but a symbolic terminal point.[19]

These events indicated the unfeasibility of further institute-type work pitched on the community level. However laudable the effort to stimulate community life or intellectual activity, it did not attract serious public support. This was Extension's experience with the Community Institutes of the prewar era, the Frank-Snell efforts to refurbish American culture by stressing a popular liberal arts program, and finally, the Citizenship Training effort. Like Extension work of the 1890's, these flourished briefly only to fade away when the novelty wore off. It seemed that the old argument over the proper starting place for reform was being settled in favor of those who would begin with the individual. University credit work was attractive.

Desire for it and accompanying anticipations of increased prestige and material advantage were socially sanctioned. For the moment, at least, Wisconsin was willing to support the Extension Centers.

Balance Sheet

I am only one.
But still I am one.
I cannot do everything.
But still I can do something.
And because I cannot do everything
I will not refuse to do the something I can do.
                    —Edward Everett Hale

Men of action who could appreciate the dreamer; idealists
who were not averse to action—together they made the
boundaries of the University of Wisconsin campus those of
the state. Together they made the University and its Extension Division known and respected wherever men sought to
master their problems through guided study and discussion.
Teacher and teamster, banker and baker, priest and prisoner—the needs and questions of these and many more were
regarded with equal respect by the men and women of the
people's school with headquarters on the Madison campus.

The extensionist did not always appreciate the problems
and outlook of the research scholar. Nor did the scholar
always appreciate the goals and the struggles of the extensionist. Although the gap has never been completely bridged,
it has been narrowed by the fact that Extension and the
twentieth century university have been shaped by similar
influences. The organization of extension work in Wisconsin
paralleled University efforts to integrate itself into a community which emphasized a certain definition of the "practical." The residence curriculum was consciously revised to
consider the plow no less than Plato or the swing of the
Pleiades. Extension went further by offering courses designed to appeal to people of all levels of academic preparation. It offered instruction to the factory worker with a
grade school education as well as aid to the graduate doing
research. As other agencies were developed for sub-Univer-
sity vocational education, Extension's existence came to
rely ever more heavily upon its credit correspondence and
class work. This made it by 1940 more of an extension of
the University than a manifestation of the University Extension movement of the early part of the century. And yet,
the early spirit of rendering broad service has not been

abandoned. In the biennium 1954–55, Extension's rolls
showed 90,000 correspondence study students, 15,000 special class students, and 2,400 Extension Center students.
At the same time, however, 30,000 people participated in
institute sessions.

Doers who were also dreamers and dreamers who tried
to translate their feelings into deeds; together they trans-
formed President Van Hise's vague reference to the "third
function" of the University into an institution, and for many,
a way of life. The men who were primarily dreamers began
with Richard T. Ely and Frederick Jackson Turner, whose
vision of a socially and culturally integrated America, however, never caused them to forget the immediate publicity
value of education for a better future. Ely's idealogical successor was William Henry Lighty, who fought against Dr.
Charles McCarthy's attempts to focus the efforts of the re-
vivified Extension movement principally upon aiding employers and increasing the earning power of the state's
workers. The home lives of McCarthy and Lighty are symbolic. Through McCarthy's windows occasionally drifted
the smoke of a Madison industry. Lighty lived in a Jeffer-
sonian manner on a farm near Middleton. It remained for
Dean Louis E. Reber, former engineer, to articulate the
view that Extension could survive as a servant of the people
of the state only if it continually adapted itself to the changing cultural foundations upon which it was built.

But the story is still incomplete. As the leaders of the
Wisconsin Dairymen's Association succeeded in having the
state University, through the Farmers' Institutes, assume
sponsorship of their program, the state's Merchants and
Manufacturers Associations provided the support necessary
for the initial financing of the general Extension Division.
This initial support gave the Division time to seek out and
organize its own constituency, to become able to appeal to
the people of the state in its own name.

The relationship between the Extension doers and dreamers was not always a pleasant one. The scars resulting from
the clashes between Lighty and Reber will persist until
those who were involved are no more. Dean Snell's often
callous attempts at efficiency have left a similar story. The
points of view articulated by Lighty and McCarthy represent
poles in an argument as heated today as it was during the
first decade of the century. It is futile now to argue what
the Extension Division might have been had other men occupied the deanship. The Division's program has never been

without the stamp of certain forceful personalities —
McCarthy, Lighty, Reber, Snell, Holt. But the program has
been more than the work of any single individual. One re-
calls the decision of the University regents who, after hearing charges against Reber, concluded that while he had
made the professional careers of some of his subordinates
uncomfortable, that fact had not interfered with the attain-
ment of the Division's goals. The Division has been more
than the magnification of any one man; it has been a manifestation of industrialism, of social uplift, of man's search
for order in a superficially chaotic world.

In 1930, Dr. Abraham Flexner accused the work of the
Extension Division of robbing the University of the "unity of
purpose" and "homogeneity of constitution" which he deemed
the prerequisites of a true university. The specific examples of Extension interference he selected, however,
were largely outdated. Under the leadership of President
Frank and Dean Snell, the allegedly offending courses in
rural school cooking and aid to prospective mothers were
gradually withdrawn from circulation. The Center program,
moreover, was but a few years away. However, Flexner
showed his concern to be for the work of the University, per
se, while the Extensionists whose work he questioned had
been concerned with state-wide unity. Much of the work of
the early Farmers' Institutes was directed toward imbuing
the farmer with the businessman's ideology. Ely's Extension activities had been carried on in large part in terms of
the Social Gospel and refutation of alien ideologies.
McCarthy feared repetition in America of the revolution of
1848, and saw in the average man's material well-being a
means of guaranteeing against such upheavals. In 1926,
Lighty noted that extension work had mentally disciplined
the English working classes to the point that they did not
turn to violence in their disputes with management. University of Wisconsin President Birge saw in extension activities a means of preventing the crystallization of the classes
and the threat that such carried for America. During the
depression of the 1930's, the Extension program became a
means of preventing the unemployed and thwarted from
sinking into despair and turning to irresponsible political
leaders. The extensionists were concerned with integrating
the various groups comprising the population of the state no
less than with the unity of purpose of the University. They
defined the relationship of the University and the people of
the state as bilateral.[1]

And yet, was the Extension Division harmful to the University? With the development of a special Extension staff, it ceased being one of the drains on the academic and physical vitality of the residence faculty. Financially, Extension work became in large part self-supporting. When Extension did become a legislative or political issue, it was not solely in terms of itself, but often as a symbol over which contending forces could come to grips. As McCarthy had foreseen, the Extension Division was to become at times a pawn in the relationships of the University and other state agencies.

The development of the extension work of the University of Wisconsin occurred amidst similar developments elsewhere. During the 1890's, eleven universities experimented with extension programs, although in going beyond agricultural instruction, the Universities of Chicago and Wisconsin proved pioneers.[2] The similarity is not accidental, for their leaders shared a common intellectual background. Inability to hold popular interest in a program having but vague goals and marked administrative and instructional shortcomings, doomed Wisconsin's initial efforts to dormancy. F. W. Speirs hit upon the formula for keeping efforts alive by redirecting them, but he addressed unsympathetic administrators. When in the years 1906–7 the work was revived and refurbished by McCarthy and the Milwaukee manufacturers, the contributions of Hutchins, Turner, Lighty and Reber gave it the broad base and administrative structure necessary for a prolonged and useful existence.

There is little question of Wisconsin's leadership in developing extension programs. Lighty felt that this leadership was the result of working the Wisconsin Idea into education, and that it was this which drew hundreds of observers to the Division. Nowhere, he concluded, had "the vision of a state-wide campus been more fully realized."

Among those who came were members of an "Expedition" of the City Club of Philadelphia. In May, 1913, East Coast educational and civic leaders and their wives journeyed to Madison to see what in the Wisconsin experiment could be applied in Philadelphia. After several days of motor tours, luncheons, banquets, receptions, and addresses, a committee issued a report. Wisconsin was commended for its "State-wide dissemination of knowledge in a form accessible to the public." On the other hand, the committee concluded, Philadelphia had already made strides in public education which surpassed those in Wisconsin. School Superintendent,

Dr. Martin G. Brumbaugh, feared that application of Wisconsin's methods would harm the adult education efforts already undertaken by his department. And had not Philadelphia already made use of experts in government by sponsoring a two-year study before deciding upon its garbage disposal system? Wisconsin seemed to have little to offer the city through which English-type extension had been imported into the United States, the committee concluded.[3]

Perhaps both guests and hosts missed the significance of the Expedition's discovery. The Wisconsin effort was built around problems peculiar to Wisconsin. In the absence of other institutions to carry on many of the aspects of extension instruction, the Division was filling local needs. In the absence of local means of financing the work, the state had assumed responsibility for part of the costs. That these have not been too high is seen in the steady support accorded the Extension Division by generations of state legislators.

While there were those who failed to find inspiration in Extension's idealism and efforts, many more turned to the Division for administrative and instructional advice. Requests of this kind were legion, coming from such scattered institutions as Cornell, Brigham Young University, Southwest Louisiana Institute, the Universities of North Carolina, California, and Minnesota. Similar requests came from schoolmen of other nations, as well—Canada, Australia, Germany, China, Esthonia, Palestine. The Russians, especially, were interested in the Extension program, seeing in it seeds for similar work made possible by the abatement of revolutionary turmoil.

What was the effect of the Wisconsin example and advice? In his tape recorded memoirs, Professor Lighty noted, in effect, that men of "vision" profited from their contact with Extension; those with lesser endowments did not. This conclusion does not allow for the variables which each man had to face in his own community. It ignores the question of what success attended the Wisconsin program. It was easy for Farmers' Institute leaders to present statistics concerning the increased yields per acre resulting from the advocacy of use of barnyard fertilizer. It is harder to estimate the success of the various general Extension programs. Did Community Institutes lessen inter-group tensions? If such tensions were decreased, what other factors might have been partially responsible? Was it the knowledge gained from correspondence study that made prisoner students less likely to be recidivists than were nonstudents,

or were the men who had the best chances for leading socially approved lives after release prone to take correspondence courses? Did the center program enable more youths
to gain University educations? If so, might not competing
educational agencies have done a similar job in limiting the
number of the state's "mute, inglorious Miltons?" The list
of possible claims and challenges is endless. The fact remains, however, that whatever the Division defined as an
educational problem, it attacked vigorously and with all of
the resources of the state and its University that it could
command.

Not all of the Division's problems were of a local nature.
The matters of transferring correspondence study credits
from one school to another alone necessitated the development of a national organization of extension divisions. Problems regarding the instruction of special groups and the
nationwide fight against unscrupulous private correspondence schools and adult education movements deemed in
error, also necessitated concerted action. J. J. Pettijohn,
extension director of the University of North Dakota, and
formerly on the Wisconsin staff, suggested that Dean Reber
spark such a movement. Most extension directors responded
favorably to the suggestion. Although the Chancellor of
Washington University at St. Louis doubted that anything of
value could be achieved by such activity, he agreed that
Wisconsin's leadership in extension work made Madison the
logical place for a first conference. In March, 1915, representatives of coöperating universities assembled on the
Wisconsin campus. The result was formation of the National
University Extension Association.[4]

For many years Lighty served as secretary of the Association, playing a leading role in its discussions of radio in
education, instruction of veterans, academic standards, and
unethical advertising of correspondence courses. In 1926,
almost as compensation for his decreasing role in the Wisconsin Extension Division, he was elected president of the
Association, the first man who was not head of a division to
be elected to the post. Wisconsin's contributions to N.U.E.A.
conferences were so marked during these years that care
had to be exercised lest the Division seem to dominate them.

Such were the Extension Division's contributions. But in
its efforts to provide educational opportunities and establish
the standards and conditions conducive to productive community and academic relationships, it occasionally stumbled,
a victim of the defensive attitudes built up during its endless

struggle for a "room in the sun." The attempted suppression
of unfavorable aspects of the Allen report represents one
such episode. So, too, was Lighty's attempt to use his position in the N.U.E.A. to quash publication of Alfred Hall-
Quest's study, The University Afield.[5] While both publications had pronounced blind and weak spots, and seemed to
threaten the future of important aspects of the Division's
work, attempted censorship but weakened Extension's moral
position. Both studies were published; eventually they had
to be met squarely and publicly. Well might the Division
have capitalized upon Governor Woodrow Wilson's statement made at the First National Conference on Civic and
Social Development held at Madison in 1911: "The treatment
for bad politics is ... exposure to open air."

    Dr. Lorenz H. Adolfson, who has headed the Extension
Division since 1945, summarized its work and indicated its
future in a recent public address. Fittingly, he spoke in re-
sponse to the thanks of the people of Racine for the Division's
efforts in their city. " ... the University of Wisconsin has a
great tradition and a great means of answering the educational needs of Wisconsin citizens wherever and whenever they
arise .... A university—like any type of enterprise—like a
business—cannot stand still. It either goes forward, or it
goes backward...."[6] Certainly the Division has never gone
backward in its major effort: making the state University
the university of the state.

REFERENCE MATTER

List of Manuscript Sources

The following manuscript collections will be cited in abbreviated form in the Notes.

Papers of Richard T. Ely, State Historical Society of Wisconsin, Madison, Wisconsin.

Papers of William H. Lighty, State Historical Society of Wisconsin, Madison, Wisconsin.

William H. Lighty, "Memoirs," Tape Recording Reels, State Historical Society of Wisconsin, Madison, Wisconsin.

Papers of Charles McCarthy, State Historical Society of Wisconsin, Madison, Wisconsin.

Papers of Francis McGovern, State Historical Society of Wisconsin, Madison, Wisconsin.

Papers of Frederick Jackson Turner, State Historical Society of Wisconsin, Madison, Wisconsin.

Papers of the Deans of the Extension Division, the University Extension Division, Madison, Wisconsin.

Papers of the Presidents of the University of Wisconsin, President's Office, University of Wisconsin, Madison, Wisconsin. Within this collection there is a group of papers marked "Extension." In the notes which follow, references to this second group of papers are cited, "Presidents' Papers, Extension."

Notes

Chapter I

1 John S. Noffsinger, Correspondence Schools, Lyceums, Chautauquas (New York, 1906), pp. 3-4.

2 Herbert Baxter Adams, "University Extension and Its Leaders," Review of Reviews, 4 (July, 1891), 591; George C. T. Bartley, The Schools for the People, Containing the History, Development, and Present Working of Each Description of English School for the Industrial and Poorer Classes (London, 1871), pp. 393-94; R. St. John Parry, ed., Cambridge Essays in Adult Education (Cambridge [England], 1920), pp. 41-43; Herbert Baxter Adams, "Summer Schools and University Extension," James Russell Parsons, Jr., ed., Professional Education, (Monographs on Education in the United States, Commission to the Paris Exposition of 1900), p. 512; George Henderson, Report Upon the University Extension Movement In England (Philadelphia Society for the Extension of University Teaching, Philadelphia, n. d.), pp. 3-9; H. B. Adams, "University Extension in England," University Extension, (Johns Hopkins University Studies in Historical and Political Science, Fifth Series, XI, November, 1887), p. 29.

3 H. B. Adams, in University Extension, pp. 41-43, 32.

4 Alfred Charles True, A History of Agricultural Education in the United States, 1789-1925 (United States Department of Agriculture Miscellaneous Publication, No. 36, Issued July, 1929, U.S. Government Printing Office, Washington, D.C., 1929), p. 9, pp . 40-42; Merle Curti, The Growth of American Thought (New York, 1943), p. 112.

5 Elwood P. Cubberly, The History of Education, Educational Practices and Progress Considered as a Phase of the Development and Spread of Western Civilization (Boston, 1920), p. 801.

6 Josiah Holbrook, American Lyceum of Science and Arts Composed of Associations for Mutual Instruction and Designed for the General Diffusion of Useful and Practical Knowledge (Worcester, November, 1826), pp. 1-7.

7 Curti, American Thought, pp. 367, 366; Henry Reeve (Trans.), Alexis de Tocqueville, Democracy in America (New York, 1900), pp. 18,272.

8 Waterman Thomas Hewett, Cornell University, A History (4 vols.; New York, 1905), I, 134-35; Samuel Fallows to C. K. Adams, November 4, 1895, Presidents' Papers; Noffsinger, Correspondence Schools, pp. 4-5; Robert Case and Victoria Case, We Called It Culture, The Story of Chautauqua (New York, 1948), pp. 12-13; H. B. Adams, in Professional Education, pp. 3-4.

9 H. B. Adams, "University Extension in America," Forum, 11 (July, 1891), 510, 515-16; Catalogue of the System of Study at Chautauqua (New York, 1893), p. 12; Alfred Lawrence Hall-Quest, The University

Afield (New York, 1926), p. 13; Henderson, Report on University Extension, p. 3.

10 H. B. Adams, in _Forum_, 11: 510; George F. James, ed., University Extension, The Official Organ of the American Society for the Extension of University Teaching (n. d.), p. 55; Richard George Moulton, Professor Moulton on University Extension (American Society for the Extension of University Teaching, November, 9, 1899), p. 3; John H. Vincent, The Chautauqua Movement (New York, 1886), p. 3.

11 University Record (University of Chicago, August 11, 1895), pp. 334-35.

12 H. B. Adams, in _Forum_, 11: 510-13; Edward Bemis to Richard T. Ely, November 19, 1888, Ely Papers

13 Richard T. Ely, French and German Socialism in Modern Times (New York, 1883), "Prefatory Note," p. 261; H. A. Schauffler to Ely, May 21, June 12, 1884, Ely Papers.

14 H. B. Adams, in _Forum_, 11: 512; Josiah Strong to Ely, November 17, 1888, Ely Papers.

15 Vincent, Chautauqua Movement, pp. xii-xiv; H. B. Adams, in Professional Education, p. 5.

16 George Herbert Palmer, "Doubts About University Extension," The Atlantic Monthly, 70 (March, 1892), 367-74. Robert Wilson to Ely, November 1, 1883; Bemis to Ely, November 19, 1888; George E. Vincent to Ely, October 19, 1888.—Ely Papers.

17 George E. Vincent to Richard T. Ely, October 19, 1888, Ely Papers.

Chapter II

1 William Dempster Hoard, Transactions of the Wisconsin State Agricultural Society (Madison; February, 1885), p. 160.

2 Ibid., p. 160.

3 Merle Curti and Vernon Carstensen, The University of Wisconsin, A History (2 vols.; Madison, 1949), I, 78; Charles Alfred True, A History of Agricultural Education in the United States, 1789-1925 (United States Department of Agriculture Miscellaneous Publications, Number 36, Issued Washington; July, 1929), p. 75.

4 M. V. O'Shea, "The University and the State," in Conrad E. Patzer, Public Education in Wisconsin (Madison, 1924), pp. 280-303.

5 The Cultivator and Country Gentleman, July, 1889, p. 1692; Curti and Carstensen, University of Wisconsin, I, 461-62, 464; University of Wisconsin Catalogue, 1883-84, p. 35;

6 Transactions of the Wisconsin State Grange (Madison; February, 1885), p. 160.

7 W. H. Glover, "The Agricultural College Crisis of 1885," in Wisconsin Magazine of History, 32 (September. 1948), 19-23.

8 University Catalogue, 1887-88, p. 153.

9 Laws of Wisconsin, 1885, Chap. 9; Ibid., 1867, Chap. 62; [Farmers'] Institute Handbook, 1895, 21-22.

10 University Catalogue, 1889-90, p. 171; 1991-92, p. 181; 1893-94, pp. 158-59; 1898-99, pp. 243-45. Wisconsin Farmers' Institute for 1910-11 (University of Wisconsin).

11 E. L. Luther, How to Secure and Hold a Successful Farmers' Institute (n. d).

12 Proceedings of the Twenty-Sixth Annual Session of the Wisconsin State Grange of Patrons of Husbandry, Held at Marshfield, Wisconsin, December 14, 15, 16, 1897, p. 14; Transactions of the Wisconsin

State Agriculture Society (Madison, February, 1885), pp. 221-24; First Annual Report of the Utah Farmers' Institute for the Fiscal Year Ending June 30, 1897 (Salt Lake City), p. 26.

13 George B. Smith to Editor, Wisconsin Farmer, April 2, 1892, p. 201.

14 Chetek Alert (Wisconsin), November 22, 1889.

15 Charles H. Everett, "Farmers' Institute in the Old Days, How There Started in Wisconsin a Movement Which Became World Wide," Wisconsin Agriculturist, January 21, 1922.

16 Curti and Carstensen, University of Wisconsin, I, 715.

17 University Catalogue, 1887-88, pp. 152-53.

18 Wisconsin Farmer, W. H. Cole to Editor, April 2, 1892.

19 Governor W. H. Upham, Institute Handbook, 1895, pp. 40-41.

20 C. K. Adams, "The Farmer in the University," Institute Handbook, 1892, pp. 201-6.

21 True Republican, November 25, 1885.

22 Institute Handbook, 1905, p. 177.

23 Free Press (Beloit), March 1, 1888.

24 Institute Handbook, 1886-87, pp. 17-19; Wisconsin Farmers' Institute, Women's Bulletin, No. 8, 1915; The Farmers' Voice and National Rural, March 26, 1904.

25 Farmers' Institute Bulletin, No. 29, 1915, p. 20.

26 Free Press (Beloit), March 1, 1888; True Republican, November 25, 1888; Wisconsin Farmer, April 2, 1892, p. 198.

27 Hon. George H. Buckstaff, "The Common-Sense Farmer," Institute Handbook, 1895, p. 291; J. H. Hale, "The Business Farmer," Institute Handbook, 1889, pp. 172-73.

28 Menomonie Times, December 5, 1889.

29 Frederick Jackson Turner, "The Extension Work of the University of Wisconsin," in George F. James, ed., Handbook of University Extension (Society for the Extension of University Teaching: Philadelphia, 1893), p. 312; Curti and Carstensen, University of Wisconsin, I, 713.

30 Elmer Bradford, "Farming and the Mercantile Business—Their Relation to Each Other," Institute Handbook, 1888, pp. 118-19; H. C. Adams, "Farmers, Businessmen and Citizens," Institute Handbook, 1888, p. 201.

31 Charles Beach, "What Can the Government Legitimately Do for the Farmers?" Institute Handbook, 1891, pp. 769-82.

32 Institute Handbook, 1895, p. 82; David F. Sayre, "Hard Times on the Farmer," Institute Handbook, 1896, p. 245.

Chapter III

Opening quotation. Professor J. C. Freeman, quoted in the Sunday Sentinal (Milwaukee), December 29, 1895.

1 Hontas P. Daniells, Report of the Monday Afternoon History Class, 1889-1890, pp. 1-3.—Madison, Wisconsin, Collection, State Historic Society of Wisconsin, Madison, Wisconsin.

2 W. C. Whitford, Historical Sketches of Education in Wisconsin (Madison, 1876), p. 106; Wisconsin Journal of Education, 22 (October, 1892), 218-19.

3 Merle Curti and Vernon Carstensen, The University of Wisconsin, A History (2 vols.; Madison, 1949), I, 494-98; Wisconsin Journal of Education, 21 (January, 1891), 16.

4 Frederick Jackson Turner, "The Extension Work of the University of Wisconsin," in George Francis James, ed., Handbook of University

Extension, (Philadelphia: Society for the Extension of University
Teaching, 1893), p. 316.

5 Wisconsin Journal of Education, 21 (January, 1891), 16; University
   of Wisconsin Catalogue, 1890-91, pp. 61-63.

6 Frederick Jackson Turner to Richard T. Ely, February 1, 1892, Ely
   Papers.

7 Milwaukee Journal, Editorial, September 20, 1887; Frederick
   Jackson Turner, "The Problem of the West," The Atlantic Monthly,
   78 (September, 1896), 189, 187.

8 George Herbert Palmer, "Doubts About University Extension,"
   Atlantic Monthly, 70 (March, 1892), 371.

9 Northwestern Chronicle (Oshkosh), July 5, 1895; Turner to Ely,
   March 31, 1892, Ely Papers; Daily Northwestern (Oshkosh), July 15,
   1895.

10 Wisconsin Journal of Education, 21 (November 18, 1891), 242.

11 Turner to Ely, February 1, 1892; Chamberlin to Ely, January 22,
   1892; Turner to Ely, November 25, 1891 and passim; Turner to Ely,
   March 20, 1892.—Ely Papers.

12 Robert C. Spencer, The People's Institute (Formerly the Working
   People's Reading Club), What It Is—What it Proposes—What It Needs
   (Milwaukee, n. d.); Wisconsin Journal of Education, 21 (January,
   1891), 16; Turner to Ely, April 14, 1892 and passim, Ely Papers.

13 Spencer to Ely, April 17, 1892; George E. Herron to Ely, March 29,
   1892.—Ely Papers.

14 University Catalogue, 1896-97, pp. 259-61.

15 University Catalogue, 1891-92, pp. 65-66; 1895-96, p. 40. Biennial
   Report of the Regents, 1894-95, 1895-96, pp. 27-31. F. W. Speirs
   to Ely, October 10, 1892; Speirs to Ely, November 2, 1892.—Ely
   Papers.

16 R. H. Halsey to Raymond, October 23, 1895, Presidents' Papers,
   Extension; Milwaukee Sentinel, October 11, 1895; Daily Northwestern (Oshkosh), Editorial, July 17, 1895; B. S. Stevens to Professor J. W. Stearns, December 23, 1892, Presidents' Papers.

17 "University Extension Lectures, Introductory Remarks, August 15-
   19, 1892," Ely Papers. University Catalogue, 1892-93, pp. 31-36;
   1896-97, pp. 258, 264.

18 Wisconsin Journal of Education, 23 (January, 1893), 17.

19 University Catalogue, 1891-92, pp. 46, 47-48.

20 Marion Connel to Jerome Raymond, 1897 and passim, Presidents'
   Papers; Benjamin W. Snow to Raymond, November 30, 1895, Presidents' Papers, Extension; Curti and Carstensen, University of Wisconsin, I, 621.

21 R. H. Baron to Raymond, December 9, 1896, Presidents' Papers;
   M. V. O'Shea, "Physical Training in the Public Schools," Atlantic
   Monthly, 75 (February, 1895), 254; "University Extension Syllabus
   Number 2;" "University Extension Syllabus Number 1."

22 Florence G. Buckstaff to Ely, January 3, 1895; Lynn S. Pease to Ely,
   January 13, 1895.—Ely Papers. Ely to C. K. Adams, June 7, 1895,
   Presidents' Papers; "Twenty Years, Wisconsin University Settlement, Anniversary Edition of Club Life," Milwaukee, 1922, pp. 10-
   14; "University Extension Syllabus, Number 41."

23 Henry Whipple to Ely, May 13, 1895; "University Extension Lec-
   tures," August 15-19, 1892.—Ely Papers. Richard T. Ely, Socialism,
   An Examination of Its Nature, Its Strength and Its Weakness, with
   Suggestions for Social Reform (New York, 1894), pp. 302, 352-53,

325, 327, 312; Richard T. Ely, "Fundamental Beliefs in My Social Philosophy," in Forum, 17 (October, 1894), 183.

24 Curti and Carstensen, University of Wisconsin, I, 288.

25 Speirs to Ely, January 2, 1893, Ely Papers.

26 Chris O. Mericee to Ely, May 9, 1895, Ely Papers.

27 Milwaukee Advance, August 6, 1892; Evening Wisconsin (Milwaukee), April 12, 1893.

28 Evening Wisconsin, April 6, 1893; The American Fabian, July and August, 1895, p. 7; January, 1896, p. 10. M. J. Kent to Ely, January 14, 1895; John J. McLaughlin to Ely, January 3, 1895; Ely to Adams, June 7, 1895.—Ely Papers.

29 Curti and Carstensen, University of Wisconsin, I, 509; Nation, July 12, 1894; Gregory to Ely, July 19, 1894, Ely Papers.

30 Curti and Carstensen, University of Wisconsin, I, 516-23; "The Ely Investigation, Communication of Superintendent Wells and the Investigatory Committee," August 20-23, 1894, p. 2, Ely Papers.

31 Milwaukee Journal, December 31, 1895, February 24, 1896.

32 Professor E. A. Birge in Daily Northwestern (Oshkosh), March 9, 1896; Rienow to Raymond, November 20, 1895, Presidents' Papers, Extension.

33 "Press Report of Regents on the Charges Against President C. K. Adams by County Superintendent Pederson," January 22, 1896, Ely Papers.

34 L. S. Hanks to Raymond, January 16, 1897, Presidents' Papers, Extension.

35 University Catalogue, 1898-99, p. 144; 1903-4, p. 276.

36 G. W. Paulus to Raymond, November 3, 1895, Presidents' Papers, Extension.

37 Magill to Raymond, April 13, 1896; G. S. Albee to Bennie Meyer, October 16, 1897.—Presidents' Papers. Estella Broomhull to Raymond, December 12, 1897; C. M. Maxow to Raymond, October, 1895 and passim.—Presidents' Papers, Extension.

38 R. H. Halsey to Raymond, September 21, 1895; Incomplete Letter to B. H. Meyer, November 18, 1897; Theodore Jackson to Raymond, September 7, 1896.—Presidents' Papers, Extension.

39 Luise Haessler to Raymond, November 14, 18, 1895; J. C. Jamiesen to Raymond, December 6, 1895; J. E. Collins to Raymond, September 1, 1896, and passim.—Presidents' Papers, Extension.

40 Whitewater Register, November 4, 1897; H. A. Simonds to Professor Hearns, November 16, 1897; W. H. Hickhok to Raymond, October 19, 1895.—Presidents' Papers. Albee to Meyer, October 16, 1897, Presidents' Papers, Extension; Daily Northwestern (Oshkosh), January 9, 1897.

41 Charles R. Van Hise to Raymond, September 2, 1895, Presidents' Papers, Extension.

42 J. W. Livingston to Raymond, May 16, 1897, Presidents' Papers, Extension; Speirs to Ely, April 13, 24, 1893, Ely Papers.

43 Milwaukee Sentinel, May 14, 1893; Wisconsin Journal of Education, January, 1891, p. 16; "The Summer School for Artisans," 1904, Presidents Papers, Extension; The Wisconsin Woman, 1 (January, 1901), 90.

Chapter IV

Opening quotation. Charles R. Van Hise, November, 1905, quoted in

Merle Curti and Vernon Carstensen, The University of Wisconsin, A History (2 vols.; Madison, 1949), II, 554.

1 Evening Wisconsin (Milwaukee), January 5, 1907.

2 Proceedings, State Federation of Labor, 1907, p. 38.

3 National Education Association, Report of the Committee on the Place of Industries in Public Education to the National Council of Education, July, 1910, published by the Association, 1912, pp. 6, 3, 8, 4, 15.

4 S. H. Goodnight, "Lessons from German Schools," Wisconsin Journal of Education, 40 (October, 1908), 273.

5 Milwaukee Journal, July 26, 1914; "Remarks of W. H. Lighty at the Frank A. Hutchins Memorial Dinner, January 13, 1913," Lighty Papers.

6 Wisconsin State Journal, June 25, 1913; Sir Horace Plunkett, "McCarthy of Wisconsin, The Career of an Irishman Abroad as it Appears and Appeals to an Irishman at Home," The Nineteenth Century American, June, 1915, p. 56; Dr. Charles McCarthy to William Tollman, April 24, 1909, McCarthy Papers.

7 The German Rundschau, February 18, 1914, McCarthy Papers.

8 Charles McCarthy in "Frank A. Hutchins' Worth and Work, Volume of Letters from His Many Friends" (1912), State Historical Society of Wisconsin, Entry of May 6, 1911.

9 William H. Lighty, "Memoirs," Tape 1.

10 Robert M. La Follette, in Ellen Torelle, ed., The Political Philosophy of Robert M. La Follette as Revealed in His Speeches and Writings (Madison, 1920), p. 294.

11 Charles Richard Van Hise, "Inaugural Address of Charles Richard Van Hise, Ph.D., LL.D., as President of the University of Wisconsin, Madison, June 7, 1904," pp. 24-25, 28, 29, 31, Presidents' Papers.

12 Van Hise in the Daily Cardinal (Madison), February 23, 1938.

13 McCarthy to Van Hise, August 6, 1907, McCarthy Papers; Merle Curti and Vernon Carstensen, The University of Wisconsin, A History (2 vols.; Madison, 1949), II, 554.

14 Curti and Carstensen, University of Wisconsin, I, 554-55; President Charles Van Hise, in Regents' Biennial Report, 1905-6, p. 35.

15 Edward A. Fitzpatrick, McCarthy of Wisconsin (New York, 1944), p. 249.

16 McCarthy to Van Hise, May, 1906, McCarthy Papers; Fitzpatrick, McCarthy, p. 250.

17 Lighty, "Memoirs," Tape 1; Legler to Van Hise, August 4, 1906, Presidents' Papers, Extension.

18 William H. Lighty, A Sketch of the Revivification of University Extension at the University of Wisconsin (University Extension Division, the University of Wisconsin, 1938).

19 Lighty, Revivification, p. 10; Lighty, "Memoirs," Tape 1. O. H. Longwell to Lighty, October 15, 1906, and passim, Lighty Papers.

20 A. J. Lindemann to Legler, March 4, 1907, McCarthy Papers; Carroll Quimby to Legler, n.d., Presidents' Papers, Extension.

21 McCarthy to George Hambrecht, 1909, McCarthy Papers.

22 "Memorandum," April 27, 1909, McCarthy Papers.

23 Legler to Van Hise, July 13, 1907, Presidents' Papers.

24 Legler to Van Hise, July 13, 1907; McCarthy to Van Hise, July 29, 20, 1907; Van Hise to Legler, July 16, 26, 1907; E. A. Birge to Van Hise, July 22, 30, 1907; Van Hise to Birge, July 22, 27, 1907.—Presidents' Papers.

25 William H. Dudley, Ed., Historical Sketch of University Extension,
    The University of Wisconsin and Reminiscences of Associates of
    Louis Ehrhart Reber, Dean 1907-1926 (Published by Friends of the
    University Extension in the University of Wisconsin, 1944), pp.
    21-22.
26 "Memorandum," 1911, Lighty Papers; Report of the Director of the
    Extension Division, 1908, pp. 7-8, 9; William H. Lighty, "Carrying
    the University to the Worker, How the Man in the Shop May Learn
    What He Needs to Know," The Designer, January, 1910, pp. 160-92.
27 Supplement, Extension Director's Report, 1908, pp. 3-4; Fred
    Brockhausen to McCarthy, November 12, 1908, McCarthy Papers.
28 W. N. Fitzgerald to Governor Davidson, copies to Reber and
    McCarthy, December 24, 1908; Reber to McCarthy, February 17,
    1909.—McCarthy Papers. Bill 146A, Assembly Journal, 1909.
29 G. D. Jones to Van Hise, March 25, 1909, Presidents' Papers;
    William D. Hoard to James O. Davidson, January 5, 1906, Papers of
    Governor James O. Davidson, State Historical Society of Wisconsin,
    Madison, Wisconsin. Van Hise to McCarthy, April 26, 1909;
    McCarthy, "Memorandum," April 27, 1909.—McCarthy Papers.
30 McCarthy, "Memorandum," April 27, 1909, McCarthy Papers.
31 McCarthy to August B. Lindemann, April 30, 1909; McCarthy to
    George Hambrecht, 1909.—McCarthy Papers.
32 McCarthy to W. H. Halton, March 20, 1911; McCarthy, "Notes on the
    Seventh Draft," 1911; Reber to McCarthy, January 10, 1911.—
    McCarthy Papers.

Chapter V

Opening quotation. William Kittle to William H. Lighty, December 4,
    1911, Lighty Papers.
 1 G. D. Jones to Van Hise, March 25, 1909, Presidents' Papers.
 2 Samuel A. Sparling, "League of Wisconsin Municipalities," Iowa
    Journal of History and Politics, 2 (April, 1904), 199-217.
 3 Marvin Wachman, History of the Social-Democratic Party of Mil-
    waukee, 1897-1910 (Illinois Studies in the Social Sciences, XXVIII,
    1, Urbana, 1945), pp. 1ff; Bayard Still, The History of a City (Madison,
    1945), pp. 515ff; Milwaukee Journal, August 28, 1906; Wisconsin
    Journal of Education, 37 (January, 1905), 3.
 4 John R. Commons, "Eighteen Months of Work of the Milwaukee
    Bureau of Economy and Efficiency, Bulletin 19," April 1, 1912, p. 6.
 5 The Reverend Frederick Jacobs in the Free Press (Milwaukee),
    October 25, 1910; Milwaukee Journal, January 16, 27, 1911.
 6 Milwaukee Journal, January 30, 1911; John F. Putnam, "The Mil-
    waukee Citizens' Bureau of Municipal Efficiency," Municipal Record,
    n. d., pp. 74-75; Merle Curti and Vernon Carstensen, The Univer-
    sity of Wisconsin, A History (2 vols.; Madison, 1949), II, 552.
 7 Charles McCarthy, "Memorandum," December 3, 22, 1909, McCarthy
    Papers; La Follette's Weekly Magazine, January 30, 1909, p. 3.
 8. Free Press (Milwaukee), May 2, 6, 1912; "Office of the State Super-
    intendent to Teachers and the General Public," Newsletter, Novem-
    ber 21, 1911; Daily News (Milwaukee), January 9, 1912.
 9 Paul H. Neystrom to William H. Lighty, February 21, 1912, Lighty
    Papers.
10 Edward A. Ross to George F. Vincent, February 8, 1912; Evan A.
    Evans to J. J. Pettijohn, February 29, 1912; Pettijohn to Evans,

February 29, 1912; Evans to Lighty, February 21, 1912; President
George Vincent, "What Has a State a Right to Expect of its University?" Saturday Lunch Club, March 9, 1912.—Lighty Papers.

11 President Charles Van Hise, quoted in Albert O. Barton, La Follette's
Winning in Wisconsin, 1894-1904 (Madison, 1912), p. 26.

12 James G. Monahan, Milwaukee Journal, June 23, 1914.

13 Milwaukee Journal, April 6, 1915, Thomas J. Neacy, quoted; Free
Press (Milwaukee), January 13, 1913; Milwaukee Sentinel, May 25,
1911.

14 Karl B. Weinman, Wisconsin State Journal, August 24, September 7,
27, 1914; W. D. Hoard to Governor Philipp, March 24, 1915, Papers
of Emanuel L. Philipp, State Historical Society of Wisconsin,
Madison, Wisconsin.

15 Samuel Plautz to Governor Philipp, April 15, 1915, and passim,
Philipp Papers.

16 Free Press (Milwaukee), July 31, 1915; Milwaukee Journal, June 12,
1915; Wisconsin State Journal, July 29, 1915; Milwaukee Leader,
July 3, 1915.

17 Laws of Wisconsin, 1917, Chapter 496.

Chapter VI

Opening quotation. Charles R. Van Hise, quoted in Milwaukee Sentinel,
June 23, 1916.

1 Handwritten notes, n.d., Turner Papers.

2 "Attitude of the Residence Faculty Toward Correspondence-Study
Teaching and the Reorganized Extension Work," 1909, Lighty Papers.

3 Report of the Director of the Extension Division, 1908, p. 28.

4 "Debating and Public Discussion Department and the Package Library," May 20, 1914, Lighty Papers.

5 Director's Report, 1908, p. 40.

6 Report of the Dean of the Extension Division, Biennial Report Ending
July 1, 1922, p. 26.

7 Francis McGovern, quoted in William H. Dudley, ed., Historical
Sketch of University Extension, The University of Wisconsin and
Reminiscences of Associates of Louis Ehrhart Reber, Dean, 1907-
1926 (Published by Friends of the University Extension in the University of Wisconsin, 1944), pp. 44, 23.

8 Louis E. Reber, "Carrying Knowledge to the People," University of
Pittsburgh Bulletin, December 1, 1913, pp. 3-5.

9 "Dean's Office Conference to Consider Having Weekly Conferences
Regarding Problems of Common Interest," May 20, 1914, Lighty
Papers; Charles R. Van Hise to Louis E. Reber, June 7, 1918,
Presidents' Papers; Lighty, "Memoirs," Tape 2.

10 Charles McCarthy to Sir Horace Plunkett, January 22, 1913;
McCarthy to Chester Allen, May 3, 1912.—McCarthy Papers.

11 McCarthy to McGovern, March 14, 1914, McCarthy Papers.

12 Daily Northwestern (Oshkosh), April 26, 1915.

13 Report Upon the Survey of the University of Wisconsin, Findings of
the State Board of Public Affairs and Its Report to the Legislature,
(State Board of Public Affairs, Madison, 1914), p. 209.

14 Lighty to Reber, January 19, 1915, Lighty Papers.

15 Milwaukee Journal, June 1, 1915.

16 Merle Curti and Vernon Carstensen, The University of Wisconsin,
A History (2 vols.; Madison, 1949), II, 200, 281.

17 Edward M. Barrow to Reber, April 7, 1915, copy in Wisconsin Legis-
    lative Reference Library, University of Wisconsin File.
18 William H. Lighty, A. H. Melville, A. L. Scott, R. S. Butler, J. L.
    Gillin, G. A. Hoare, "The University Extension Division and Exhibit
    '16' of the Allen Survey," 1924 [sic], pp. 1-8, Deans' Papers; Mil-
    waukee Journal, June 1, 1914.
19 M. V. O'Shea to Reber, November 17, 1913, Lighty Papers.
20 Copies of Extension ads are scattered throughout the Lighty Papers.
21 E. B. Norris to Reber, January 17, 1922, Lighty Papers.
22 William H. Lighty, quoted in The University Extension News Bulle-
    tin, March 1926.
23 Lighty to Gillin, December 31, 1948, Lighty Papers.
24 Lighty to Reber, January 15, 1936, Lighty Papers.

Chapter VII

Opening quotations. Charles R. Van Hise, address before the Merchants
    and Manufacturers Association of Milwaukee, April 14, 1908, quoted
    in the Association's Bulletin, May, 1908, p. 15; Extension student to
    Lighty, April 13, 1916, Lighty Papers.
1   Report of the Dean of the Extension Division, 1914, p. 169.
2   "An Incident Showing How Correspondence-Study Teaching May be
    Used by Well-Educated and Well-Trained People as Well as Those of
    Little Education or Training Who Desire to Come Abreast and Keep
    Abreast of the Times," January 22, 1925, and passim, Lighty Papers.
3   Thomas J. Neacy to McCarthy, January 27, 1912, McCarthy Papers;
    Extension student to University Extension Division, June 26, 1916,
    Lighty Papers; Mary Burchard Orvis, "The University That Goes to
    the People," Review of Reviews, 45 (April, 1912), 460.
4   Report of the Dean of the Extension Division, 1920, p. 166; "Regis-
    tration of Evening Students in Credit Courses," 1925, Lighty Papers.
5   Charles McCarthy to George Hambrecht, 1909, McCarthy Papers.
6   Lighty to Morse Salisbury, July 9, 1926, Lighty Papers.
7   George H. Johnson to R. S. Trent, September 19, 1914; Frederick
    F. Zepp to S. H. Van Dusen, August 17, 1914.— Lighty Papers.
8   "Summary Record of Registration, Comparing Biennium," Dean's
    Report, 1922, p. 7.
9   Louis E. Reber to President Charles Van Hise, June 13, October 8,
    1910; Lighty to Reber, July 11, 1910.—Lighty Papers. Dean's
    Report, 1910, p. 240.
10 "Lecture and Entertainment Courses, University List," University
    Bulletin 706-510 (January, 1915); "Lectures and Entertainments,
    Non-University List," University Bulletin, 713-517 (January, 1915)
11 Milwaukee Journal, May 29, 1914; Daily Northwestern (Oshkosh),
    April 23, 1915; Republican and Press (Neillsville), December 30,
    1915, February 24, 1916; Dean's Report, 1922, p. 15.
12 Lighty to Reber, February 24, 1925, Lighty Papers.
13 "University Extension Division Faculty—Madison—1925-1926,"
    Lighty Papers; Capital Times (Madison), April 1, 1925.
14 William H. Lighty, "Report to the Dean," 1912, Lighty Papers.
15 William H. Lighty, "Memoirs," Tapes 1, 2, 4; Lighty to Edward T.
    Adams, March 23, 1909, Lighty Papers.
16 Lighty, "Memoirs," Tapes 1, 2, 12; Professor E. B. Skinner to
    Lighty, September 15, 1922, Lighty Papers.
17 Annie M. Pitman to Lighty, April 24, 1922; Lighty to Reber, February

29, 1922.—Lighty Papers. Zona Gale to Miss Waters, April, 23, 1925, Papers of Zona Gale, State Historical Society of Wisconsin, Madison, Wisconsin; Birge to Reber, May 13, 1925, Presidents' Papers.

18 Reber to Birge, March 24, 1922, Presidents' Papers. "Numbers of Courses Taught by Each Instructor, 1913–1914"; Annie Pitman to Lighty, February 8, 1924.—Lighty Papers.

19 Lighty to Reber, January, 1924; "Report of the German Department in the Extension Division of the University of Wisconsin for the Biennium July 1, 1912 to July 1, 1914," pp. 1–5.—Lighty Papers.

20 Miss Edwards to Margaret Race Ross, November 18, 1922 [?], Lighty Papers.

21 Dean's Report, 1922, p. 10. Lighty to Chester Snell, May 12, 1925; Lois Crawford to Miss Pitman, January 22, 1924.—Lighty Papers.

22 M. J. Haire to Reber, December 29, 1911; Lighty to Reber, May 11, 1925; W. K. Halt to Lighty, February 3, 1925.—Lighty Papers.

23 Lighty to W. G. Carpenter, March 27, 1926, Lighty Papers.

24 Allen to Reber, November 30, December 5, 1925, Lighty Papers; University Extension News Bulletin, March, 1920.

25 Dean's Report, 1910, pp. 251–52.

26 Marshall Graff to Reber, January 24, 1924, Lighty Papers.

27 Lighty to Walter Piersen, February 21, 1925; Estelle A. Freu to A. S. Bow, March 1, 1926; J. P. O'Connor to Lighty, November 26, 1923.—Lighty Papers.

28 Free Press (Milwaukee), August 4, 1909; The Evening Wisconsin (Milwaukee), October 6, 1909.

29 Reber to Van Hise, March 21, 1910. Letter not sent. Lighty Papers.

30 Dean's Report, 1922.

31 Extension Handbills and Announcements, 1923, Lighty Papers.

32 Edward A. Fitzpatrick to Senator Teasdale, February 18, 1925, copy to Dean Reber, Lighty Papers.

33 Capital Times, editorial, January 20, 1926.

34 Edward A. Fitzpatrick to Senator Teasdale, February 18, 1925. Copy in Dean's Files.

35 University Extension News Bulletin, December, 1926.

Chapter VIII

Opening quotation. William H. Lighty, Miscellaneous Manuscripts, 1912, Lighty Papers.

1 Report of the Dean of the Extension Division of the University of Wisconsin, 1914, pp. 165, 166; Dean's Report, 1912, p. 3.

2 William H. Lighty, "Report on Correspondence-Study," 1914, Lighty Papers.

3 William H. Lighty, A Sketch of the Revivification of University Extension at the University of Wisconsin (University Extension Division, the University of Wisconsin, Madison, 1938), p. 14.

4 Percival Chubb, The Larger Fellowship, An Ethical Tract for the Times (n. d.), pp. 6, 4; News Letter of the International Union of Ethical Societies, November, 1913, February, 1914.

5 William H. Lighty to W. A. Brandenburger, October 19, 1910; Lighty to Anna Garlin Spencer, June 8, 1911.—Lighty Papers.

6 Daily Northwestern (Oshkosh), January 11, 1915, Professor John Gillin, "Causes of Poverty;" Dean's Report, 1922, p. 26.

7 "Wisconsin Baby Week Campaign," 1917, University Bulletin, 847–641 (March, 1917); also Bulletin 816–612 (November, 1916). Lighty

to Reber, October 18, 1919; "Public Health Nursing," n. d..—Lighty Papers.

8   McCarthy to Housman Brewing Company, July 26, 1907, Papers of Charles McCarthy, State Historical Society of Wisconsin, Madison, Wisconsin. E. B. Norris to Reber, August 28, 1914; E. M. Jenison to Norris, April 22, 1914; Lighty to B. E. McCormick, February 3, 1925; M. F. Rueping to E. B. Norris, August 12, 1914.—Lighty Papers.

9   "Tuberculosis or Consumption, The Problem," University Bulletin 291–165 (April, 1909); Edward F. McSweeney to McCarthy, November 16, 1911, McCarthy Papers; John R. Commons, "A Reconstruction Health Program," University Bulletin, 1055–8992 (June, 1920).

10   William G. Haber to Lighty, January 3, 1926, and enclosures, Lighty Papers.

11   Haber to Lighty, January 3, 1926, Lighty Papers; Mary B. Orvis, "Workers' Education Growing," N.U.E.A. News Bulletin, September, 1924; Haber to Lighty, January 3, 1926, and enclosures, Lighty Papers.

12   Lighty to Morse Salisbury, July 9, 1926, Lighty Papers.

13   "The Extension Division and Commercial Education," May 13, 1915, Lighty Papers.

14   Lighty to Extension fieldmen, February 21, 1922, and passim, Lighty Papers.

15   E. J. Demsey quoted in Allen to Reber, September 27, 1922, Presidents' Papers.

16   Herbert Croly, The Promise of American Life (New York, 1909), pp. 138–40; William P. Bowen and Elmer D. Mitchell, The Theory of Organized Play, Its Nature and Significance (New York, 1928), pp. 24, 26; Josiah Strong, The Twentieth Century City (New York, 1890), pp. 124–25, 280–81.

17   J. H. Puelicher to Reber, June 17, 1910; E. J. Ward to Reber, June 13, 1910; Reber to Van Hise, May 24, 1911, and passim.—Lighty Papers.

18   Lighty, "An Independent Budget," January 15, 1924, Lighty Papers.

19   Clarence A. Perry, "Social Center Development to Date and the Schoolhouse as a Recreation Center," University Bulletin 474–314 (February, 1912).

20   Edgar B. Gordon, "Community Music and Drama," University Bulletin 920–708 (April, 1918), pp. 3–6; Milwaukee Journal, June 22, 1914, Margaret Wilson.

21   Kaukauna Times, February 26, 1915.

22   Charles Joseph Galpin, Rural Life (New York, 1922), pp. 62–63, 61; The Press (New London), March 12, 1914; Kaukauna Times, June 19, 1914.

23   Kaukauna Times, January 29, 1915, January 15, 1915.

24   Brown County Democrat, February 13, December 18, 1914; Kaukauna Times, November 27, 1914, January 22, 1915; Brown County Democrat, December 4, 11, 1914.

25   B. W. Faast to Lighty, April 7, 1916, Lighty Papers.

26   Dean's Report, 1922, pp. 27–28; Milwaukee Journal, November 2, 1924; Capital Times (Madison), April 1, 1925.

27   "Proceedings of the First National Newspaper Conference, Madison, Wisconsin, July 29, August 1, 1912," University Bulletin 561–386 (April, 1913), p. 1; "War Emergency Service Available Through the University Extension Division," 1917, Lighty Papers.

Chapter IX

1 William H. Lighty, "Carrying the University to the Worker, How
   the Man in the Shop May Learn What He Needs to Know," The De-
   signer, January 1910, pp. 160-92; Report of the Director of the University Extension Division, The University of Wisconsin, 1908, p.
   15; Reber to McGraw-Hill Company, 1910, Lighty Papers; F. L.
   Gilbert to Van Hise, March 10, 1910, Presidents' Papers; Reber to
   Martin Foss, March 14, 1910, Lighty Papers.
2 Lighty to Reber, April 18, 1911, Lighty Papers; Report of the Dean
   of the Extension Division, 1910, pp. 239-40. J. M. Wilkinson to
   Reber, May 31, 1910; W. D. Hoard to L. S. Hanks, May 31, 1910.—
   Lighty Papers.
3 Reber to Van Hise, June 10, 1910; A. C. McClurg and Company to
   Reber, September 13, 1910, and passim.—Lighty Papers.
4 Biennial Report of the Civil Engineering Department, University
   Extension Division, July 1, 1914; James S. Thompson to Lighty, February 27, 1923; "Review of Electrical Meters by C. M. Jansky,"
   Electrical Review, London, April 17, 1914.—Lighty Papers.
5 Dean's Report, 1922, p. 12; "Distribution of Royalties Among the
   Instructional Force of the University Extension Division," May 2,
   1922, Presidents' Papers; "Extension Memorandum Number 40,"
   July 1, 1922, Lighty Papers. Chester D. Snell to President Glenn
   Frank, December 13, 1932; Snell to Ben Faast, July 3, 1931; Norris
   to Snell, April 9, 1935.—Deans' Papers.
6 Harold A. Engel, "WHA, Wisconsin's Pioneer" (Unpublished manuscript, March 5, 1936, Wisconsin State Historical Society), pp. 1-3.
7 William H. Lighty, "Memoirs," Tape 14.
8 Engel, "WHA", p. 4, and passim; Mrs. F. N. Peters to C. V. Hibbard,
   February 16, 1925, Lighty Papers.
9 W. S. Bittner to Lighty, April 4, 1923; "Educational Radio Broadcasting," a paper read before the Eighth Annual Convention of the
   University Extension Association, St. Louis, Missouri, April, 1923.
   —Lighty Papers.
10 Lighty, "Memoirs," Tape 14. E. M. Terry to Lighty, December 12,
   1924; Lighty to W. L. Miller, January 22, 1925.—Lighty Papers.
11 Mrs. A. Cadman to Lighty, February 11, 1925, and passim, Lighty
   Papers.
12 Milwaukee Journal, April 24, 1924. Lighty to Marshall Graff, April
   26, 1924; Lighty to Reber, October 21, 1924; Lighty to F. B. Swingli,
   November 21, 1924.—Lighty Papers.
13 Lighty to M. A. Davidson, February 4, 1925; Lighty to L. R.
   Alderman, September 8, 1925; A. C. Watson to Lighty, April 21,
   1923.—Lighty Papers.
14 G. A. Thompson to Radio Department, University of Wisconsin,
   October 3, 1922, Lighty Papers; "University Extension Instruction
   Service by Radio Broadcast," n.d., Presidents' Papers.
15 Lighty to Maurice W. Weseen, November 21, 1925; "Questionnaires
   Sent to City Superintendents, City Grade Principals, Supervisors
   and Acting Superintendents, County Superintendents and Principals
   of State Graded Schools," 1925.—Lighty Papers.
16 Lighty to Hugh S. Bonar, May 12, 1925, and passim, Lighty Papers.
17 Elmore Pederson to Lighty, April 3, 1922; Chester D. Snell to Lighty,
   April 10, 1923; W. D. Henderson to Lighty, April 5, 1924; J. W.
   Scroggs to Lighty, April 7, 1924; B. C. Riley to Lighty, July 7, 1922.
   —Lighty Papers.

18 Lighty to Professor R. V. Achatz, September 12, 1924, Lighty
    Papers; Lighty, "Memoirs," Tape 14; Lighty to Miss J. M.
    Wilkinson, March 30, 1926, Lighty Papers.
19 John Guy Fowlkes, "The Wisconsin Experiment in Radio," Wiscon-
    sin Journal of Education, 63 (December, 1930), 167-69.
20 Harold B. McCarthy, "The Wisconsin School of the Air," Wisconsin
    Journal of Education, 53 (November, 1921), 136-37. "Can Radio
    Supplant the Classroom Teacher?" Wisconsin Journal of Education,
    64 (December, 1931), 188-89; Malcolm S. MacLean to Dean, March,
    December 31, 1931, Deans' Papers.
21 F. O. Holt to O. H. Planzke, March 21, 1940; H. B. McCarty, State-
    ment, March 29, 1940.—Deans' Papers.
22 WHA File, 1932-33, Deans' Papers.

Chapter X

Opening quotation. President Charles R. Van Hise, "What the University
    Can Do for the State," address before the Canadian Club, Toronto,
    October 21, 1913, Presidents' Papers.
 1 Louis E. Reber to President E. A. Birge, September 18, 1922, Pres-
    idents' Papers.
 2 John Collier to Charles McCarthy, April 13, 1911, McCarthy Papers;
    G. D. Jones to M. E. McCaffrey, April 10, 1917, Presidents' Papers.
 3 Wisconsin Journal of Education, 49 (November, 1917), 251, 244.
 4 Mary B. Orvis to Lighty, January 17, 15, 1927, Lighty Papers;
    "American Ideals in Citizenship," Department of Group and Com-
    munity Development, August 15, 1920, p. 2.
 5 "Lecture Outlines," School of Citizenship, Conducted by the Univer-
    sity Extension Division in Coöperation with the National League of
    Women Voters, July 18, 1920.
 6 Richard T. Ely, "Political Economy in the High School," March,
    1895, Ely Papers; Daily Northwestern (Oshkosh), editorial, May 1,
    1915.
 7 Chester Allen and Carl E. Johnson, "An Adult Education Program
    for Prisoners Operating in Wisconsin Prisons Through the Coöper-
    ation of the University of Wisconsin Extension Division, State De-
    partment of Public Welfare, Division of Corrections and Other State
    Departments," University Bulletin 2486-2270 (September, 1940);
    Lighty to Reber, January 5, 1920, Lighty Papers.
 8 Inmate of State Prison to Extension Division, 1924; Number 14184,
    "Prison," Ms., July 25, 1925.—Lighty Papers.
 9 Chester Allen to Lighty, March 1926, and enclosures; Allen and
    Johnson, in University Bulletin, pp. 17ff; Lighty to Chester Snell,
    May 12, 1925.—Lighty Papers.
10 J. W. Livingston to Van Hise, September 17, 1906; Legler to
    McKenny, September 29, 1906.—Presidents' Papers.
11 Report of the Dean of the Extension Division, 1910, p. 246; Wiscon-
    sin Alumni Magazine, February, 1914, p. 211; Dean's Report, 1922,
    p. 17; Wisconsin Journal of Education, 55 (October, 1923), 8.
12 Dean's Report, 1910, p. 238. Benjamin Frey to E. B. Norris, Novem-
    ber 11, 1912; Lighty to Professor F. G. Hubbard, September 19,
    1916.—Lighty Papers. Wisconsin Journal of Education, 53 (March,
    1921), 90; Miss Leila Bascom to Lighty, October 11, 1926, Lighty
    Papers; Allen to Reber, May 7, 1926, Deans' Papers. K. G. Smith to

Lighty, March 26, 1926; Allen to Reber, June 24, 1926, and enclosures.—Lighty Papers.

13 Wisconsin Journal of Education, Editorial, 55 (January, 1923), p. 3; Lighty to N. A. Anderson, et al., October 31, 1923, Lighty Papers; Madison Democrat, January 13, 1907.

14 C. J. Cary, et al., "Wisconsin's Most Pressing Educational Needs," Wisconsin Journal of Education, 40 (November, 1908), 307; C. E. Patzer in the Free Press (Milwaukee), December 1, 1909; M. V. O'Shea, "The Teachers' Institute," Wisconsin Journal of Education, 40 (November, 1908), 339.

15 Dean E. A. Birge, "The University and the High School," Wisconsin Journal of Education, 38 (September, 1906), 248; Brown County Democrat, June 5, 1914; Milwaukee Journal, January 5, 1913; Free Press (Milwaukee), January 8, 1913; Daily Cardinal (Madison), May 25, 1920; Wisconsin Journal of Education, 53 (January, 1921), 1.

16 Lighty to M. E. Hazeltine, September 2, 1925; Lighty to Reber, January 11, 1917, February 7, 1924; Marshall Graff to Lighty, April 9, 1924; "Extension Course Number 91 in Education," June, 1914. —Lighty Papers.

17 Lighty to Reber, January 11, 22, 16, 1917; John Callahan to J. E. Giessel (copy), February 17, 1923; Callahan to William A. Derthick, October 24, 1923.—Lighty Papers. "State Requirements for Teachers' Certificates and Licenses," University Bulletin, 1963-1747 (March, 1934).

18 Dean's Report, 1922, pp. 13-14. Lighty to Harry P. Woost, December 6, 1923; Executive Committee, State Normal School, La Crosse, to Lighty, October 16, 1924; Lighty to Field Representatives, October 18, 1924.—Lighty Papers.

19 Lighty to Reber, January 17, 1922, Lighty Papers.

20 Lighty to J. P. O'Connor, December 12, 1923; Graff to Lighty, October 18, 1923; O'Connor to Lighty, January 6, 1924. — Lighty Papers.

21 O'Connor to Lighty, January 1, 1924; Lighty to O'Connor, January 23, 1924; Marshall Graff to O'Connor, February 11, 1924. — Lighty Papers.

22 Allen to Lighty, December 7, 1923; Lighty to Allen, December 3, 1923; G. M. Osborne to Lighty, February 22, 1926; Lighty to Allen, December 3, 1923.—Lighty Papers.

23 Lighty to Allen, January 23, 1924; Allen to Lighty, April 13, 1926.— Lighty Papers. Wisconsin Journal of Education, 58 (March, 1926), 284. Lighty to Allen, March 13, 1926; Lighty to Henmon, October 6, 1925.—Lighty Papers. Silas Evans to Allen, May 15, 1926, Deans' Papers.

24 Biennial Report of the Regents, 1916-1918, p. 215; Dean's Report, 1922, p. 19; William H. Dudley, ed., Historical Sketch of University Extension, The University of Wisconsin and Reminiscences of Louis Ehrhart Reber, Dean, 1907—1926 (Published by Friends of the University Extension in the University of Wisconsin, 1944).

Chapter XI

1 Louis E. Reber to Chester D. Snell, Papers of the Dean of the Extension Division of the University of Wisconsin, Madison, Wisconsin. Glenn Frank to Snell, November 27, 1925; Snell to Frank, December 10, 1925; Frank to Snell, April 6, 1926.—Presidents' Papers.

2 The University Extension News Bulletin, September, 1926; Snell to
   Reber, March 2, 1925, Deans' Papers.
3 Wisconsin Journal of Education, Editorial, 59 (September 1926), 7;
   "Number of Lessons per Registration," 1928, Deans' Papers.
4 Louis E. Reber, "Memorandum for Mr. Snell," n. d., Deans' Papers.
5 Snell to Frank, October 7, 1927; Snell to Ben Faast, November 3,
   1930.—Deans' Papers.
6 Reber, " Memorandum."
7 "Reorganization," Budget Folder, 1931-32; Snell to Faast, June 21,
   1927.—Deans' Papers. Snell to Frank, April 4, 1935, Presidents'
   Papers.
8 Capital Times (Madison), January 17, 1930; "Change of Duties,"
   Budget Folder, 1931-32, Presidents' Papers.
9 Donald C. Broughton to Snell, June 4, 1934, and enclosures, (Copy
   of Snell to Broughton, January 19, 1934), Deans' Papers.
10 Milwaukee Journal, September 21, 1935; Snell to Frank, April 4,
   1935, Deans' Papers.
11 Snell to Frank, April 4, 1935, Presidents' Papers.
12 Frank to Senator C. F. Brunette and enclosures, April 24, 1935,
   Presidents' Papers.
13 "The Snell Case," 1935, Presidents' Papers; Lighty "Testimony Before the Board of Regents," Lighty Papers.
14 M. V. O'Shea, "Editorial Comment," Wisconsin Journal of Education,
   47 (November, 1915), 243; "The New Education," Editorial, Wisconsin Journal of Education, 58 (April, 1926), 7.
15 Glenn Frank, quoted in Milwaukee Journal, February 29, 1928; Glenn
   Frank, "A Prayer for Teachers," Wisconsin Journal of Education,
   59 (September, 1926), 11.
16 Chester D. Snell, "Future Trends in University Extension," enclosed,
   Snell to Frank, March 2, 1927, Deans' Papers; Milwaukee Journal,
   March 31, 1927; M. S. Dudgeon to Snell, April 13, 1928, Deans'
   Papers.
17 Snell to Frank, et al., and enclosures, January 19, 1928; "Minutes of
   Adult Education Conference," December 10, 1927.— Deans' Papers.
18 "Comparison in Enrollments in Liberal Education Courses, 1928-
   1929 and 1929-1930"; Malcolm S. MacLean to Senator Edward P.
   Costigan, March 9, 1931.—Deans' Papers.
19 MacLean to Snell, March 6, 1931, Deans' Papers; A. J. Dorr to Snell,
   February 12, 1931.—Deans' Papers.
20 "Ethel T. Rockwell and Committee on Cultural Possibilities, 1935,"
   Deans' Papers.
21 "Memorandum of Meeting of Field Representatives, Held in Dean
   Snell's Office on Saturday, April 2, 1932; "Coöperative Plan with
   Wisconsin High Schools," 1932.—Deans' Papers.
22 Snell to C. M. Purin, November 17, 1932; Budget Folder, 1934-35;
   "Educational Plans for High School Granduates, Prepared by a State
   Committee Composed of John Callahan, Chairman, State Superin-
   tendent of Public Instruction, George Hambrecht, Director, State
   Board of Vocational Education, E. G. Doudna, Secretary, Board of
   Regents of Normal Schools, Chester D. Snell, Secretary, Dean of
   University Extension Division."—Deans' Papers.
23 "A Field Program," 1928; "Minutes of the Meeting of the Vocational
   Directors Committee with the Dean of the Extension Division, Held
   in the Dean's Office, Thursday, January 12, 1928, at 2:00 P.M.—
   Deans' Papers.

24 Snell to Charles C. West, November 12, 1928; Snell to Frank, March 25, 1931.—Deans' Papers.

25 George Hambrecht to Vocational School Directors, June 8, 1932, copy enclosed, Hambrecht to Snell, June 8, 1932, Deans' Papers.

26 Snell to All Field Representatives, June 15, 1932, Deans' Papers.

27 Glenn Frank to the University Faculty, an address, March 5, 1934, Deans' Papers.

Chapter XII

Opening quotations. Frank O. Holt to the Principal Addressed, form letter, November 11, 1940, Deans' Papers; Capital Times (Madison), January 29, 1931, Governor Phil La Follette quoted.

1 Dean Frank O. Holt to Members of the Extension Staff, October 8, 1941, Deans' Papers.

2 Curtis Merriman to Principals of Wisconsin High Schools, May 12, 1936; Holt to President Glenn Frank, July 1, 1936.—Deans' Papers.

3 Chester Allen to Holt, June 28, 1935, and enclosure, "Memorandum of Conference of City Superintendents and Vocational Directors," June 20, 1935, Deans' Papers.

4 Professor Paul Knaplund to Holt, December 4, 1935, May 5, 1937, Deans' Papers.

5 "University Extension College Classes, Analysis of Day Program Enrollments, 1936-1937, 1937-1938, First Semester Registrations"; Marshall Graff to Holt, 1938; Graff to Miss Katherine McMullen, August 15, 1942; Graff to Chester Allen, August 15, 1942.—Deans' Papers.

6 Charles McCarthy to the Honorable Josephus Daniels, June 25, 1913, McCarthy Papers. William H. Lighty to J. S. Thompson, January 11, 1918; Lighty to Louis E. Reber, July 13, 1917; Major John F. Landis to Lighty, October 15, January 26, January 6, 1927.—Lighty Papers.

7 Holt to General Ralph M. Immel, September 20, 1940; Major General E. S. Adams for the Chief of Staff to Holt, October 10, 1940.—Deans' Papers. Laws of Wisconsin, 1943, Chapter 410, p. 736.

8 A. N. Smith to Armed Forces Institute Instructor, March 27, 1944, Deans' Papers.

9 News Letter, Number 1, July 20, 1945, Deans' Papers.

10 Daily Cardinal (Madison), editorial, September 24, 1946; Milwaukee Journal, editorial, October 20, 1946.

11 "The Snell Case," President's Papers; Milwaukee Journal, September 21, 1935; Herald (Washington, D.C.), September 22, 1935; Press Gazette (Green Bay), November 6, 1935; Milwaukee Sentinel, November 9, 1935; Free Press (Burlington), editorial, May 23, 1935.

12 Wisconsin State Journal, June 9, 1935; Leader (Eau Claire), May 17, 1935.

13 President Van Hise, quoted in Albert O. Barton, La Follette's Winning of Wisconsin, 1894-1904 (Madison, 1912), p. 26.

14 Graff to Holt, May 27, 1937; "Mr. Lowe's Report on Employing Alien Instructors," 1937.—Deans' Papers.

15 "Report on Mr. Crofts' Case at Fond du Lac, Respecting Religious Teachings," April 7, 1933, and passim, Deans' Papers.

16 Daily Record (Wausau), November 11, 12, 1936; Record (Spencer), November 12, 1936; News (Rhinelander), November 13, 1936; Post-Crescent (Appleton), November 16, 1936.

17 Capital Times, editorial, November 16, 1936. O. E. Olson to Holt,

November 16, 1936; "Memorandum, Department of History," 1936.
—Deans' Papers.

18 Pertinent correspondence will be found after the dates November 30,
    December 3, 6, 16, 1940; January 10, 21, 1941, March, 1941, Janu-
    ary 8, 1941, Deans' Papers.

19 "First Narrative Report, University of Wisconsin Forum Project,
    October 1, 1939—June 18, 1940, Auspices of the University of Wis-
    consin Extension Division, United States Office of Education, the
    W.P.A. and the N.Y.A.," Deans' Papers.

Chapter XIII

1 Abraham Flexner, Universities, American, English, German (New
   York, 1930), pp. 216ff.; Capital Times (Madison), November 23,
   1930; "Cost of Courses by Correspondence," University Bulletin,
   1472-1248 (March, 1927), p. 17; "List of Courses in Correspondence"
   Correspondence-Study Bulletin of the University of Wisconsin, 1836-
   1620 (April, 1932), p. 17.

2 Louis E. Reber, "University Extension in the United States" (U.S.
   Bureau of Education, Bulletin, 1914, No. 19, Whole Number 592,
   Government Printing Office, Washington, D.C., 1914).

3 Philadelphia Inquirer, May 27, 1913. For a sympathetic interpretation of the Wisconsin Idea in education, see "The Next Step for Pennsylvania, Program of Conference on Educational Extension, Philadelphia, November 21-22, 1913."

4 William H. Lighty, "Memoirs," Tapes VII, VIII. J. J. Pettijohn to
   Dean Louis E. Reber, August 23, 1913; G. F. Reynolds to Reber,
   March 6, 1914; De Witt C. Croissant to Reber, March 6, 1914, and
   passim; Frederick A. Hall to Reber, March 6, 1914.—Lighty Papers.

5 M. S. Dudgeon to Lighty, November 1. 1924; Lighty to H. F. Mallory
   February 17, 1925; Lighty to T. H. Shelby, March 20, 1926; Lighty
   to H. G. Ingham, and passim, May 19, 1926.—Lighty Papers. Joseph
   K. Hart, Adult Education (Crowell Social Science Series, New York,
   1927), p. 181.

6 Dr. Lorenz H. Adolfson, November 11, 1954, quoted in Inside Extension, November 16, 1954.

Index

ADAMS, Charles Kendall, 21
Adams, H. C.: farm institute
speaker, 20; and Beach debates,
23
Adams, H. S., 25
Adams, Herbert Baxter: on mass
education, 4; on English extension work, 7; and library extension courses in 1897, 10; advocates University Extension, 11;
mentioned, 38
Addams, Jane: School of Ethics
lecturer, 98; philosophy, 105
Adler, Felix, 98
Adolfson, Lorenz: appointed Dean
of Extension Division in 1945,
169; address at Racine, 178
Adult education: at Cornell University in 1869, 10; Chautauqua,
Monona Lake Assembly, 13 ff.
passim; Hutchins and Mc-
Carthy, 47; use of traveling lecturers, 113 ff.; University Experimental School, 146; at University of California, 151. See
also Worker education
Agassiz, Louis, 10
Agricultural education: early colonial, 7; Farmers' College,
Ohio, 8; early courses in, 16–17;
Farmers' Institutes, 17 ff. passim, 44; legislative appropriations for, 51; mentioned, 56. See
also Farmers' Institutes
Agricultural societies, 8, 16
Agriculture, College of: established at University of Wisconsin,
17; waning influence, 54; advocates mail order house buying,
62; and Charles Galpin, 109; and
dissension with Extension Division, 111
Agriculture, State Department of,
117
Agriculture, U.S. Department of,
101

Albee, G. S., 39
Ali, Mohammed, 83
Allen, Chester: and scholarships
for Waupun inmates, 127; and
high school level correspondence
courses, 131; appointed Director
of Field Organization, 139; promoted to assistant professor,
140; urges expanding of field
service, 155
Allen, William F., 29
Allen, William Harvey: heads municipal survey of Milwaukee, 60;
and survey of University, 63, 71
ff. passim. See also Allen Survey
Allen Survey: attempted supres-
sion of findings, 73, 178; cited by
McCarthy, 104
American Economics Association:
organized by Ely and others, 13;
as manifestation of Progressivism, 96
American Ethical Union, 97
American Federation of Labor,
103
American Federation of Teachers,
142
American Home Missionary Society, 13
American Legion, 153
American Library Association,
52
American Lyceum movement:
established by Josiah Holbrook,
7–8; purposes, 8–9; conservative
aspects, 9; deterioration of, 9–
10; and Farmers' Institutes, 21
American Magazine, 60
American Society for the Extension of University Teaching, 84
Amherst University, 103
Andrews, Charles M., 12
Antigo Plan, 157
Anti-Tuberculosis Association:
and Extension, 96, 99, 101; Wisconsin Anti-Tuberculosis Associ-

Anti-Tuberculosis Assn.. (cont.):
ation Apprentice School, 102
Appleton, D., and Company, 115
Appleton Post-Crescent, 166
Appropriations, Legislature: for
    Farmers' Institutes in 1885, 17-
    18, 54; agriculture, 45, 54; Ex-
    tension, 49, 53, 63-64, 51
Armour Institute, 41
Army and Navy Journal, 159
Army Institute, 159, 160

BABCOCK, Stephen Moulton: Farm
    Institute speaker, 19; mentioned,
    144
Badger, The (Yearbook), 129
Bakers' Institute of 1908, 101
Balmer's Kaffir Boys' Chorus, 83
Barnes, Charles Reid, 31
Barr, Arvil S., 135
Bascom, John: supports use of
    strike, 36; on public service, 45,
    47; mentioned, 20, 56, 144
Bascom, Leila: and correspond-
    ence course work, 85; on Carne-
    gie Foundation, 86-87; number
    of courses taught, 88; urges high
    school level correspondence
    work, 131; on Snell, 139
Beach, Charles: Farm Institute
    speaker, 20; and Adams debates,
    23; opposes Populist movement,
    25
Beatty, Arthur, on English faculty,
    82, 85
Beecher, Henry Ward, 10
Bemis, Edward, 12, 14, 35
Bennett, Edward, 116
Better Baby Weeks: sponsored by
    Extension, 99
Big Sisters, 107
Birge, Edward A.: as University
    Extension lecturer, 31, 41; on
    Extension faculty status, 87; and
    Milwaukee Branch of University,
    95; appoints Lighty chairman of
    committee on educational broad-
    casting, 116; succeeded by Glenn
    Frank, 120; and School of Citi-
    zenship, 126; on teacher training,
    132
Birkbeck, George, 5
Bliss, W. D. P., 97
Board of Regents. See Regents,
    Board of

Bolshevism, 153
Boston Trade Union College, 103
Bradley, W. C., 23
Brigham Young University, 176
Broadcasting. See Educational
    broadcasting; WHA
Brockhausen, Fred, 53
Brook Farm, 97
Broughton, Donald C., 142
Brown University, 115
Bruce, William George, 59
Brumbaugh, Martin G., 176
Brunette, E. F.: criticizes Univer-
    sity, 162; investigation of subver-
    sive activity at University, 163
Bryn Mawr, 103
Bureau of Community Music and
    Drama, 108
Bureau of Dramatic Activities,
    155
Bureau of Economy and Efficiency,
    58
Bureau of Industrial Relations,
    112
Bureau of Visual Education, 130
Business administration, 112
Butler, R. Starr, 104

CALIFORNIA, University of: and
    worker education, 103; and adult
    education, 151; requests advice
    from University Extension, Wis-
    consin, 176
Callahan, John: approved Exten-
    sion courses for teachers in
    1923, 134; and community serv-
    ice programs, 150
Capital Times (Madison): opposed
    Milwaukee branch of University,
    95; on function of University, 161;
    on subversion charges against
    University, 167
Carnegie Foundation, 86-87
Cary, Charles P., suggested as
    gubernatorial candidate, 60-61;
    on teacher education, 132
Catholic Social Union, 60
Central Council of Philanthropy,
    59
Chamberlin, Thomas C.: interest
    in English extension, 20; sug-
    gests establishment of Mechan-
    ics' Institute, 21; on teacher
    training, 29; growing interest in
    off-campus work, 29-30; sees

Extension as advertising University, 30; and Ely, 32; and Mechanics' Institutes, 41; and cultural courses, 56; mentioned, 144

Chapple, John, 162-63

Chase, Wayland, 82

Chautauqua: origins, 7; growth, 10; standards, 11; and Ely, 13

Cheever, W. H., 132

Cheyney, E. P., 12

Chicago, University of: extension work inaugurated in 1891, 11; and University of Wisconsin, 66; and educational broadcasting, 120; lecturers at Wisconsin, 146; and Charles R. Walgreen, 154; and freshman center class programs, 156; as Extension pioneer, 175

Chicago Concert Company, 83

Chicago Federation of Labor, 103

Chicago Operatic Company, 83

Christian Socialists: and University Extension, 4; on popular education, 6

Christmas seals, 102

Citizenship training: more formalized, 123; courses, 124; and National League of Women Voters, 126; in Manitowoc, 170

City Club of Milwaukee: sponsors municipal survey in 1912, 60; initiates lecture series, 83-84

City Club of Philadelphia, 175-76

City clubs: and civic reform, 57

Civic and Social Conference, Madison, in 1911, 108, 178

Civic centers. See Community service.

Civic reform, Milwaukee, 57-58

Civil Conservation Corps, 149

Colbert, R. J., 170

College of Agriculture. See Agriculture, College of

Colorado, University of, 120

Columbian Catholic Summer School, at Madison, 31

Committee to Avoid Duplication of Effort, 97

Common Council, Milwaukee, 58

Commons, John R.: conducts economic survey of Milwaukee, 58; on health education, 101-2

Communism: charges of subversion at University, 162-64

Community Institutes: shortcomings, 100; Extension welfare effort, 109; patterned after Farmers' Institutes, 110; waning influence, 111-12; effectiveness evaluated, 176

Community service: civic centers and settlement house work, 35, 58, 105-6, 107, 112-13, 125; experiments in, 57; health programs sponsored by Extension, 96-100 ff. passim; criticism of Extension programs, 97; smoke pollution, 100; Food and Drugs Commission, 101; legislature approves use of schools for community programs in 1911, 106; Big Sisters, 107; and Municipal Reference Bureau, 108; Civic and Social Conference in 1911, 108; Bureau of Community Music and Drama, 108-9, 148; Wisconsin Bankers' Association and Milwaukee Chamber of Commerce, 110 ff. passim; rehabilitation programs, 123-24, 150-51; health education, 137. See also Settlement house work

Compulsory School Attendance law, 55

Comstock, George C., 35

Comte, Augustus, 4

Contemporary Club of Madison, 29

Convict labor, 127-28

Cornell University: extension program of 1869, 10; and Wisconsin University Extension, 176

Courses, Extension: of general nature in early years, 12

Courses, Lecture: social criticism, 1887-88, 12-13; Monona Lake Assembly, 31; for University credit, 34; fees, 34; evaluation of, 34-35, 40; on social reform, 35-36; for electric and steam plant managers, 41; engineering, 49; use of traveling instructors, 53; cultural, 56; effect of Allen Report on, 73-74; enrollments, 76, 81, 136; Instruction by Lecture, instituted 1909, 82; decline of, 84; busi-

Courses, Lecture (cont.):
ness, 104; for trade unionists,
125
Courses, Correspondence: agriculture, 17–18; first offered,
1896, 34; failure of early efforts,
34; evaluation of, 34, 53, 85, 90;
specialized faculty needed, 1908,
67, 84–85; students, 78–80, 89;
increase in instructional staff,
1906–26, 84; percentage of
course completions, 89–90;
scope extended, 91 ff. passim;
French and Spanish language,
104; for law officers, 108; encouraged in 1922, 112; study
guides, 113; shop and technical,
113; business, 123–24; for prisoners in state institutions, 127–
28; high school level, 131–33;
for teachers and administrators,
133–34; enrollments, 136, 149–
50; for unemployed, 148; for
Civil Conservation Corps, 149;
advised for remote areas, 156;
for armed services, 158–59
Crane, Frank, 86
Croft, Albert E., 165–66
Croly, Herbert, 106, 111
Cutler-Hammer Corporation, 64

DAILY Cardinal, 49
Daily Northwestern (Oshkosh),
127
Davidson, James O., 51
Dearholt, Hoyt: heads Health Bu-
reau in 1913, 99; and anti-tuber-
culosis campaign, 101
Debating and Public Instruction,
department of: created by
Hutchins, 67–68; effectiveness
evaluated, 89; and citizenship
training, 124
Dewey, John, 106
Doudna, E. G., 131
Drake, L. E., 142
Drama, 108
Drexel Institute, 41
Dudgeon, Matthew, 146
Dudley, William H., 130
Dwight, Theodore, 10
Dykstra, Clarence, 156

EDUCATION, Department of: Extension included in, 38, 47

Education, School of: and educational broadcasting, 120; and
Extension, 135; and teacher
training, 136. See also Teacher
training
Educational broadcasting: Committee on, 116; WHA, "Wisconsin School of the Air," 117, 121;
use in high schools, 119; evaluation of, 119–20; use by other
universities, 120; recognized by
Federal Communication Commission, 120; recognized by National University Extension Association, 120; and Schools of
Education and Music, 120; criticism of, 121–22
Edwards, Reverend Frederick,
59
Edwards, Martha, 88–89
Eliot, Charles W., 130
Ellingwood, R. E., 140
Elliot, Ben G., 85, 100
Elliott, Edward C., 66
Ely, Richard T.: pioneered extension work at Wisconsin, 4,
12, 13 ff. passim; and Social
Gospel, 14, 32, 35, 36; and Socialism, 36–37; attack on, 36–
38, 40, 43; and McCarthy, 46–
47; and Van Hise, 53; and
League of Wisconsin Municipali-
ties, 57; and Turner, 66; and re-
vival of platform lectures, 68;
and social service, 107; and
citizenship training programs,
124; and Elmira Program,
127; mentioned, 115, 167,
169, 173
Emerson, Ralph Waldo, 10, 97
Engel, Harold E., 121
Engineering, School of, 100
Engineering Education Series,
114
Enrollments, Extension, 38–39,
94, 136, 158, 172–73
Ernst, A. B., 86
Estabrook, C. E., 16
Ethical movement: and Lighty,
97; waning influence of, 98;
Ethical Society's Self Culture
Hall Association, 50
Evans, Evan A., 61
Evans, Silas, 83
Everett, Charles, 19

Executive Committee, University: on Extension textbook publication, 114

FABIANS, 35
Fairchild, Lucius, 25
Farmers' College, Ohio, 8
Farmers' institutes: first held in Hudson, 17, 21–22; attendance at, 17–18; legislative appropriations for, 17–18, 54; Institute Proceedings, 18; nature of programs, 18 ff. passim; speakers and conductors, 19–20, 23; criticism of, 19; advocate diversified farming, 22–24; as conservative influence, 22–23, 25–26, 45; farmer compared to businessman, 24–26; oppose Populist movement in Wisconsin, 25; lose influence before World War I, 26; popularity, 27; and Chamberlin, 29; economy, 101; as community service, 109; influence evaluated, 173–74; mentioned, 30, 41, 176
Farrell, Mary, 91
Federal Children's Bureau, 99
Federal Communication Commission, 120
Federal Reserve System, 104
Fees, correspondence course, 34
Field Organization, 139
Field service: importance of, 134–36; expanded, 155
Fish, Carl Russell, 82, 84
Fish, Hamilton, 162
Fiske, John, 31
Fitzpatrick, Edward A., 94–95
Flexner, Abraham, 174
Flisch, Julia, 50, 84
Food and Drugs Commission, 101
Fowlkes, John Guy, 117
Frank, Glenn: and educational broadcasting, 120; and Snell, 138, 140, 143, 144; and University educational policy, 145, 146, 161; on adult education, 150; on vocational education, 152; replaced by Dykstra, 156; on charges of subversion at University, 163; and Williams affair, 167; mentioned, 170
Fred, Edwin Broun, 160
Free Library Commission, Wisconsin: created, 45; and Hutchins, 46, 67; and Henry Legler, 48–49; office moved to Bascom Hall, 86
Freeman, J. C., early Extension lecturer, 12, 31, 41; quoted, 27
Freeman, J. R., 49
Free Press (Burlington), 163
Freshman centers, 156, 157, 160, 161

GALE, Zona, 87
Galpin, Charles, 107
Geltch, Waldemar von, 83
General Information and Welfare, department of, 68, 106
George, Henry, 6
G.I. Bill, 160
Gillin, John Lewis: and Committee to Avoid Duplication of Effort, 97; address at Oshkosh, 98–99; and State Conference on Charities and Correction, 107; and scholarship fund for Waupun prisoners, 127
Gilman, Stephen W.: and John R. Commons, 58; and public lectures, 82
Girls' Industrial Home, 127
Gladden, Washington: Chautauqua lecturer, 13; and Monona Lake Assembly, 31; mentioned, 35
Goodnight, Scott Holland, 44, 47
Gordon, Edgar B.: and Bureau of Community Music and Drama, 108; and community service programs, 109; group singing programs, 131; and correspondence courses in physical education, 133; mentioned, 121
Gould, F. J., 98
Graff, Marshall: urges leniency in Extension course work, 92; on freshman center program, 158; on Williams affair, 168
Granger movement, 24
Green Bay Power and Light Company, 165
Guyer, Michael F., 82

HALE, Edward Everett: quoted, 172
Hall-Quest, Alfred, 178
Hambrecht, George P., 151–52
Hapgood, Norman, 158

Harper, William R., 4, 11, 12, 30
Hatch, Kirk L., 78
Hayakawa, S. I.: as Extension
    lecturer, 164-65; on Williams
    affair, 167
Health Bureau, 99
Health education. See Community
    service
Henry, William A., 16
Herron, George, 33
Hesseltine, William B., 157
High school level correspondence
    courses, 131-33
History, Department of, 156,168
Hoard, William D.: quoted, 15;
    and rural education, 16; as
    Farmers' Institute speaker, 20;
    criticizes Extension, 53; op-
    poses private publication of Ex-
    tension texts, 114
Hohlfeld, George, 67
Holbrook, Josiah, 4, 16
Holst, H. Von, 10
Holt, Frank O.: quoted 153; and
    changing nature of Extension,
    154; depression measures, 155;
    and correspondence study for
    armed services, 159; heads Uni-
    versity Committee on Public
    Relations, 161; and Williams
    affair, 167; answers criticism
    of English instructor, 169; men-
    tioned, 144, 174
Holt, Harriet, 86
Hool, G. A., 85
Huber, Lt. Governor Henry, 162
Hull House, 105
Hutchins, Frank R.: and Wiscon-
    sin Free Library Commission
    in 1895, 45; background and edu-
    cation, 46; and adult education,
    47, 65; and McCarthy, 47, 48,
    53; and Legler, 48; and Depart-
    ment of Debating and Public Dis-
    cussion, 67, 124; methods at-
    tacked, 69; and anti-tuberculosis
    campaign, 102
Huxley, H. E., 18

ILLINOIS, University of, 115
Indiana, University of, 117, 120
Industrial education, 55, 114
Industrial Education, State Board
    of, 64
"Industrial Relations Bulletin," 105

Institute Handbook, 26
Institute of Municipal and Social
    Service, Milwaukee, 59
Institute Proceedings, Farmers'
    Institute, 18
Instruction by Lectures, 82
Interchurch World Movement, 138
International Correspondence
    School: methods studied by
    ry, 91, 131; and shop level text-
    books, 113
International Ladies' Garment
    Workers University, 103
Iowa, University of, 120

JACOBS, H. H.: and settlement
    house in Milwaukee, 35; and
    Milwaukee city parks, 58; and
    Institute of Municipal and Public
    Service, 59; heads University
    Settlement House, 106
Jansky, C. M.: as correspondence
    course instructor, 85, 88; shop
    textbooks, 115; and Army Insti-
    tute, 159
Jastrow, Joseph, 82
Job training program. See Worker
    education
John Bascom College, 47
Johns Hopkins University, 12
Jones, G. D.: criticizes Exten-
    sion, 53; conflict with Van Hise,
    56; opposes University men in
    politics, 60; opposes use of Uni-
    versity buildings for forum, 125
Jones, Jenkin Lloyd, 98
Jones, Nellie Kedzie, 119

KANSAS, University of, 83
Kaukauna High School, 110
Kelly, W. W., 150
Kenosha Civic Council, 169
Kenosha Extension Center, 168
Kewaunee High School, 162
Kiekhofer, William H., 82-83
Kingsley, Charles: quoted, 113
Kittle, William: quoted, 56
Knaplund, Paul, 156, 167
Kuney, Bernice D., 86

LABOR unions, 53
La Follette, Phil: quoted, 153; on
    function of University, 161
La Follette, Robert M.: influ-
    enced by John Bascom, 36; and

1905 agricultural education appropriation, 45

La Follette's Weekly Magazine, 60, 68

Land Grant College Act of 1862, 8, 16

Langerscheidt, Gustav, 4

Lawrence University, 36-37, 40

League of Wisconsin Municipalities, 57, 107

Lear, Lt. Gen. Ben, 159

Legislative Reference Library: initiated by Charles McCarthy, 45-46; and Hutchins, 46; attacked by Stalwarts, 60; and social service, 107

Legler, Henry E., 48-49, 66

Leonard, William Ellery, 117

Library Commission, 45-49 passim, 67, 86

Lindemann, August S., 54

Lighty, William Henry: heads Correspondence-Study Department, 50; and Wisconsin Conference of Charities and Correction, 59; answers Cary attack, 61; and cultural education, 65; on correspondence work, 66, 67, 74, 78, 90, 128, 135, 158; and Reber evaluated, 69, 76-77; and Reber controversy, 70, 76; and English adult education, 80; and McCarthy goals compared, 81; and cultural lecture series, 83-84; cites need for specialized correspondence study faculty, 85; demands equal status for Extension faculty, 86-87; quoted, 96; and worker education, 96, 103-4; and Anna Garlin Spencer, 98; and State Conference on Charities and Correction, 107; and educational broadcasting, 113, 116-20; supervises textbook publication, 115; and Wisconsin Journal of Education, 131; on teacher training, 134-35; briefs Snell, 140; in Reber memorandum, 141; relieved of duties, 142; and Snell investigation, 144; elected president of National University Extension Association, 177; mentioned, 173, 174

Little, Malcolm G., 142, 149

London Society for the Extension of University Teaching, 6-7

London Workingmen's College, 4

Loomis, H. B., 31

Lowell, James Russell, 10

Lowell Lectures, 83

Luther, C. L., 19

MABIE, Hamilton W., 31

MacLean, Malcolm S., 147-48

McCarthy, Charles: and worker education, 4, 47, 65-66, 80, 174; and Free Library Commission, 45, 48-49; and Legislative Reference Library, 45-46; background and education, 46-47; and reviving Extension, 50; and Lighty, 53, 76, 81; studies German technical education, 54; and Institute of Municipal and Public Service, 59; and legislation-drafting department attacked by Stalwarts, 60; identified with Extension, 62; and Sub-Committee on Credit for University Extension Work, 66; and Hutchins, 67; and Reber, 69; and vocational schools, 71; advocates practical courses, 72, 98; urges industrial smoke control program, 100; evaluated, 102, 175; advises elementary business subjects, 104; urges development of community centers, 108; on debate and public discussion, 125; and vocational school law in 1911, 151; on correspondence study for armed services, 158; mentioned, 148, 173, 174

McCarthy, H. R., 122

McGovern, Francis, 60-61

McGraw-Hill Book Company, 114, 115

McGuffy Readers, 153

McKenzie, Frederick, 52

McKinley, William, 12

McSweeney, Edward F., 101

Malthus, Thomas, 4

Manitowoc Vocational School, 157

Marietta College, 119

Marquette University, 124

Maryland Agricultural College, 115

Marx, Karl, 35

Mechanics' Institutes, England, 5, 21, 41
Medical Extension, 145
Meikeljohn, Alexander, 146
Merrill City Hall, 157
Meyer, Benno W., 91
Michigan Central Normal School, 90
Miles, H. E., 63
Miller, H. L., 135
Milwaukee branch of University, 93
Milwaukee Chamber of Commerce, 110
Milwaukee County Federation of Teachers, 143
Milwaukee Electric Railway and Light Company, 64
Milwaukee Extension Center: day classes opened, 94; freshman and sophomore classes, 121, 123; evaluation of instruction, 124; brought under supervision of Madison office, 139; building project, 141; and Snell, 142; and adult education program, 146–47; courses for unemployed, 148; autonomy, 161; faculty criticized, 162–63
Milwaukee Journal: on immigration problems in 1887, 30; on civic reform in 1906, 57; commends Extension lyceum series, 83; supports Extension community program in 1910, 106; on educational broadcasting, 118; and WTMJ, 121; on Extension center program, 160
Milwaukee Labor College, 145
Milwaukee Leader, 64
Milwaukee Merchants' and Manufacturers' Association: and industrial training school, 43–44; and Extension courses for workers, 51; endorses Extension appropriation of 1909, 53; withdraws support of appropriation bill, 54; backs Seidel for Mayor, 58; and anti-tuberculosis campaign, 102; mentioned, 56, 173
Milwaukee Normal School, 124, 129, 136
Milwaukee School Board, 101
Milwaukee Workers' College, 103
Minnesota, University of: adopts

Extension texts, 115; requests advice from Wisconsin Extension, 176
Mission House, 156
Monona Lake Assembly, 31
Morrison, William H., 19, 24
Municipal Reference Bureau, 108
Music, School of, 120
Muzzey, David S., 98

NATION, The, 168
National Education Association, 44
National Manufacturers' Association, 43
National Newspaper Conference, 112
National Society of Stationary Engineers, 53
National Woman's Suffrage Association, 126
National University Extension Association: and educational broadcasting, 120; formed, 177; Lighty elected president of, 177
Neacy Thomas J., 62
Nearing, Scott, 125
Nebraska, University of, 120
New Masses, The, 168
New Republic, The, 168
New York, University of State of, 130
New York Bureau of Municipal Research: model for Milwaukee Bureau of Economy and Efficiency, 58; conducts survey of Milwaukee, 60; and Allen, 71. See also Allen Survey
New York School of Philanthropy, 59
Neystrom, Paul H.: answers Stalwart attack on University Extension, 61; advocates statistical defense of Extension, 63; and Allen Report, 72; first correspondence student under Lighty program, 78
Norgord, C.P., 19
Normal School Board, 28
Normal schools: and Extension relations with, 127–30, 133–34, 136
North Carolina, University of, 138, 176

North Dakota, University of, 120, 177

Nye Committee, 166

OLSON, Julius, 31
Olson, Orvil E., 156
Oregon, University of, 120
Orwell, George, 121
O'Shea, M. V.: Extension lecturer, 35, 49; on University policy, 131; on teacher training, 132
Oshkosh Chamber of Commerce, 105
Oshkosh State Normal School, 39, 40
Otto, Max, 146, 169

PACKAGE libraries, 112, 124
Page, Herbert, 117
Pahlow, Edwin H., 49
Palmer, George Herbert, 30-31, 40
Parkinson, J. B., 31
Paxson, Frederic Logan, 82
Pederson, Oscar, 37
Penal reform: and Jacob Riis, 127; correspondence courses for prisoners, 127-28
Pennsylvania, State College of, 120
Pennsylvania, University of, 115
People's Institute, Milwaukee, 32, 33
Pereles, Nathan, 59
Pettijohn, J. J., 82, 177
Philipp, Emanuel L.: selected to oppose McGovern, 61; elected governor of Wisconsin, 63; and school consolidation program, 131
Phillips, Wendel, 10
Pitman, Annie M., 85, 88, 89
Pittsburgh, University of, 115
Platteville Normal School, 129
Populism: as political movement, 15; opposed by Farmers' Institute speakers, 24-25; growing popularity of, 36; and Ely, 37
Powderly, T. V., 35
Powell, John W., 94
Powell, Lyman B., 33
Pratt Institute, 115
Pray, Theron B., 129, 136
Progressives: La Follette elected governor, 45; use of Univer-

sity specialists, 60; and University Extension, 96, 125
Pulver, H. E., 85
Purdue University, 90
Pure History Law, 125

RADIO. See WHA; Educational broadcasting
Rastall, B. M., 58
Raymond, Jerome T., 38-39
Reber, Louis E.: as Dean of University Extension, 4, 52; and G. D. Jones, 53, 54; advises on health and sanitation problems in Milwaukee, 58; attacks Allen Survey, 63; coördinates worker education program, 65; and administrative policy, 68-71; work evaluated, 71-73; memorial volume of 1948, 76; and Lighty evaluated, 77 ff. passim; on correspondence study, 85, 90-91, 131; and retirement pension question, 86; and Extension faculty status, 87; report of 1910, 91; and Milwaukee Extension, 93, 94; and community programs, 96; and widened University scope, 99; and Edward J. Ward, 106; suggests need for retrenchment, 112; and Extension textbooks, 113-15; and educational broadcasting, 116, 118; on debating and public discussion, 124; and William H. Dudley, 130; and medical courses, 137; retires, 138; and Snell, 140, 141; and community service, 145; and vocational school law of 1911, 151; mentioned, 123, 143, 173, 174
Redpath Agency, 40
Regents, Board of: agrees to limited extension program in 1891, 30; and Ely investigation, 37; on Extension textbooks, 114; and Snell administration, 141-44; mentioned, 19
Rensselaer Polytechnic Institute, 8
Republican State Convention, 62
"Retail Bulletin," 105
Reynolds, R. L., 157
Rice, C. S., 132
Riis, Jacob, 127

Ripon, Wisconsin, model com-
munity experiment, 57
Ripon College, 131
Rockefeller, John D., Jr., 46, 66
Rockwell, Ethel, 145, 148
Roosevelt, Theodore, 14
Rose, David, 57–58
Ross, E. A.: Extension lecture
series, 82–83; criticized, 162–
63; mentioned, 166
Rugg Social Science Series, 154
Rusk, Jeremiah, 16
Russell, Harry L., 58
Russell Sage Foundation Survey,
133

SADLER, William, 83
Salisbury, R. D., 31
Sanborn, A. W., 59
Saturday Evening Post, 168
Saturday Lunch Club, 61, 68
Schlatter, E. B., 86
School for Workers in Industry,
162
School House Community Center,
Milwaukee, 125
School of Citizenship, 126
School of Ethics, 98
Schwartztrauber, E. N., 162
Science and Art of Teaching,
chair of, 29
Scott, Almere, 67, 124
Scott, William A., 35, 41
Seidel, Emil, 58, 101
Settlement house work: N. H.
Jacobs, 35, 58; Lighty, 50, 52,
66; as conservative influence,
105; University Settlement
House, 106. See also Community
service
Sheldon, Anne, 28
Smith, Kenneth G., 93, 131
Snell, Chester D.: appointed Director of Extension Division,
138; and centralization of Extension activities, 139; and Milwaukee center, 142; and faculty
policy, 141–43; and Regents' investigation, 141, 143–44; and
educational policy, 145, 146;
opposes community drama program, 148; and high school level
work, 149–50; and junior college
work, 151; on vocational education, 151–52; charges subversion

at University, 163; mentioned,
120, 170, 173, 174
Snow, Edgar B., 67
Social centers, Milwaukee, 58
Social Democrats, 58, 59, 106,
125
Social Gospel, 96, 174
Social Service Institute, in Mil-
waukee, 107
Society to Encourage Studies at
Home, 10
Southwest Louisiana Institute,
176
Speirs, F. W.: and People's Insti-
tute, Milwaukee, 33, 39; and
Socialism, 36; and Ely, 37;
leaves Wisconsin, 41; and shop
courses, 55–56
Spencer, Anna Garlin: brought to
Madison, 98; and Social Service
Institute in Milwaukee, 59, 107
Spencer, Herbert, 13
Spencer, R. E., 32
Stalwarts: attack University par-
ticipation in government, 62;
mentioned, 125
State Agricultural Society, 15
State Board of Control, 59, 127
State Conference of Charities and
Corrections, 35, 48, 59
State Industrial Commission, 148
State Library Commission, 45–
49, 67, 86
State Park Service, 46
State Reformatory, 127
State Teachers' Association, 29
Steffens, Lincoln, 60
Stout Institute, 55
Strong, Josiah: as Chautauqua
lecturer, 13; and community
programs, 97; and Christian
Socialism, 106
Stuart, James, 4
Sub-Committee on Credit for Uni-
versity Extension Work, 66
Sumner, William Graham, 13, 31
Superior Normal School, 136

TAFT, William Howard, 158
Teacher training: summer classes instituted in 1888, 29; backgrounds of, 129; Extension
courses, 132–36; Extension efforts increased, 149
Teachers' Institutes, 28

Terry, E. M., 116, 117
Textbooks, 89, 113–16
Thatcher's Metropolitan Orches-
  tra, 83
Thomas, C. W., 169
Thorp, Charles, 19
Thwaites, Reuben Gold, 29
Tillman, Ben, 24
Tocqueville, Alexis de, 10, 14,
  40
Tolman, H. C., 31
Toussaint, Charles, 4
Toynbee, Arnold, 6
Tressler, A. W., 47
Turneaure, Frederick E.: and
  League of Wisconsin Municipalities, 57; advises in state government, 58; supports Extension
  program, 67
Turner, Frederick Jackson:
  pioneered University Extension,
  4, 12; lecture series of, 29, 41;
  and Ely, 32; and industrial
  teacher training, 65; urges revival of lecture-correspondence
  work, 65–66; and correspondence courses, 88; and citizenship programs, 124; on teacher
  training, 129; mentioned, 43,
  144, 173
Turnverein, 106

UNDERWOOD Tariff, 96
United States Armed Forces In-
  stitute, 159, 160
University Committee on Public
  Relations, 161
University Experimental School,
  146
University Radio Research Com-
  mittee, 120–21
University Settlement House, 106

VAN Cleef, Frank Louis, 31
Van Hise, Charles R.: refuses to
  give Extension lectures, 41;
  quoted, 43, 65, 76, 78, 123, 164;
  inauguration of, 47; on function
  of University, 48, 86, 173; on reorganizing extension work, 49;
  appoints Lighty, 50; appoints
  Reber, 52; and 1909 Extension
  appropriation, 53; and compulsory school attendance law, 55;
  accused of socialistic tendencies,
  56; defends role of experts in
  government, 61; blocks move for
  Milwaukee branch of University,
  95; School of Ethics lecturer, 98;
  and Wisconsin Idea, 122; as
  president of Wisconsin Teachers' Association, 131; and vocational school law of 1911, 151;
  mentioned, 140, 144
Vilas, William F., 16
Vilture Manufacturing Company,
  64
Vincent, George E., 61
Vincent, Bishop John H.: ob-
  serves English extension, 7;
  pioneers Chautauqua movement,
  10, 11, 14
Visual aids, Extension's use of,
  129–30
Vocational education: schools,
  55; texts, 114. See also Worker
  education
Walgreen, Charles R., 154
Wallace, Henry, 19
Ward, Edward J.: and Milwaukee
  city parks, 58; and Institute of
  Municipal and Social Service,
  59; and Milwaukee community
  program of 1910, 106, 107
Ward, Lester, 105–6
Washington, Booker T., 40
Washington University, 177
Waukesha, Wisconsin, model
  community experiment, 57
Waupun State Penitentiary, 127
Wausau Vocational School Board,
  167
Webster, Daniel, 10
Weinman, Karl B. (pseud.), 63
Wells, Oliver E., 37
WHA: licensed, 116; sports events
  broadcasted, 117; audience re-
  action, 118; high school broad-
  casts, 119; acceptance of non-
  University broadcasting, 119–
  20; "Wisconsin School of the
  Air," 121; influence evaluated,
  121–22; attempts to transfer to
  private control, 122
White, Andrew D., 12, 50
Wilcox, Ella Wheeler, 31
Wilder, Amos P., 35
Williams, T. Harry, 166–67, 168
Wilson, Margaret, 109
Wilson, Woodrow, 178

Wisconsin Anti-Tuberculosis As-
sociation Apprentice School, 102
Wisconsin Bankers' Association,
110
Wisconsin Conference of Chari-
ties and Corrections, 57
Wisconsin Conference on Social
Work, 107
Wisconsin Dairymen's Associa-
tion, 16, 23, 51, 173
Wisconsin Farmers' Institutes.
See Farmers' institutes
Wisconsin Federation of Catholic
Societies, 59
Wisconsin Federation of Teach-
ers, 167
Wisconsin Idea: attacked by Stal-
warts, 60; defended by Lighty,
61; Reber's attitude toward, 69,
77; interpreted, 175
Wisconsin Journal of Education:
attacks Teachers' Institutes, 28;
criticizes Rose administration,
57–58; reflects postwar conser-
vatism, 125; and University ar-
ticles, 131
Wisconsin Medical Society, 137
Wisconsin School of the Air, 121
Wisconsin State Federation of
Labor, 53
Wisconsin State Journal, 63, 136
Wisconsin State Library Commission, 89. See also Free Library
Commission
Wisconsin Teachers' Association,
131, 132–33

Wolfe, Thomas, 168
Women's Self Government Association, 162
Women's Trade Union, 103
Worker education: in England, 6;
early extension efforts, 32;
People's Institute, Milwaukee,
33; need for, 43, 44 ff. passim;
objections to, 44; University
Extension enters field of, 44–
45; German influences on, 47–
48; and McCarthy, 51 ff. passim;
shop courses, 55–56; at University of California and Bryn
Mawr, 103; increasing interest
in, 103; at Boston Trade Union
College, 103; economic rewards
cited, 104–5; textbooks for, 114;
classes for trade unionists, 125.
See also Adult education
Working People's Reading Room,
32
World War I: changes in Extension activities, 112, 123; veteran
rehabilitation programs, 123;
conservative reaction following,
125
WTMJ, 121
Wylie, George, 19

YMCA, and Extension coöperation, 158

ZIMMERN, Alfred, 102